Christian Realism and Liberation Theology

p.61 – problem of evil
p.127 – Psychology of the Oppressed
p.142 – "Reformists" & "Militants" in L. America
p.143 – "conscientization"
p.146 – "Elitism" & "Consumerism" & "Capitalism"

*To my teachers
at St. Charles Borromeo Seminary, Columbus, Ohio (1963–1967),
this book is dedicated with gratitude and respect,
especially to
James F. Cooney and Thomas F. Duffy,
who first got me to think about these things*

Christian Realism and Liberation Theology

Practical Theologies in Creative Conflict

Dennis McCann

ORBIS BOOKS
Maryknoll, New York 10545

The Catholic Foreign Mission Society of America (Maryknoll) recruits and trains people for overseas missionary service. Through Orbis Books Maryknoll aims to foster the international dialogue that is essential to mission. The books published, however, reflect the opinions of their authors and are not meant to represent the official position of the society.

Copyright © 1981 Orbis Books, Maryknoll, NY 10545

Manufactured in the United States of America

Library of Congress Cataloging in Publication Data
McCann, Dennis.
  Christian realism and liberation theology.

  Bibliography: p.
  1. Sociology, Christian—History—20th century.
2. Christian ethics—History—20th century. 3. Social
ethics—History—20th century. 4. Niebuhr, Reinhold,
1892-1971. 5. Liberation theology. I. Title.
BT738.M25   261.8   80-23163
ISBN 0-88344-086-5 (pbk.)

Contents

82574

Introduction

This book is about practical theology. More specifically, it is about practical theologies locked in conflict, and what we are to make of them. Latin American liberation theology has triggered a crisis for many North American Christians. For some it has meant a reawakening of conscience, a disturbing cry from oppressed peoples, calling this nation into account for the consequences of its policies. For others it has confirmed a sense of the intellectual and moral bankruptcy of North American theology. The latter have interpreted the Latin American challenge as an invitation to create their own theologies of liberation.

The full dimensions of the conflict became apparent in the fall of 1973. At that time *Christianity and Crisis* published an exchange of views on "Liberation Theology and Christian Realism," involving an attack on liberation theology made from a perspective identified with Reinhold Niebuhr's Christian realism. Since by all accounts Niebuhr's work was the major influence shaping the practical theology of Christian social activists in the United States prior to his death in 1971, this exchange served as a call to arms. Thomas G. Sanders, invoking Niebuhr's authority, criticized liberation theology as "Christian utopianism." The Latin American liberation theologian Rubem A. Alves responded by denouncing Christian realism as an "ideology of the Establishment." With these polemics the issue was joined: North Americans were summoned to choose between two models of practical theology.

Sanders was not mistaken in recognizing the tensions between Niebuhr's Christian realism and liberation theology. He argued that liberation theology is a "moralistic" ideology which, in reacting against the "legalistic and conservative" ethic once typical of Catholicism in Latin America, effectively obscures the complexities of the political situation there (Sanders, 1973:170). Since the meaning of liberation, in Sanders's view, is based on an interpretation of history and social conflict inspired by Marxism, liberation theology is properly criticized as a form of "soft utopianism." Thus Sanders invoked Niebuhr's later work, which had used "soft utopianism" and "hard utopianism" to catalog the "illusions" of religious liberals and secular intellectuals. While both errors were based on theologically inadequate views of human nature and history, "soft" utopians were distinguished by their naiveté; the "hard" ones, by their ruthlessness. Thus secular liberals, the remnants of the noncommunist Left, and Protestants still clinging to the theology of the Social Gospel, were "soft"; while

1

Marxist-Leninists were "hard." In numbering Latin American liberation theologians among the "soft" utopians, Sanders remarked that they reminded him most of the partisans of the Social Gospel. In other words, Latin Americans were merely going through a phase that North American Protestantism experienced in the first quarter of this century. This somewhat patronizing suggestion was matched by an unsolicited piece of advice: if liberation theologians are serious about the problems of Latin American development, they will do well to rethink their position in light of Christian realism.[1]

It is not difficult to imagine Alves's response to Sanders. Alves took up the charge of utopianism and made it a point of honor. Although Christian realism imagines that utopian thinking is "sinful," this interpretation is based not upon the Bible, but upon an acquiescence in "the revolt against transcendence that characterizes Western civilization" (Alves, 1973:175). Christian realism, in other words, is spiritually bankrupt. It has ratified a set of "silent agreements" with pragmatism and positivism, philosophies clearly discredited as ideologies of the Establishment. Indeed, Christian realism is merely the "American ideology" decked out in religious symbols. That being the case, Latin Americans would be fools to judge liberation theology by its categories. Alves was particularly incensed by the charge that liberation theology is a "moralistic" ideology. "Morality," as far as he is concerned, "ignores all pragmatic issues and is solely concerned with the will of God." Since Christian utopianism is based on a vision that all social systems are under God's historical judgment, liberation theologians happily wear that label as proof of their fidelity to the Bible. While Alves directed most of his fire against Sanders, he did mention Niebuhr at one point: Christian realists should, he suggested, go back and read Niebuhr's *Moral Man and Immoral Society*. Thus Alves implied that Niebuhr's earlier work, at least, is congenial to liberation theology.

As it turned out, Sanders and Alves fired the opening rounds in a battle that continues intermittently to this day. In subsequent issues *Christianity and Crisis* presented a range of responses to that first skirmish. Most contributors wanted to have it both ways, expressing appreciation for Niebuhr's position but also welcoming liberation theology. Thus Robert McAfee Brown tried to dissociate Niebuhr from Sander's criticisms, speculating that given Niebuhr's flexibility and perceptiveness he probably would be a supporter of liberation theology were he alive today (Brown, 1973:199). Thomas Quigley made a similar point by quoting from Niebuhr's *Moral Man and Immoral Society* (Quigley, 1973:201). Other sympathizers suggested that Niebuhr's later realism cannot be understood apart from his earlier radicalism, and vice versa. John C. Bennett, for example, argued that "Christian realism is not a self-sufficient theology, but a corrective theology that at its best incorporated something of the dynamism of the Social Gospel and the Christian Socialism of the Niebuhr of *Moral Man and Immoral Society*" (Bennett, 1973:197). But John Plank reminded Alves— and, by implication, Quigley and Bennett—that Niebuhr also wrote *The*

Children of Light and the Children of Darkness (Plank, 1973:199), a work
that criticizes both Marxism and liberalism while proposing a new vindication of democracy. Still others tried to clarify the political situation in Latin
America, so that the practical consequences of this dispute might better be
understood. While each of these responses opened up important questions
of interpretation, as a whole they succeeded only in publicizing the conflict,
but not in resolving it.

In the years since that initial exchange, the discussion has broadened to
include a variety of theological perspectives, Catholic as well as Protestant,
Latin American and North American. A new stage was reached with the
"Theology in the Americas" conference held in Detroit, Michigan, in
August 1975. There the discussion centered on the prospects for North
American liberation theologies committed to dismantling "the American
Empire" (Torres and Eagleson, 1976:7). Latin American liberation theol-
ogy was to be taken as a "new way of doing theology," for which the
process leading up to the conference and beyond was to serve as a model.
But there have also been less enthusiastic responses. Peter Berger and
Richard Neuhaus have followed up the "Hartford Declaration," a conservative theological manifesto calling Christians to be "against the world for
the world," by expressing skepticism about liberation theology's adequacy
for either North America or Latin America. Berger in particular denounced
its method of "conscientization" as an "elitist" exercise in political indoc-
trination (Berger, 1974:129–44). Most recently, Edward R. Norman's
Christianity and the World Order has ignited further controversy by rejecting liberation theology as a "politicization" of Christian values (Norman,
1979:19–25). Thus a certain polarization has occurred among Christian
theologians and social activists.

The question is, of course, whether this polarization can be overcome, or
is it irresolvable? Apparently some have decided that there is no point in
attempting to adjudicate conflicts of this sort. A person simply makes a
commitment for or against the oppressed, and the choice of theological
models follows inevitably. In fact, there are those who insist on a public
confession of one's "oppressorhood" as a precondition for serious
dialogue on the subject of liberation. But it is precisely this sort of posturing
that has provided many others with an excuse for dismissing liberation
theology entirely. There are a few, however, who still think that rational
discussion is possible. Among them, Schubert Ogden has tried to offer a
firmer metaphysical foundation for liberation theology (Ogden, 1979).
Whatever the merits of Ogden's proposal, his work does proceed on the
assumption that theological criticism has an integrity of its own, and need
not be reduced to ideological polemics. While the political implications of
this conflict cannot be ignored, any resolution of the theological issues can
only come by proceeding on the common ground that all theologians share:
a common commitment to a common task involving common standards of
theological discourse.[2]

What follows is presented in the hope that it will contribute to a rational discussion of this theological dispute, and perhaps even to its resolution. In answer to the challenge of liberation theology, I propose to return to its conflict with Christian realism and to analyze the merits of both positions as models for practical theology. I do so because, after watching the controversy unfold, I am convinced that the best way to advance the discussion is to reexamine Niebuhr's Christian realism in light of liberation theology, and vice versa. In that way several issues crucial for the future of practical theology in the United States may be opened up for critical reflection.

The most important of these is the nature of religious transcendence and its role in Christian social action. Is Christianity's distinctive contribution to politics a spirit of "religious disinterestedness" capable of exorcising the demonic aspects of the social struggle, as Reinhold Niebuhr thought? Or is it a sense of "solidarity with the oppressed" based on faith in "Christ the Liberator," as liberation theologians insist? Is the meaning of Christianity immanent to history, or does it transcend history in any meaningful way? After wrestling with this issue for a number of years, I conclude that Niebuhr's "paradoxical vision" of the Hidden God's relationship to human history is a more adequate basis for practical theology and Christain social action than the vision of Christ the Liberator proclaimed by Latin Americans like Gustavo Gutiérrez. While Niebuhr's vision is more promising, the theology and ethics that he develops from it are not without their deficiencies. I shall try to show what these are and why they give the charge "ideology of the Establishment" some plausibility. But I shall also argue that in light of the even more severe problems facing liberation theology, these deficiencies do not warrant the repudiation of Christian realism. For Gutiérrez's vision is of dubious origin, and his theology consequently is vitiated by a critical ambiguity: a failure to clarify the theological relationship between "liberation" and "salvation." As liberation theologians continue their "critical reflection on praxis," Gutiérrez's ambiguity becomes a dilemma: either the content must be politicized or the method trivialized. I shall give reasons why this dilemma rules out liberation theology, as it stands, as an alternative to Christian realism. Its structural failure means that this theology possesses no theoretical resources for distinguishing religious transcendence from political enthusiasm, a distinction that practical theologians and Christian social activists must make if they are to remain recognizably Christian.

The point to the analysis that follows is a limited one. It is not to say that Christian realism is right and liberation theology is wrong, nor to say that liberation theology is inadequate simply because it disagrees with Christian realism. It argues, rather, that while the one exhibits some serious weaknesses, the other is faced with a perhaps insuperable dilemma. If that point can be made convincingly, then North American theologians and social activists should not respond to this dispute by abandoning the legacy of Reinhold Niebuhr for the false promise of liberation theology. Instead, we should take liberation theology as a sincere but confused protest, a call to conscience that challenges us to rethink the theory and practice of Christian realism in light of the problems that await us in the 1980s.

NOTES

1. Christian realism's perspective on Latin America should not be a matter for speculation. In a book coauthored with Reinhold Niebuhr, Paul E. Sigmund analyzes the prospects for democracy in Latin America: *The Democratic Experience: Past and Prospects.* A synopsis of the argument of this book is presented in Chapter 5, below.

2. The analysis that follows assumes that something like David Tracy's *Blessed Rage for Order: The New Pluralism in Theology* provides an adequate description and analysis of the standards of theological discourse in general, and that practical theology can proceed only by adhering to those standards. Tracy's own sketch for a "revisionist" practical theology is given in Chapter 10 of that book, "History, Theory and Practice." While his work has inspired some of the concerns expressed in my analysis, he can in no way be held responsible for the conclusions I have reached about either Christian realism or liberation theology.

1

Christian Realism in Context

It is difficult to know whether the criticism of both liberal and Marxist views of human nature and history was prompted by a profounder understanding of the Biblical faith; or whether this understanding was prompted by the refutation of the liberal and Marxist faith by the tragic facts of contemporary history which included two world wars and the encounter of a liberal culture with two idolatrous tyrannies, first Nazism and then Communism, resting respectively upon the foundations of moral cynicism and moral utopianism. About the circular relation between the presupposition of faith and the facts of experience I must say more presently.
　　　　—Reinhold Niebuhr, "Intellectual Autobiography," 1956

Reinhold Niebuhr refused to be known as a theologian. He preferred to think of himself as a preacher, "a kind of circuit rider" commuting between the ecclesiastical and academic communities of the United States. While he claimed little competence in "the nice points of pure theology," he charged himself with "the defense and justification of the Christian faith in a secular age" (Niebuhr, 1956:3). His writings—in fact, his best writings—for the most part were occasional pieces, more bent on presenting a Christian perspective on some current political issue than on explaining the theological rationale behind his analysis. Nevertheless, he succeeded so well in engaging the attention of the theologians and social activists of his generation that he is credited with "the most important American contribution to Protestant theological ethics in the first half of this century" (Gustafson, 1971:31).

Niebuhr's contribution rests on his ability to make a theological interpretation of human events plausible to a wide audience as a basis for political action. His observations on American life and thought stemmed from a historical consciousness nurtured and sustained by his Christian faith. Theology therefore became a mode of reflection based on his sense of contemporary events, ever changing in response to his intuitions—the second-guesses as well as the flashes of insight—by which he tried to discern the meaning of this faith for historically decisive action. Instinctively pragmatic in his approach to theology, Niebuhr characterized this historic consciousness as "experience" and proposed to keep his theological speculations faithful to it.

If Niebuhr's achievement is to have relevance beyond its original audience, it must be reconstructed as a model for practical theology. In short, the basic principles of his Christian realism must be identified and criticized systematically. Any exercise in model-building runs the risk of abstraction, and in Niebuhr's case this means emphasizing the general features of his historical consciousness while neglecting its richness as a personal witness to Christian faith. What follows in this chapter is meant to minimize this risk. It introduces the agenda for Christian realism in the context of Niebuhr's lifelong struggle with modernity: his search for insight into what it means to be a modern Christian, and what it takes for a modern Christian to contribute to the common effort for justice and peace. While this context is illuminated primarily by the contours of Niebuhr's biography, it also has important sociological, ideological, and theological dimensions. These will make it possible to see Niebuhr's perspective as a model for practical theology.

A Theologian's Experience

Karl Paul Reinhold Niebuhr was born in Wright City, Missouri, on June 21, 1892. His father, Gustav Niebuhr, the son of a wealthy landowner, was a preacher, and his mother, Lydia Hosto, a preacher's daughter. Gustav had immigrated to America in 1878 from Hardissen bei Lage in northwestern Germany (Stone, 1972:17). In leaving the old country he was rebelling against the authoritarianism of his father and Prussian life in general (Merkley, 1975:4). Once in America he soon found a home among the German-American communities of the Midwest, many of which had been settled by the Forty-Eighters—men like Carl Schurz—who had fled Germany after the failure of the Revolution of 1848. After finding work as a fieldhand near Freeport, Illinois, young Gustav was soon on his way to the seminary, with help from the farmer who employed him.

Eden Theological Seminary, located at Webster Groves, Missouri, served as the denominational seminary for the German Evangelical Synod of North America. Already well established in Gustav's day, the Synod represented the tradition of the *Kirchenverein*, the 1817 union of the Prussian Reformed and Lutheran churches, inspired by the liberal theology of Frederich Schleiermacher and the political interests of the Prussian monarchy. Once transplanted to the United States, the supporters of this Evangelical Church of the Prussian Union gradually formed a more or less coherent denomination, embodying the religious traditions of the Reformation but in a "distinctly American" form of church organization (Chrystal, 1977:21).

Gustav Niebuhr completed his studies at Eden and was ordained in 1885 to assist "the Synod's pioneer missionary" in California, Edward J. Hosto. Soon thereafter he married Hosto's daughter, Lydia. After serving in various parishes in California, Utah, and the Midwest, Gustav was called in 1902 to the pastorate in Lincoln, Illinois, where the Niebuhrs finally settled. Along the way in Wright City the family was completed with the birth of Reinhold in 1892, and H. Richard two years later. The Niebuhr brothers were to dominate the American theological scene at midcentury.[1]

By the time the family got to Illinois, young Reinhold had acquired a deep respect for his father and his father's calling. As he later remembered, he thought his father the most interesting man in town. And very likely he was right. Gustav was a man of intense personal piety and intellectual vigor. He daily read the Bible both in Hebrew and in Greek and kept up on the latest in German theology, works from scholars like Adolf von Harnack, who represented the culmination of German liberal Protestantism. Gustav also aligned himself politically with American Progressives and greatly admired Teddy Roosevelt. In a community of conservatives for whom ethnic loyalties were paramount, he considered himself an American and a liberal. These were the values that he shared with his children. Thus it was not surprising that in 1912 Reinhold followed his father's footsteps to Eden Seminary.

After his graduation a year later, the Niebuhr family decided that Reinhold needed a graduate school education. Consequently, he petitioned the denomination to defer his call to a pastorate so that he could attend the Yale Divinity School. At Yale Reinhold became acutely aware of the deficiencies of his previous training. In a letter to his former teacher, Dr. Samuel Press, he declared, "Everywhere around here they not only assume that you have a B.A. but they assume a fundamental knowledge of these college courses. I have bluffed my way through pretty well by industrious reading, but I feel all the time like a mongrel among thoroughbreds . . ." (Merkley, 1975:7). Apparently, his was no mean talent for "bluffing," for he managed to acquire the Yale B.D. at the end of his first year, and the M.A. at the end of the second, both with excellent marks. His graduate education, however, went no further than the two years at Yale. In view of the family's financial situation after Gustav's death in 1913 and his own disenchantment with formal study, Reinhold now accepted a pastorate. The experience at Yale confirmed the theological liberalism that he had learned from his father and exposed him to the ways of American academia, but his future awaited him in Detroit.

The Mission Board of Niebuhr's denomination sent him to Detroit in 1915 as pastor of the Bethel Evangelical Church, where he was to serve for thirteen years. On his arrival the congregation numbered only sixty-five, but during his tenure that number would increase tenfold (Merkley, 1975: 9). Niebuhr's success at Bethel was part of a larger trend. The great migration from the farms to America's industrial heartland had begun, and Detroit was fast becoming a major center for automobile manufacturing. In the midst of these changes Niebuhr soon earned a local reputation as a preacher and progressive clergyman, and the size of his congregation grew accordingly.

The pastorate at Bethel also awakened the social activist in Niebuhr. In the early years he was confronted by a congregation made up mostly of German-Americans, who had resented the hysterical patriotism aroused by World War I and had reacted with a tendency toward cultural isolation. Niebuhr's response was characteristically blunt: he urged his people to set aside their defensiveness and contribute their best to the American nation in the making (Merkley, 1975:17–18). After the Great War the economic and social changes accompanying rapid industrialization in Detroit began to occupy the pastor. Thus in the 1920s he became an outspoken critic of Henry Ford's American utopia. Along with Episcopal bishop Charles D. Williams and lawyer Fred M. Butzel, Niebuhr campaigned for a guaranteed annual wage and other benefits for workers. Frequently he turned his pulpit over to A.F. of L. organizers in their drive to unionize the automobile industry. In 1926 he took his case to the public in a series of articles in *The Christian Century*. There he debunked the myth of Ford as "a great benefactor of the working man" by documenting the inhuman conditions created by the assembly lines and erratic employment practices (Stone, 1972:28–29).

The picture of Niebuhr's pastoral ministry would not be complete without mention of Sherwood Eddy's role in it. An officer of the YMCA and an ardent Social Gospel radical, Eddy was impressed by the young preacher turned social activist. In 1923 he invited Niebuhr to participate in his European Seminar, which allowed American intellectuals, politicians, and church leaders to meet to discuss social issues with various influential Europeans. The 1923 seminar visited both Britain and Germany. Conditions in Germany's Ruhr Valley under French occupation dismayed Niebuhr sufficiently to reinforce his pacifism, adopted in disgust after World War I (Niebuhr, 1957:67–69). The visit to Britain gave him cause for hope. He saw in the British Labour party and its commitment to social democracy "a political policy which approximates the Christian ideal" (Merkley, 1975:19). The European Seminar of 1923 thus galvanized Niebuhr's perspective on international politics. He became a Europeanist, who looked to Britain and to Germany for possible clues concerning the American future. But Eddy's role was not limited to the seminar. During the 1920s he persuaded the Bethel congregation to accept an assistant pastor, so that Niebuhr would be free to preach in other pulpits and do some weekend lecturing at colleges and universities. His eagerness to promote Niebuhr was so great that evidently he paid the assistant's salary out of his own pocket (Merkley, 1975:19). Even Niebuhr's appointment to a professorship at Union Theological Seminary in New York City in 1928, as he later remembered it, "came largely at the instigation of my friend Sherwood Eddy" (Niebuhr, 1956:8).

Before moving on to New York's Morningside Heights, Niebuhr captured the meaning of his personal experience at Bethel in a book of occasional journal entries, *Leaves from the Notebook of a Tamed Cynic*. They reveal a man of deep piety sincerely concerned not only with the major social issues of the day, but also with the spiritual perplexities of the humbler members of his congregation. Despite the fact that in later years Niebuhr regarded this book as representative of "the then typical notions of liberal Protestantism," there are passages that point in the direction of his mature theology. Thus, for example, in reflecting on the meaning of a funeral service, he compares religion and poetry in a way that anticipates the "aesthetic motif" of Christian realism (Niebuhr, 1929:50–51). Niebuhr comes across in this book not just as a good preacher and politician, but also as a sympathetic pastor. Through it all there is his quest for a politically relevant Christian spirituality.

Niebuhr's association with Union Theological Seminary began in 1928 and continued for the rest of his life. He considered himself especially ill-equipped to assume a professorship of applied Christianity, since he was all but self-taught in the field of theology. But at that time his lack of formal preparation was not unusual. Professors of applied Christianity—the term apparently was invented by the great Social Gospel preacher Washington Gladden (Hopkins, 1940:70)—were supposed to be politically experienced and effective in making Christianity seem relevant to the problems of modern society. In appointing Niebuhr to the professorship, Union probably hoped that he would initiate the next generation of Protestant clergy into the style of ministry he had developed at Bethel and the values that went along with it. They did not expect him to make an original contribution to academic theology.

The theological contribution that he did make while at Union remains closely related to his political experience. As the "Roaring 20s" collapsed into the Great Depression, Niebuhr became a leading spokesman for "religious socialism," a political ideology claiming to be grounded in substantively religious values. In effect it was the Social Gospel updated for hard times. Religious socialists were Christian social activists drawn from both clergy and laity, who took seriously both the "prophetic" moral values of the Bible and the apparently insoluble contradictions of the capitalistic system. In 1931 Niebuhr and other likeminded activists banded together to form the Fellowship of Socialist Christians (Merkley, 1975:104). The fellowship worked very closely with the Socialist party of America on various projects, including the efforts to organize the Southern Tenant Farmers' Union (Merkley, 1975:105). Niebuhr's relation to this project was typical of his activism at Union. By lending his services as a speaker at political rallies and as a journalist, he helped to publicize the violence suffered by union organizers, and tried to alert America's "community of conscience" to the meaning of the struggle. Throughout the period, Niebuhr stood very close to the militant wing of the Socialist party and the politics of its leader,

Norman Thomas. He supported Thomas's candidacy for president in 1932 and again in 1936, and he lent his everflowing pen to the socialist cause in periodicals like *The World Tomorrow* and *Radical Religion.*

But as the 1930s wore on, Niebuhr became increasingly disenchanted with socialist politics. The American Left was splintered by a host of ideological conflicts, inspired in part by events in Europe. Militant socialists, religious and secular alike, were confronted with something unforeseen, the threat of totalitarianism represented by Nazism in Germany and Stalinism in the Soviet Union. The factionalism that ensued was compounded by the demoralizing feeling that electoral politics held no promise of a socialist victory. When Norman Thomas failed in his bid to become governor of New York in 1938, Niebuhr became convinced that the Socialist party "must resign itself to the role of a socialistic educational force in the ranks of labor" (Merkley, 1975: 110). Two years later, he cast his first vote for Franklin D. Roosevelt, not because he admired the "New Deal," but because he feared the consequences of isolationism.

Niebuhr's increasingly frantic concern over the war and America's response to it marked a significant shift of perspective for him. This is not to say that before World War II Niebuhr had little interest in international politics, but that he tended to view it primarily in relation to trends in United States domestic politics. The impending catastrophe soon reversed these priorities, for Niebuhr realized that the survival of Western civilization was at stake in the struggle against Nazism. All domestic differences had to be subordinated to the common fight against fascism. After leaving the Fellowship of Reconciliation in 1934, Niebuhr had been critical of pacifism, but now he bitterly attacked pacifists for their political failure in the face of an "intolerable tyranny." His support for the war reached a climax with his resignation from the editorial board of *The Christian Century,* which in December 1940 still advocated a policy of neutrality. Within a year Niebuhr had founded another journal, *Christianity and Crisis,* where he was to develop his Christian realism.

Niebuhr's commitment to socialism was one of the casualties of the war. As he became increasingly critical of isolationism, his admiration for the foreign policies of Franklin Roosevelt and Winston Churchill grew. Eventually his support for Roosevelt became general, and thus he came to reexamine his previous hostility to the domestic New Deal. By every pragmatic test, Niebuhr admitted in retrospect, the New Deal had helped bring America through the Depression. As a socialist, Niebuhr had shared the common leftist prejudice that the New Deal was a desperate attempt to reform capitalism with no hope of success, and that Roosevelt was a muddle-headed Pollyanna, large on style but small on substance. But somehow the muddling approach had worked, and an American social democracy, neither purely capitalist, nor socialist, nor communist, nor fascist, had emerged as the last best hope of Western civilization. In light of its success, Niebuhr saw himself not simply as a critic who'd been proved wrong, but as a new convert now charged with interpreting this American "triumph of experience over dogma."

By the end of the war, there were many ex-socialists who felt as Niebuhr did. Together in 1947 they formed the Americans for Democratic Action, a "left-wing" political organization dedicated to support of the Allies, maintenance and extension of the New Deal social programs, and anti-communism (Merkley, 1975:154). As first vice-president of this organization, Niebuhr was a leading architect of the postwar democratic Left. In that same year, Niebuhr became an adviser to the State Department's Policy Planning Staff under George C. Marshall, and in that capacity he helped provide an intellectual basis for the "political realism" by which America's responsibilities in the postwar world were justified. His chief moral concern was to ward off any policies of adventurism that might develop from the frustrations of the cold war.[2]

Throughout this period of intense political involvement, Niebuhr deepened his theological reflections. As the professor of applied Christianity at Union Seminary, he conducted courses typically designated as "History of Christian Ethics" and "A Theological Framework for Social Ethics," which introduced students to his developing style of practical theology (Gilkey, 1975:56). In the several books that he wrote at this time, beginning with *Moral Man and Immoral Society* (1932) and ending with *The Irony of American History* (1952), he shared with his readers the various struggles—political, ideological, moral, and religious—in which he participated. In general his books present an increasingly penetrating criticism of the Social Gospel liberalism with which he began and a search for alternatives. His search led him for a while to project a synthesis involving various elements of Marxism and Christianity. But when both his political experience and his deepening appreciation for Christian values suggested that this synthesis was neither possible nor desirable, he returned to his desk and worked out the design for a Christian realism, grounded equally in the Augustinianism of the Reformation and his own hard-won political wisdom. A chance occasion, an invitation to deliver the prestigious Gifford Lectures in Edinburgh, Scotland, afforded Niebuhr an opportunity to distill from the political and religious tensions of the late 1930s his paradoxical vision of *The Nature and Destiny of Man*. That book came to be recognized as Niebuhr's *magnum opus*, for in it he came as close as he ever would to a systematic presentation of his practical theology.

The years of vigorous political action and theological reflection were interrupted suddenly by a series of illnesses, which began in 1952. Afterward his activities necessarily were restricted, and he never again was able to push himself as he had before. The quantity of his writings diminished— and some would say the same for their quality (Merkley, 1975: 202). But it was also at this time that Niebuhr received increased public recognition. The list of his self-proclaimed disciples reads like a "who's who" of American politics. As the "Establishment theologian" (Rovere, 1962:13),

Niebuhr was acclaimed for his role in articulating the "vital center" of American politics, Arthur Schlesinger's phrase for the consensus shared by the leadership of the Democratic party until recently. Niebuhr's blessing became a symbol of legitimation for many aspiring young politicians, John F. Kennedy among them (Merkley, 1975:205). More often than not, his blessing did not succeed in conveying the political wisdom for which it stood. This is not to say that Niebuhr's diminished physical strength meant a corresponding decline in intellectual vigor. Throughout the period from 1952 until his death in 1971, Niebuhr was constantly criticizing and revising his previous work in suggestive ways.[3] He did not want Christian realism to become a new standard of orthodoxy, and he could be sarcastic in his criticisms of those who did. The point is, rather, that he was unable to match his retractions with constructive proposals capable of meeting the challenges of the 1960s.

The biographical sketch just given presents only what is sufficient to illustrate the "circular relation" between Niebuhr's faith and his experience, and to propose it as the point of departure for understanding his theology. It suggests that Niebuhr inherited from his family an appreciation for the liberal side of the German-American tradition: a sturdy Protestant piety coupled with a refreshingly pragmatic approach to the challenges of the New World. First evident as Niebuhr began his ministry at Bethel, these qualities shaped his approach to any political and theological issue. Although his opinions on various matters were to change significantly over the years, this blend of piety and pragmatism remains characteristic. Thus the key to Niebuhr's theological development is that his political experience never ceased being challenged by his sensitivity to its religious dimension. However vague or ill-defined, Christian faith for Niebuhr always served as an ultimate norm for ordering his various commitments. But his sense of faith was not some dogmatic absolute removed from the vicissitudes of history. As he later came to recognize, it was related in a "circular" fashion to "the facts of experience." Thus what he knew personally as the "truth" of his experience had to be trusted as the guide to theology.

Niebuhr's reliance on experience, especially in an era as turbulent as the one that he lived through, meant that theological reflection for him became remarkably tentative and flexible. Gone were the predictable certainties of a dogmatic faith immunized against change. In their place was a challenge to do theology from an emerging historical consciousness based, as one wag put it, on a daily reading of the Bible and the *New York Times*. But while Niebuhr's understanding of the circle of faith and experience was pragmatic and open-ended, it was not totally amorphous. The structures underlying his theology are apparent in the "elective affinities"[4] that typify the various stages of his life and thought. These may be recognized by focusing more clearly on the sociological, ideological, and theological dimensions of his experience. From these dimensions the agenda for Christian realism begins to emerge.

The Pastor and His Congregation

The sociological dimension reflects those aspects of Niebuhr's experience as pastor and teacher indicative of significant social changes in American Christianity. It makes a difference, in other words, that Christian realism emerges from an urban rather than a rural parish, and from a nonspecialized congregational ministry rather than from a settlement house or from a denominational bureaucracy. As we have seen, Niebuhr grew up inside a denomination recently formed from German-language congregations united in a common loyalty to the *Kirchenverein* tradition of Prussia. Thus the German Evangelical Synod had a distinctive ethnic constituency and a small-town rural base. But when Niebuhr began his ministry, this denomination was expanding into urban America, a part of the great migration to the cities of an advancing industrial society. Historians tell us that generally Protestantism in this country was ill-prepared for this move (Herberg, 1960:117). While American Protestantism had flourished as a creative social movement on the everexpanding frontier, its very success there may have hampered its effectiveness in the new environment. Consequently, when Niebuhr was assigned to the Bethel congregation, there were few models for an urban ministry.

The most promising attempts to respond to this challenge had come under the auspices of the Social Gospel. Originally a somewhat naive exercise in "applied Christianity," the Social Gospel had enlisted the support of the older, more established denominations—the Congregationalists, Episcopalians, and Baptists—in organizing settlement houses, social action agencies, and urban missions. Under the influence of Episcopal bishop Williams, Niebuhr came to understand his ministry at Bethel as a form of the Social Gospel.

At the same time, he adapted this model to the distinctive needs of his congregation. Neither an ethnic enclave nor a union hall for autoworkers and their families, Bethel contained a cross-section of urban America, including two millionaires (Niebuhr, 1956:5). Its social and economic diversity is reflected in Niebuhr's developing style as a social activist pastor. Unlike other Social Gospel ministers—for example, Walter Rauschenbusch in Hell's Kitchen or Norman Thomas at the Spring Street Settlement House—Niebuhr opted for strategies not defined by the class-interests of his parishioners (Merkley, 1975:33). If, as he later recalled, "Ford made him a socialist," he was not yet a Marxist in any real sense. The class struggle between the proletariat and the bourgeoisie was foreign to both his thinking and his experience at Bethel. Instead, he understood the situation in more pluralistic terms, and regarded it as open to the influence of public opinion. As a preacher and later as an editor of *The Christian Century*, he naturally gravitated toward those strategies by which he might publicize political issues without compromising the essentially religious nature of his role in the community. The Great Depression and the intellectual ferment of New York in the 1930s were to bring some changes in Niebuhr's style, but for the most part these turned out to be variations on a pattern that was set at Bethel.

Niebuhr's approach to social questions, in short, was typically that of a preacher, and rarely if ever that of a denominational bureaucrat. While he showed little aptitude for political organizing or administrative routine (Merkley, 1975:96), the nonspecialized skills appropriate to his ministry were used to political advantage. His greatest weapons were an extension of the pulpit: his personal presence and his pen. Even after leaving Bethel for Union Seminary, Niebuhr gravitated toward those circles of socialist intellectuals and Christian social activists who showed similar traits. Thus the sociological dimension of Niebuhr's experience—his role in the pulpit, in the classroon, at the editor's desk, and on various interdenominational social action committees—is significant not because it represents a radical departure from the forms of the Social Gospel, but because it carried the seeds of Niebuhr's religious vision and its theological expression in Christian realism. As a pastor charged primarily with the nonspecialized task of interpreting the meaning of Christian faith for his congregation, Niebuhr finally broke with the Social Gospel because of its religious deficiencies. Disenchanted by its superficial moralizing, Niebuhr proposed Christian realism as a corrective.

The Making of an American Reformer

The ideological dimension reflects Niebuhr's changing views of American society and politics. More specifically it represents the question whether it is possible to connect Niebuhr's political ideas with his personal experience of faith and his social role as pastor and teacher. The previous remarks suggest that it is possible, perhaps even necessary, to do so. The point to be made here is that there is an elective affinity between religious socialism and the ideology of the militant socialists, and that increasing disenchantment with both accounts for the "piecemeal reform" strategy of Christian realism. The thread of continuity in this change is Niebuhr's instinctive pragmatism about experience. Niebuhr was a religious thinker long before he entered the seminary, but he became a socialist because of his experience in Detroit. There the ideology of religious socialism gradually took shape in his mind as a critical revision of the Social Gospel.

From this vantage point he began his lifelong intellectual struggle with Marxism. Like other religious socialists, both in this country and in Europe, Niebuhr hoped for a creative synthesis of Marxism and Christianity, but never without certain critical reservations. For many years, until the mid-1940s, Niebuhr's appreciation for Marxism took the following form:

Whatever the defects of Marxism as a philosophy and as a religion, and even as a political strategy, its analysis of the technical aspects of the problem of justice has not been successfully challenged, and every event in contemporary history seems to multiply the proofs of its validity. The political theories of the moralists and religious idealists who try to evade or transcend the technical and mechanical bases of justice are incredibly naive compared with them. The program of the Marxian will not create the millennium for which he hopes. It will merely provide the only possible property system compatible with the necessities of a technical age. [Niebuhr, 1935: 113]

This quotation illustrates what Niebuhr meant when he later recalled that he had appropriated Marxism to criticize "the individualism and optimism of the old liberalism" (Niebuhr, 1956:8). It provided the critical theory of society which allowed him to break with the moralism of the Social Gospel.

Furthermore, in the early 1930s Niebuhr saw promise in Marxism as a revolutionary social movement. When considered as "proletarian religion," a radical secularization of the biblical tradition of social protest, Marxism held certain political and religious advantages. It offered the kind of "fanaticism" that might be necessary to sustain a radical political commitment. Nevertheless, at no time did Niebuhr commit himself to fanaticism. Recognizing his own limits, he preferred instead a "parliamentary or evolutionary socialism" based on a "qualified Marxism" (Niebuhr, 1932b:200), the model for which he found in the ideology of the British Labour party. Despite this qualification he did not want to rule out the revolutionary option for others, but advocated a strategy by which proletarian radicals and middle-class parliamentarians might collaborate in a united front. Thus even at the height of his enthusiasm for Marxism, Niebuhr remained a pluralist politically as well as ideologically.

While this strategy coincided at the time with the position of the socialist militants, for Niebuhr it had deeper meaning as the point of departure for the synthesis of "religious socialism." This he proposed as a theological reflection on Christian faith and history. Historically, Niebuhr argued that authentically socialist values were biblical religious values in a secular form. The two were not identical, because religious values sounded a "dimension of depth in life" (Niebuhr, 1935:3) unavailable in the secular version. In faith Niebuhr accepted this "dimension of depth," insisting that without proper religious orientation the socialist commitment would oscillate wildly between fanaticism and apathy, and thereby defeat itself. Whatever Niebuhr's friends among the militants may have thought of this argument, they were not about to repudiate the much needed political support of religious socialists. The militants and their Christian allies shared a common loyalty to the Marxist critique of capitalism, a common perception of the need for a united front against both capitalism and fascism, and a common hostility to Stalinist infiltration from the Communist party (Merkley, 1975:96–98).

Since Niebuhr's initial reasons for adopting a Marxist perspective were pragmatic, so later were his reasons for abandoning it. Throughout his intellectual struggle, he always held it to the test of experience. In short, he judged Marxist theory by Soviet practice, and measured Marxism's relevance to American society by the vicissitudes of socialist politics. Regarding the Soviet Union, Niebuhr at least was consistent. While never sharing the enthusiasm of those Americans who responded to the Russian social experiment with "We have seen the future and it works!" still in the early 1930s he expressed a grudging admiration for the Russians' revolutionary "idealism" (Niebuhr, 1932b:191–99). But as the shape of the Stalinist tyranny became clearer, he denounced it sharply and began to put Marxism to the scrutiny for its totalitarian tendencies. The failure of the self-proclaimed "dictatorship of the proletariat" to organize a model Marxist society was attributed not merely to the eccentricities of the Russian national character but, more importantly, to certain strategic weaknesses in Marx's understanding of political power.

Niebuhr's suspicions about Soviet Marxism were reinforced by his experience with socialist politics at home. As World War II approached, the vision of a socialist America participating in a harmonious community of socialist nations had faded for Niebuhr. Earlier, in 1932, he had warned against nationalism, declaring that "international conflict grows out of intra-national injustice and the class struggle seeks to abolish such injustice" (Niebuhr, 1932b:229). After Munich in 1938, however, he became convinced that the strength of the American nation, notwithstanding its failure to achieve a greater measure of social justice, was crucial to the defeat of Nazism. Not everyone on the Left agreed with Niebuhr's new set of priorities. Those still loyal to a position similar to the one he advocated in 1932 were not about to compromise the class struggle by supporting America's new role as the Arsenal of Democracy. Others, however, adjusted their stance according to the short-term interests of Soviet foreign policy, supporting the antifascist Popular Front when it coincided with Comintern policy, but abandoning it in favor of isolationism after the Hitler–Stalin nonaggression pact of 1939. Niebuhr was particularly irked by the latter. For him this form of international solidarity became symbolic of the final bankruptcy of socialist politics.

As an ideology of reform, Christian realism emerged from Niebuhr's disenchantment with socialism and his growing appreciation for the pragmatic style of Roosevelt's New Deal. Not only did its compromises seem to work, but it also created the illusion of an end to ideology precisely at a time when Leftists like Niebuhr were fed up with ideological squabbling. Niebuhr believed that the New Deal had some undeniable achievements to its credit: real economic recovery and a significant improvement in the condition of the American working class. There was a sense that a new era had begun and virtually no one wished to go back to "the good old days" prior to 1929. Faced with Roosevelt's striking success, Niebuhr became a champion of "piecemeal reformism."

The most concise statement of this new position is to be found in *The Children of Light and the Children of Darkness*. Although the "Christianity" of his "new vindication of democracy" remains tacit,[5] Niebuhr there sets the tone for Christian realism in one of his best known epigrams: "Man's capacity for justice makes democracy possible; but man's inclination to injustice makes democracy necessary" (Niebuhr, 1944:xiii). The first clause is based on his theological understanding of human nature as made to the image of God; the second, on his understanding of sin. Democracy works, not in virtue of the utopian aspirations of its bourgeois defenders, but because in fact it has evolved a system that restrains the lust for power that lurks in every human being. Its processes may appear to be inefficient, but in fact they represent the most effective means for securing whatever justice and peace may be possible in human society. Since in Niebuhr's view persons exhibit both sinful and graceful tendencies, democracy works because it institutionalizes the conflicts of interest inherent in this paradox of human nature. Politics, the effort to seek proximate solutions to the perennial problems of life, must be predicated upon a humble recognition of limits: limits to human aspiration and achievement. The result is a way of approaching political problems, such as the search for an equitable distribution of property in the human community, that remains suspicious of the once-and-for-all promises of revolutionary change and resolves to take up the ambiguous and complicated quest for "rough justice." Consequently, Niebuhr rejects both bourgeois liberalism and Marxism on account of their "utopianism," in other words, because of their naive optimism about the chances for creating the perfect society. Although their visions of the perfect society diverge in significant ways, they are one in their utopian attitude toward them. In Niebuhr's opinion utopian thinking as such is destructive of politics.

Not surprisingly, this ideology of reform also exhibits the "circular relationship" of faith and experience. Niebuhr's Christian awareness of the paradox of human nature, its limits and possibilities, had dawned on him some ten years before, at the height of his struggle with leftist factionalism. At that time he announced his intention of combining "political radicalism with a more classical and historical interpretation of religion" (Niebuhr, 1934a:ix–x). What he had in mind was a practical theology based on a spirit of "religious disinterestedness." He was convinced that such a spirituality could be both genuinely radical and politically effective, because it alone promised to overcome the "fanaticism" and "cynicism" that he now detected at the heart of the ideological crisis among socialists. The "paradoxical vision" that sustained this spirituality, as we shall see, eventually became the nucleus of Christian realism as a theology. Its ideological consequences, however, slowly evolved over the next decade, as Niebuhr used it further to interpret his political experience. By the mid-1940s it provided him with Christian reasons for vindicating democracy as morally necessary for social justice and peace. Since democracy—especially the kind of democracy represented by the social programs of the New Deal— came closest to respecting the paradox of human nature, for Niebuhr it became the uniquely appropriate vehicle for a strategy of reform.

In the years following World War II, his further experience and reflection led him to declare that "rough justice" had actually been achieved in America. Furthermore, in the mid-1950s he conceded that since "organic" descriptions of society were truer to experience, he found himself sympathetic to the political theories of philosophers like Edmund Burke (Niebuhr, 1955:163–82). While the ideology of reform was not overcome by his intellectual drift in the direction of "neo-conservatism," it did become as tentative as the experience it was meant to interpret (Stone: 1972:125– 29). The problems implicit in this drift will have to be resolved lest this ideology of reform be mistaken for an "ideology of the Establishment."

An Agenda for Practical Theology

The origin of Niebuhr's distinctive religious vision and its role in shaping Christian realism forms the theological dimension of his experience. His reflections as a practical theologian, as we have seen, stemmed from his historical consciousness of the problem of being a modern Christian in a modern world. Given his sense of history, theology for Niebuhr is meant to interpret the "signs of the times." In other words, theology seeks to discover what God is allowing us—the individual believer, the community of faith, the community of all human persons—to be and to do in this particular historical moment.[6] All practical theologies do this. What distinguishes Niebuhr's is that God comes to be recognized as a "Hidden God" (Niebuhr, 1943:65–66) and therefore the process of discerning God's will in history remains ambiguous and difficult. God's hiddenness does not mean that history is devoid of religious and ethical meaning; it means, rather, that God's will is known indirectly, through a theological analysis of the content and structure of human experience and a pious meditation on the images of God as pictured in the Bible.

It is clear that, whatever else its merits,[7] the vision of God as the Hidden God greatly enhances the importance of religious discernment and theological interpretation. It requires the theologian to be sensitive to the vicissitudes, the ironies, even the paradoxes of historical experience. He or she must be gifted with a sure feeling for the difference between religious "truth" and the "vain imaginings" that obscure it, and must be ever alert to the possibility of self-deception. For if God is a Hidden God, then things are never quite as they seem. The task of scrutinizing the visions by which we live is difficult in any case, but the burden is doubled for the practical theologian. It calls not only for daily self-examen, but also for constant vigilance regarding the myths, symbols, and images taken for granted in society. If such a task is to be politically relevant, those images—the idols of the marketplace—will have to be criticized not simply for their religious disorders, but also for their ideological distortions. In other words, the practical theologian will have to address the concerns of critical social theory as well as therapeutic psychology. Otherwise his or her personal intuitions regarding the truth or falsity of religious images will remain incommunicable and politically without effect.

Although Niebuhr did not begin by emphasizing God's hiddenness, his first full-length book, *Does Civilization Need Religion?*, does address the practical problems of discernment. Subtitled, "A Study of the Social Resources and Limitations of Religion in Modern Life," it proceeds from a liberal Protestant definition of what it means to be a modern Christian:

> Personality is that type of reality which is self-conscious and self-determining. The concept of personality is valid only in a universe in which creative freedom is developed and maintained in individual life as well as in the universe. Religion therefore needs the support of both metaphysics and ethics. It tries to prompt man to ethical action by the sublime assumption that the universe is itself ethical in its ultimate nature whatever data to the contrary the immediate and obvious scene may reveal; and through the cultivation of the ethical life in man it seeks to make such a personalization of the universe both necessary and plausible. It teaches men to find God by loving their brothers, and to love their brothers because they have found God. It inspires a mystical reverence for human personality, prompted by the discovery and creation of a universe in which personality is the supreme power and value; and it persuades men to discover personal values in the universe because they have first come upon clues to the transcendent value of personality in the lives of their fellows. [Niebuhr, 1927:6–7]

If reverence for personality is the essence of religion, then the problem of discernment consists in making this "personalization of the universe" seem "both necessary and plausible." The imagination, in other words, must be disciplined by entering into the circle of faith and experience, so that "whatever data to the contrary" it may discern "the sublime assumption that the universe is itself ethical in its ultimate nature." Although initially accepted on faith, this truth will be confirmed in the experience of those who try to live it.

Niebuhr is not unaware of the difficulties facing modern Christians who seek to reorient their lives by this vision. Early on he remarks that it is "easier to challenge the idea of an impersonal universe than to change the fact of an impersonal civilization" (Niebuhr, 1927:7). This observation not only reflects his sense of the historic moment, but also suggests a significant polarity in his thought. "Impersonal civilization" contrasts with "personal religion."[8] Since "modern life" is an unstable synthesis of both elements, with destructive as well as creative possibilities, the theologian must use the resources of personal religion more imaginatively, if an impersonal civilization is to be overcome through effective political action. Yet Niebuhr criticizes religion—which for him at this time is synonymous with Christianity—because it lacks these resources: it suffers from "ethical impotence" in the face of the "social complexity" of modern life (Niebuhr, 1927:24). As a remedy he proposes that its "vital religious idealism" be integrated with an "astute intelligence . . . needed to guide moral purpose in a complex situation" (Niebuhr, 1927:140). The hoped-for result will be a "social imagination" capable of developing relevant strategies for "the ethical reconstruction of modern society" (Niebuhr, 1927:39).

Creating and sustaining this form of religious social imagination involves both practical and theoretical difficulties. These form the problematic for any exercise of religious discernment on the part of modern Christians:

Religion is therefore under the necessity of developing the critical faculty even while it maintains its naiveté and reverence. The necessity of cooperation between the naturally incompatible factors of reason and imagination, of intelligence and moral dynamic, is really the crux of the religious and moral problem of modern civilization. The complexity of modern life demands that moral purpose be astutely guided; but moral purpose itself is rooted in ultra-rational sanctions and may be destroyed by the same intelligence which is needed to direct it. Both humility and love, the highest religious virtues, are ultra-rational; yet they cannot be achieved in an intricate social life without a discriminating intelligence which knows how to uncover covert sins and to discover potential virtues. [Niebuhr, 1927: 222–23]

Thus the relationship between faith and experience is not only circular but paradoxical as well. A politically relevant discernment of "the signs of the times" calls for juxtaposing "the naturally incompatible factors of reason and imagination." If the resulting tensions are creative, a fresh understanding of the Christian vision may emerge.

Although this description of Niebuhr's agenda for practical theology and its difficulties is relatively abstract and devoid of sociological content (Stone, 1972:59), it does prefigure his philosophy of religion and therefore helps to account for some of the emphases characteristic of Christian realism. Niebuhr typically viewed religion in general and Christianity in particular, for example, as having meaning first in personal terms and only after that in terms of social groups and their histories. The social imagination he envisions is rooted in the personal sensibilities of individuals. Religion is valued for its capacity to create, criticize, and renew this kind of social imagination. As we shall see, the writings representative of Christian realism carry forward this agenda by offering arguments that favor the personal perspective fostered by Christianty on the basis of its relevance to politics. While this agenda does not make Niebuhr a personalist in the sense of one who is naive about society and politics, it does mean that Christianity's political relevance is understood primarily in terms of the Hidden God's disclosure in the hearts of individual believers. This focus helps explain why Niebuhr typically analyzes political problems in terms of "the heights and depths of human existence." While the formal outline of this perspective is present in his earliest work, his later works will elaborate it substantively. Christian realism represents a deeper penetration into its religious meaning and theological expression.

Faith Scrutinizing Experience?

This analysis of the context of Christian realism suggests that Niebuhr's theology is a reflection of the circle of faith and experience that he actually lived. There is nothing particularly novel about Niebuhr's personal discovery of this circular relationship; what is significant is that he adopted this perspective on thoroughly practical grounds. In the chapters that follow we shall see how Christian realism emerged from this circle, and shall assess its merits as a model for practical theology today. Before proceeding further, however, we should be aware of a theoretical difficulty implicit in Niebuhr's conception of the circle. His appeal to experience is so global and intuitive that it becomes virtually self-authenticating. But how does Niebuhr propose to criticize experience? Daily self-examen may be sufficient for the individual, but is it sufficient for the practical theologian who seeks to address the problems of politics? Does Niebuhr, in other words, provide a sufficient basis for public discourse about such problems? By no means blind to this difficulty, he called for an "astute intelligence" capable of disciplining the religious social imagination. His purpose was to formulate common principles for criticizing illusions, his own as well as others'. The analysis that follows shall seek to determine how well he succeeded in this effort. For now it is sufficient to record an initial suspicion: namely, that the very strength of Niebuhr's position may also be its chief weakness. His almost instinctive pragmatism about experience may make it difficult to achieve the theoretical perspective necessary to scrutinize either the idols of the marketplace or the vain imaginings of the human self. But such scrutiny is necessary if the vision of a Hidden God is to have the practical relevance that he claimed for it.

NOTES

1. In addition to Reinhold and H. Richard, Gustav and Lydia had a daughter, Hulda, the firstborn, and a son, Walter. Walter, the only one of the Niebuhr children who did not make a

mark in professional religious circles, became a businessman; Hulda became professor of Christian education at McCormick Theological Seminary in Chicago. With Hulda teaching at McCormick, H. Richard at Yale, and Reinhold at Union, the influence of the Niebuhr family on twentieth-century American Protestant seminary education is without parallel (Stone, 1972:17–18).

2. The significance of Niebuhr's contribution to the Policy Planning Staff for understanding Christian realism and judging its merits as a model for practical theology is discussed in Chapter 5. A more extensive presentation of Niebuhr's views on foreign policy is available in Stone, 1972:168–217.

3. The most challenging example of Niebuhr's later retractions is his admission of "a rather unpardonable pedagogical error in *The Nature and Destiny of Man*," made in the introduction to his last book, *Man's Nature and His Communities*. At that point Niebuhr was willing to forgo the analysis of original sin that stands at the heart of his theological anthropology. He reasoned that although his analysis was "historically and symbolically correct," he was unable to overcome the prejudices against the doctrine of original sin characteristic of modern culture (Niebuhr, 1965:23–24). In that final book Niebuhr tries to use the vocabulary of Erik Erikson's psychology to express the same points he had made earlier using the language of original sin. This retraction stands as a challenge because it is not clear that Niebuhr can rectify this "error" without abandoning "the mythical method" of Christian realism, which will be discussed here in Chapters 2 and 3.

4. The term "elective affinity" is a Weberian adaptation of the title of one of Goethe's works. In the language of Weberian sociology it represents a relationship between two independent variables within a context of meaning, which helps to explain the motive of an agent's action. Max Weber's formulation and analysis of the methodology of ideal types provides a point of departure for constructing "models" of practical theology. In attempting to identify the "elective affinities" linking, for example, the ideology of piecemeal reformism with the theology of Christian realism, or the ideology of "oppression/liberation" with the theology of liberation, I am not seeking to establish either a strictly logical deduction or a psychological relationship, but a meaningful correlation within a "world-vision" or framework for action holistically considered. For more on the methodology of ideal types, see Weber, 1964:87–157. For an example of its fruitful adaptation to the study of the interaction between religious belief systems and ideologies, see Geertz, 1971.

5. *The Children of Light and the Children of Darkness* (1944) must be understood as an application in the field of political philosophy of the theological perspective outlined in *The Nature and Destiny of Man* (1941 and 1943).

6. This definition of the task of practical theology echoes James M. Gustafson's formulation of an approach to Christian ethics (Gustafson, 1975: 156–57). The emphasis on interpreting the "signs of the times," however, is borrowed from Vatican II's *Gaudium et Spes*. It is used here to set up a comparison between Christian realism and liberation theology as practical theologies sharing a similar point of departure, but with substantively different views as to what the signs point to.

7. The French Marxist Lucien Goldmann a few years ago published *The Hidden God: A Study of Tragic Vision in the* Pensées *of Pascal and the Tragedies of Racine*. There he develops a challenging Marxist critique of the "tragic vision," which he rejects in favor of Marx's "dialectical vision." Despite the close relationship between Christian realism and Pascal's "tragic vision," I have not used this term, but coined another—the "paradoxical vision"—to describe Niebuhr's perspective. I have done this not in order to evade the impact of Goldmann's challenge, but in order to respect the peculiarities of Niebuhr's understanding of Christianity's relationship to tragedy (Niebuhr, 1937b: ix–xi, 153–70). Nevertheless, in their theological structure, Pascal's "tragic vision" and Niebuhr's "paradoxical vision" are virtually the same. And as we shall see, Marx's "dialectical vision" is the determining element in the method of liberation theology. Thus in offering a qualified defense of Niebuhr's "paradoxical vision" and a systematic criticism of liberation theology's "dialectical vision," I intend not only to provide some guidance to Christian theologians and social activists but also to respond to Goldmann's challenging development of Marxism's critique of religion. This point will be made explicit in Chapter 10.

8. The polarity between "impersonal civilization" and "personal religion" is twofold. It includes not only the contrast between "personal/impersonal," but also one involving "religion/civilization." Although both of these confirm the fact that Niebuhr's interest in religion is as a norm for social action, the latter is significant in that it exhibits Niebuhr's tendency to emphasize the "vertical" dimension of religious transcendence, i. e., the indi-

vidual's problematic of "selfhood" as the privileged point of encounter with God. This emphasis allows Niebuhr to discover and create an attractive personal spirituality, but it also makes it rather difficult to establish the connection between this spirituality and the structures of society—as he must do if Christian realism is to have the political relevance he claims for it. The polarity of "impersonal civilization/personal religion" in his earliest full-length work is the first indication of a problematic that runs throughout Christian realism as a whole, a problematic that represents both the strength and the weakness of this model for practical theology.

2

Christian Realism: A Method for Theological Reflection

*Religion is poetry. The truth in the poetry is vivified by adequate
poetic symbols and is therefore more convincing than the poor prose
with which the average preacher must attempt to grasp the ineffable.*

*Yet one must not forget that the truth is not only vivified but also
corrupted by the poetic symbol, for it is only one step from the vivid
symbol to the touch of magic. The priest does, after all, deal in magic.
When religion renounces magic it finds itself in the poor workaday
world trying to discover the glimpses of the eternal in the common
scene. That is not an easy task, but it is not an impossible one.
Wherefore let us envy the priest, but pity him too, meanwhile. He has
been betrayed by his magic. He has gained too easy a victory over
life's difficulties and he helps his people to find a premature peace.
The rivers of life in Protestant religion are easily lost in the sand, but if
they really run they carry more life than holy water.*

        —*Reinhold Niebuhr,* Leaves from the Notebook
of a Tamed Cynic, *from an entry dated 1920.*

While Niebuhr had little interest in "the nice points of pure theology," he
had even less interest in questions of theological method. Given his almost
instinctive pragmatism about both faith and experience, this is not surprising. After all, Niebuhr's concern was to criticize political and religious
"illusions," while defending the "abiding truth" of Christianity as a practical alternative to them. Such a task requires a kind of prophetic intuition
that is quick to grasp the religious meaning of any social conflict.
Methodological reflection in such circumstances could be seen as an evasion, a tempting way of avoiding the pressing demands of the historical
moment. In that case concern for theological method would signify an
apathy born of self-deception rather than the reflective distance inspired by
a true spirit of "religious disinterestedness."

Despite the fact that Christian realism thus harbors a suspicion against
method—a suspicion at once both pious and pragmatic—inevitably
Niebuhr did address questions at this level of inquiry. The complexities of
modern civilization and the ideological conflicts that they generate, as well

25

as the theoretical sophistication of theological perspectives that differed from his own, both worked to ensure that Niebuhr would have to offer more than just a promising agenda for practical theology. His reflections that reach a methodological level of inquiry consist, no doubt, in a few occasional essays and a number of tantalizing aphorisms. Nevertheless, if Christian realism is to be reconstructed as a model for practical theology, these will have to be identified and analyzed for their continued relevance.

The most familiar of these aphorisms is the typically paradoxical utterance found in *The Nature and Destiny of Man:* "It is important to take Biblical symbols seriously but not literally" (Niebuhr, 1943:50). While this assertion is introduced somewhat offhandedly in a discussion of the meaning of the kingdom of God—specifically, "the New Testament idea of *parousia*"—its significance as a formulation of the method for Christian realism is evident from the explanation that follows: "If they are taken literally the Biblical conception of a dialectical relation between history and superhistory is imperiled; for in that case the fulfillment of history becomes another kind of time-history. If the symbols are not taken seriously the Biblical dialectic is destroyed, because in that case concepts of an eternity are connoted in which history is destroyed and not fulfilled." Abstracted from its context—and perhaps even in context—Niebuhr's aphorism and the explanation that accompanies it may seem needlessly dense. Even so, its density reflects a methodological purpose, which is to give a rule for interpreting the "paradoxical vision" of humanity's conversation with a Hidden God.

For as we shall see, this vision communicates a sense of the Infinite in the finite, the transcendent in the immanent, the Eternal One in the historic many, which—while neither confusing nor separating the two—definitively represents them as a tension awaiting resolution in the figure of Christ on the cross. In light of this paradoxical vision, the Bible becomes a privileged source of religious symbols in need of interpretation. If they are interpreted literally, they no longer symbolize the hiddenness of God in history, but falsely designate his presence as a fulfillment in history. If they are not taken seriously, the opposite mistake is made: history becomes meaningless in comparison with the paramount reality of Eternity. Both of these fundamental errors are recognizable for their practical consequences: a false literalism regarding the kingdom of God inspires political "fanaticism"; and a lack of seriousness, "cynicism." The spirit of religious disinterestedness that Niebuhr contrasts to both can be sustained in a Christian "social imagination" only by taking the biblical symbols seriously but not literally.

In this chapter we shall reconstruct the emergence of this paradoxical vision and Niebuhr's attempt to formulate its meaning in a "mythical method" of interpretation. While these proposals represent one possible way of fulfilling the agenda with which Niebuhr began, they remain rather unexpected. For the substantive meaning of this paradoxical vision at first appears somewhat alien from the liberal Protestant perspective which he assumed in proposing that an "astute intelligence" be united with "vital religious idealism." Indeed, Christian realism rests on a vision which itself represents a dramatic rediscovery of the spirituality of the Reformation. But while some of Niebuhr's contemporaries in Europe—notably Karl Barth[1]—were making a similar rediscovery, his is distinctive in that it was based on thoroughly American and pragmatic grounds. As a result, the method of Christian realism remains relevant today for practical theology in the United States.

Marxism and Christianity: "A Frank Dualism in Morals"

Niebuhr's first proposed agenda for practical theology, as presented in *Does Civilization Need Religion?*, sought to graft an "astute intelligence" onto a "vital religious idealism" so that Christianity might contribute to "the ethical reconstruction of modern society." "Astute intelligence," in itself a rather vague notion, meant for Niebuhr some sort of critical social theory capable of explaining the dehumanizing effects of industrial capitalism. Such a theory was necessary, he reasoned, so that the naive and often sentimental political strategies usually inspired by the Social Gospel might be overcome. Marxism, of course, presented itself as one possible way of filling the need for "astute intelligence." The effort to bring Marxism and Christianity together in some sort of creative synthesis marks the point of departure for the method of Christian realism.

The Great Depression convinced Niebuhr that Marxism offered the only realistic framework for criticizing capitalism and for working toward socialism. As he declared later in 1935, "its analysis of the technical aspects of the problem of justice have not been successfully challenged, and every event in contemporary history seems to multiply the proofs of its validity." This much we have learned by retracing the circle of Niebuhr's faith and experience. But the question here is what impact Marxism made on his deepening insight into the meaning of Christianity. In what way did his struggle with Marxism help trigger his paradoxical vision of humanity before a Hidden God?

Early on, Niebuhr's experience suggested that Marxism was not just an "astute intelligence" but itself a form of "vital religious idealism." For his political activities in New York placed him in personal contact with Marxists who displayed all the symptoms of religious conversion. Impressed by their zeal, he saw that Marxism "is more than a doctrine. It is a dramatic, and to some degree, a religious interpretation of proletarian destiny. In such insights as this, rather than in his economics, one must discover the real significance of Marx" (Niebuhr, 1932b:154). The fact that Marxism called for a militant atheism, insisting that "the critique of religion is the beginning of all critique," did not disqualify it as a religion. Ever the student of the Social Gospel, Niebuhr knew that the Hebrew prophets had linked the denunciation of idolatry to the demand for social justice. Thus he was prepared to admit that both Marx and the Bible present a revolutionary "transvaluation of values" (Niebuhr, 1932b:154). At the same time, he did recognize a tension between these two "religions," which he tried to explain in various ways.

His first effort is formulated in terms of the question of religion and class-consciousness. In *The Contribution of Religion to Social Work*, a series of lectures delivered within a year of his appointment to Union Seminary, Niebuhr outlines a typology of three class-related religious perspectives: (1) "classical" or "orthodox" religion encapsulating the remnants of the feudal order, (2) "liberal Christianity" representative of the middle classes, and (3) "communism" identified as "proletarian religion" (Niebuhr, 1932a:68). This typology represents one form of "astute intelligence" insofar as it allows a more concrete definition of the "vital religious idealism" discussed in *Does Civilization Need Religion?* The social imagination sustained by religion differs from one class to another, and may be analyzed sociologically. Thus Niebuhr is in a position to explore his deepening disenchantment with the "sentimentalities" of liberal Christianity and to propose practical alternatives:

> Whatever may be the weaknesses of proletarian religion, it does have the vision of a just society to spur human effort, and the tremendous moral energy which that vision inspires is proof of the fact that men do not move toward high goals without religious passion. Their religion may be good or bad, judged from varying perspectives, but like all vital religions, it does create an energy which is beyond the capacities of rationalists. That fact can best be proved by comparing a modern communist, with his almost demoniac passion, with a typical liberal intellectual. If a new society is to be built, we may be sure that religion will have a hand in building it. Only religion has the power to destroy the old and to build the new. Whether that new creative religion will be absolutely destructive of the values incorporated in classical religion, or whether it will learn how to appropriate what is best in the insights of the past for its own uses, will depend to a large degree upon the ability of classical religion to come to terms with the ethico-political problems of modern industrial society, out of which proletarian religion is being born. [Niebuhr, 1932a:92–93]

While this passage suggests that Niebuhr was groping toward a sociological mode of analysis based on the recognition that religious differences seem to have a class-related basis, its overriding intention reflects the general tendency of his religious socialism: a desire for some sort of creative synthesis that will overcome the "ethical impotence" of liberal religion.

As a stage in the development of Niebuhr's theological method, this passage marks a subtle shift away from the category of "vital religious idealism" to that of "religious passion." Although both categories reflect Niebuhr's emphasis on personal religious dispositions, there is a significant difference between them. "Idealism" stresses conscious—perhaps even rational—motivations, whereas "passion" suggests a subterranean depth of religious "energy," a mood or quality of experience. As a result of this shift, the semantics of Niebuhr's religious "social imagination" appears more deeply rooted in the psychosomatic reality of human nature. The formalism of "personal religion" with which he began now opens up to substantive interpretation. Suggestive of this new direction is the fact that both Marxism and Christianity are commended for their "effective religious paradoxical attitude toward human nature."

At this time Niebuhr also experimented with other ways of comparing Marxism and Christianity as religions. If *The Contribution of Religion to Social Work* understands religion as an embodiment of class-consciousness, his next book, *Moral Man and Immoral Society*, compares them as religious ideologies proclaiming a "millennial hope." This may seem like another new departure, but in fact it is rooted in his continuing exploration of the religious social imagination. Echoing his initial understanding of "personal religion," Niebuhr redefines religion as "the poetry of the absolute": "It uses the symbols derived from human personality to describe the absolute and it finds them morally potent" (Niebuhr, 1932b: 53). This new definition allows Niebuhr to overcome the polarity of "personal religion/impersonal civilization" implicit in *Does Civilization Need Religion?* by investigating the symbolic dimension of religion. The symbols derived from human personality generate not only an uncompromising reverence for personality, but also a vision of the "absolute society."

The "millennial hope" sustained by this poetry of the absolute proclaims a state of perfect justice and peace. Niebuhr recognizes this hope in three typical moments in the history of religion in the West: (1) ancient Israel, (2) primitive Christianity, and (3) modern communism (Niebuhr, 1932b:61). Common to all three is an emphasis on "catastrophe" that encourages "fanaticism" in one form or another:

> It does not see the new society emerging by gradual and inevitable evolutionary processes. It is pessimistic about the present trends in society and sees them driving toward disaster; but its hope, as in all religion, grows out of its despair, and it sees the new society emerging out from catastrophe. [Niebuhr, 1932b:62]

Despite its catastrophism, this millennial hope is politically relevant because it creates a "social imagination" from which "present.social realities are convicted of inadequacy, and courage is maintained to continue in the effort to redeem society of injustice" (Niebuhr, 1932b:61).

While Niebuhr is not unaware of the "perils" of catastrophism, he finds the liberal's "sweet reasonableness" even more distressing. In comparison, the fanaticism of the "true proletarian" has its attractions. It may be the only "passion" capable of sustaining the struggle for a just society:

> The temptation to inertia and opportunism which the rationalistic radical faces is no less perilous. The history of parliamentary socialism is filled with evidences of it, and Christian history offers interesting analogous instances. There is only one step from a rationally moderated idealism to opportunism, and only another step from opportunism to dishonest capitulation to the *status quo*. The absolutist and fanatic is no doubt dangerous; but he is also necessary. If he does not judge and criticize immediate achievements, which always involve compromise, in the light of his absolute ideal, the radical force in history, whether applied to personal or to social situations, finally sinks into the sands of complete relativism. [Niebuhr, 1932b: 222]

The torturous paradoxes of radical politics, however, are never resolved entirely in favor of fanaticism. Even in desperate circumstances Niebuhr remained a pluralist for whom the contributions of both proletarian revolutionaries and evolutionary socialists are necessay if the goal of an absolute society is to be approximated. In practice, he hoped they would work together to resist each other's "temptation." Reflecting on the theoretical implications of this call for collaboration, Niebuhr proposed "a frank dualism in morals." Instead of the hoped-for synthesis of Marxism and Christianity, he was now willing to settle for an uneasy juxtaposition of the two, one which accepts Christian idealism as the basis of one's personal ethics, and Marxist fanaticism as the key to the social struggle.

Not surprisingly, such a frank dualism helps to focus Niebuhr's understanding of religion in a particular direction. Here Marxism and Christianity are compared as forms of "millennial hope," "apocalyptic vision," and "eschatology." In each case these categories reflect a "catastrophic" perspective and reinforce a militant social imagination. Although Niebuhr continues to note their class-related basis, he is more concerned to distinguish them according to ideological differences:

> In the eschatology of the true Christian, virtue will ultimately triumph by the power of its own strength, or by the strength supplied by God's grace. In the eschatology of the true Marxian, justice will be established because weakness will be made strong through economic forces operating with inexorable logic in human history. [Niebuhr, 1932b:155]

This comparison, of course, helps give some plausibility to Niebuhr's "frank dualism in morals." The "eschatology of the true Christian" addresses the spiritual conflicts characteristic of personal morality, while the "eschatology of the true Marxian" explains the material conflicts shaping the social struggle.

But instead of showing how it is possible to reconcile each eschatology with the other, Niebuhr reflects on their common status as meaningful illusions. The "poetry of the absolute" is subject to the paradoxical logic of religious visions, which become true by being acted upon:

> Furthermore, there must always be a religious element in the hope of a just society. Without the ultra-rational hopes and passions of religion no society will ever have the courage to conquer despair and attempt the impossible; for the vision of a just society is an impossible one, which can be approximated only by those who do not regard it as impossible. The truest visions of religion are illusions, which may be partially realized by being resolutely believed. For what religion believes to be true is not wholly true but ought to be true; and may become true if its truth is not doubted. [Niebuhr, 1932b:81]

Such "illusions," however, are politically effective only if they are taken seriously. The disenchanted radical is no radical at all. Since these illusions are cast in the form of millennial hope, their plausibility is preserved by the pull of the future. Niebuhr's frank dualism means that at this point both Marxism and Christianity are regarded in this way.

"The Problem of Communist Religion"

But such a frank dualism could not and did not last long. The uneasy juxtaposition collapsed because proletarian fanaticism proved to be a political liability. Experience convinced Niebuhr that the perils of fanaticism in fact were greater than the pitfalls of compromise. In an article, "The Problem of Communist Religion," written for *The World Tomorrow* at a time when factionalism was at a fever pitch within the Socialist party (Merkley, 1975:96), Niebuhr declared that "communism is bad religion," and bad religion "precisely because it is a political religion." Communists now are to be condemned for introducing "a demonic cruelty into social life" and for fostering "blind politics," certainly not the role envisioned earlier for "proletarian religion." In response to the ideological squabbling among American Leftists and the ominous turn of events in Europe, Niebuhr declared that something demonic had been let loose in the struggle for justice. Leftist fanaticism along with fascist cynicism were now regarded as no different from the idolatry denounced by the prophets. Since idolatry is a religious problem, it requires a religious solution:

> If the demonic enters into human life through the religious sanctification of partial and relative values it can be exorcised from social life only by the worship of a God who transcends all partial and imperfect

values. This accounts for the inability of Christianity at its best to identify itself completely with any political movement, a hesitancy which makes radicals so impatient and which deserves some of this impatience because it is frequently the screen for the social fears of privileged classes. Nevertheless life would sink to a consistent inhumanity if men did not have an object of worship and a source of meaning which transcended the values and objectives which any particular human social group may be able to project. Nor can this function of high religion be performed by critical skepticism. The worship of demons can be destroyed only by the worship of God. A negative skepticism toward unworthy objects of worship can hold religious hysteria in check only for a short time. This accounts for the fact that academic liberalism succumbed to the Nazi religion in Germany while the Church, in spite of its moribund character, resisted it. It is therefore only religion, the high religion which worships a holy God before whom all men feel themselves sinners, that can maintain the elements of decency, pity and forgiveness in human life and can resist the cruelty and inhumanity which flow inevitably from the process that absolutizes some human values and identifies others with the very source of all evil. [Niebuhr, 1934b: 379]

This insight, coming as it did after a period of intensely frustrating political activity, represents the closest thing to a religious conversion in Niebuhr's experience. Cast aside is the effort to bring together two different class-related "idealisms," "passions," or "illusions," in either a creative synthesis or a frank dualism. Instead, their incompatibility is stressed: "bad religion" must give way to "high religion," implying a decision for the one and a renunciation of the other. The worship of "a holy God before whom all men feel themselves sinners" is embraced as "a source of meaning which transcends the values and objectives which any particular human social group may be able to project." Here lies the dawning of Niebuhr's paradoxical vision of humanity before a Hidden God. Out of his felt need for "exorcism," he rediscovers the reason why "Christianity at its best" cannot "identify itself completely with any political movement."

In that moment of recognition, Niebuhr took the decisive step toward Christian realism. Without abandoning his political commitment to socialism, he now qualified it with a religious reservation. Although he had experimented with the vision of an "absolute society," he now recognized that absolutes in politics lead to the creation of "political religions." By exorcising these false absolutes, he hoped to convince others that "all human morality consists in choosing relative excellencies." Sustained by the "elements of decency, pity, and forgiveness," he now renounced the "perils of fanaticism," while still hoping to avoid the "temptation of inertia." His new agenda would involve showing how a commitment to social justice might be sustained in the labyrinth of "sober social and political judgments."

Christianity Rediscovered

The methodological implications of Niebuhr's paradoxical vision surface occasionally in *Reflections on the End of an Era*.[2] The book begins by announcing a new strategy to take the place of the discredited "frank dualism in morals":

> In my opinion adequate spiritual guidance can come only through a more radical political orientation and more conservative religious convictions than are comprehended in the culture of our era. The effort to combine political radicalism with a more classical and historical interpretation of religion will strike the modern mind as bizarre and capricious. It will satisfy neither the liberals in politics and religion, nor the political radicals nor the devotees of traditional Christianity. These reflections are therefore presented without much hope that they will elicit any general concurrence. [Niebuhr, 1934a:ix–x]

Whatever the merits of Niebuhr's suspicions about his readers, it is clear that the spiritual counsels he is about to offer will be difficult to understand, let alone to practice. For they will depend upon a recognition of the "aesthetic motif in religion" which enables Christians to perceive "the assurance of grace." Thus, Niebuhr hopes, "adequate spiritual guidance" will emerge from the paradoxical vision.

By proposing a radical spirituality centered on conservative religious convictions, Niebuhr could only have created controversy. Remember, this is an American liberal Protestant theologian speaking, albeit a socially radical one. Pious talk about an "assurance of grace" coming from such a person risks being misunderstood as obscurantism, a regression to the realm of superstition and magic. Faced with the frustrations of radical politics, was Niebuhr retreating into a supernaturalism, long before discredited among liberal Protestants? If not, then what did he mean by these "more conservative religious convictions" and this "assurance of grace"? Furthermore, how do they clarify the methodological structure of Christian realism?

Niebuhr's "assurance of grace" in effect redefines the contribution of religion to politics. The complex problems of modern civilization cannot be solved simply by juxtaposing the "naturally incompatible factors of reason and imagination, of intelligence and moral dynamic." Both "religious idealism" and "astute intelligence" must be criticized from a transcendent perspective of "pure disinterestedness." Experience suggested to Niebuhr that, left to its own resources, politics cannot comprehend this perspective. Oscillating wildly from fanaticism to cynicism on a personal level, the radical's political commitment veers back and forth between the twin perils of tyranny and anarchy (Niebuhr, 1934a:274). All too often the pendulum comes to rest in an apathetic withdrawal from the struggle. Niebuhr's diagnosis indicated that to embrace fanaticism under such circumstances through a sheer act of will was self-defeating. How then might a radical's commitment be sustained? Niebuhr's answer:

> Some way must be found to relax these tensions without destroying the validity of the absolute ideal or without tempting too premature compromises with historical forces. Whenever the tension between spirit and nature is fully felt the aesthetic motif in religion arises to compete with the ethical urge. Men find it necessary not only to approximate perfection ethically but to adjust themselves to an imperfect world in terms of aesthetic insights which, in classical religion, are expressed in the experience of grace. There is no place in either radical or liberal utopianism for the "experience of grace." The hope of realizing perfection in history has made such an experience unnecessary. When the hard realities of history have once again dissipated the utopian dreams of the present the emphasis of classical religion upon the experience of grace will find its way back again into the moral and religious life of the race. [Niebuhr, 1934a:274–75]

In other words, the frustrations of radical politics require the social activist to achieve some measure of detachment from the struggle precisely in order to be more effective in it. Religion, as it turns out, better serves as a resource for achieving "religious disinterestedness" than as a torch for rekindling the dampened fires of fanaticism.

In defining this "experience of grace," Niebuhr avoids the traditional categories of supernaturalism. He refers, instead, to an "aesthetic motif in religion." What he has in mind is a quality of religious imagination arising out of "the tensions between spirit and nature":

> Essentially the experience of grace in religion is the apprehension of the absolute from the perspective of the relative. The unachieved is in some sense felt to be achieved or realized. The sinner is "justified" even though his sin is not overcome. The world, as revealed in its processes of nature, is known to be imperfect and yet it is recognized as a creation of God. Man is regarded as both sinner and child of God. In these paradoxes true religion makes present reality bearable even while it insists that God is denied, frustrated and defied in the immediate situation. [Niebuhr, 1934a:281–82]

These "paradoxes" represent an imaginative transformation of the tension between spirit and nature based on Jesus' "religio-poetic conceptions of life and the world." Niebuhr elaborates:

> In Jesus' religio-poetic conceptions of life and the world the impartiality of nature, which to the humanist presents nature's injustice and

indicates her inability to support the moral values conceived by man, is regarded as a relevation of divine mercy which "maketh his sun to rise on the evil and the good and sendeth rain on the just and the unjust." The conception here is of a God who, in spite of his transcendence, does not negate the forces of nature but reveals himself in them. Here religious faith transmutes nature's unconcern for the moral distinctions between human good and evil into a revelation of the highest spiritual achievement: forgiving love. The very pinnacle of the spirit is found in the broad basis of natural process. The whole world process is endowed with spiritual meaning which reveals both the judgments and the mercy of God. In this imaginative insight the relation of the assurance of forgiveness to the demand for perfection in high religion is revealed at its best. Nothing in conceptions of orthodox and conventional religion approaches this profundity. [Niebuhr, 1934a:282]

Thus the religious imagination learns to see the Infinite in the finite, the transcendent in the immanent, the morality of persons in the nature of things.

The practical advantages of this "assurance of grace," however, are clearer than its "aesthetic" dynamics. Niebuhr proposes it as the key to a radical political commitment: a religious disinterestedness born of the experience of grace "guarantees the ethically striving soul a measure of serenity and provides the spiritual relaxations without which all moral striving generates a stinking sweat of self-righteousness and an alternation of fanatic illusions and fretful disillusionments" (Niebuhr, 1934a:296). It does not promote indifference to the social struggle, the kind of tired wisdom that slips into "hypocrisy" out of disgust with the bloody excesses of "vengeance." On the contrary, religious disinterestedness allows the radical to exorcise the idols of political absolutism with an assurance that overcomes the paranoid fear of compromise. Granted that this experience of grace is desirable, how is it to be made available? Where does Niebuhr find the "religio-poetic" perspective from which to imagine it? Very simply, he finds it in what he now calls Christian "mythology": "The idea of grace can be stated adequately only in mythical terms" (Niebuhr, 1934a: 290). The apprehension of grace "in mythical terms," therefore, is what constitutes "the aesthetic motif in religion."

By introducing the category of "myth" into his analysis of religion, Niebuhr adds an essential element to the methodological structure of Christian realism. The new category is introduced almost casually, but his previous work does move in that direction. Just as the transition from "vital religious idealism" to "religious passion" marked a significant shift in meaning, so does the shift from "religious passion" to religious "myth." The two are linked by the discussion of politically meaningful "illusions" in *Moral Man and Immoral Society*. With each shift in categories, Niebuhr has attempted to express the contribution of the religious imagination to

politics. Although his focus has fixed consistently on the personal dispositions motivating social activists, the trend has been to abstract these
dispositions from class-consciousness and to interpret them, first, as embodied in the psychosomatic constitution of human nature and, second, as
reflected in illusions or mythologies about history. This trend allows
Niebuhr methodologically to formulate an anthropological theory about
these dispositions that is not derived from Marxist analyses of class-
consciousness. Such a theory permits Niebuhr to represent his normative
moral and religious considerations without contradicting himself. The correlation between mythology and moral psychology provides a set of
theoretical reference points against which to map his paradoxical vision of
humanity before a Hidden God, as well as the "prophetic" insights into the
"end of an era" that are inspired by it.

Niebuhr defines myth as an integrating "vision of the whole" that
discloses the meaning of history and interprets the "signs of the times."
Such visions are available only in religion, since philosophy has become
"too empirically rationalistic." Nevertheless, there are rational criteria for
judging the success of myth in conveying the "vision of the whole":

> An adequate mythology of history must be able to do justice to the
> suggestions of meaning in momentary chaos. It must be able to realize
> that forces which are not immediately conscious of purpose, at least
> not of ultimate purpose, may be used to weave meaning into the
> strands of history. It must not be assumed that any mythology of
> history can do justice to all of its detailed facts nor that it will be
> absolutely true in the sense that it is the only possible interpretation of
> all the facts. [Niebuhr, 1934a:124]

Thus, many myths may be told, and many may appeal to the imagination;
but a successful myth must convey a transcendent meaning to history as a
whole, while remaining immanent in the structure of particular historical
events.

To illustrate this point, Niebuhr discusses three visions that compete for
the soul of modern civilization. What once were compared as "idealisms,"
as "passions," and as meaningful "illusions," are now analyzed as
"myths": the bourgeois mythology of progress, the communist mythology
of social catastrophe, and the Christian mythology of grace and atonement.
Niebuhr hopes to clarify the choices among them, since decisive action in
history is impossible apart from the assurance of meaning provided by
myth. But which myth is most appropriate? The mythology of progress in
which "human history is portrayed as the gradual triumph of mind over
impulse" (Niebuhr, 1934a:123) has been discredited by the more than
"momentary chaos" of the Great Depression. Its passing marks the end of
an era. The two remaining mythologies, Marxism and Christianity, are
interrelated because they have a common source in "Jewish apocalyp-

tic."[3] They differ in that Marxism develops the apocalyptic perspective into a dialectical vision of catastrophe and utopia, while Christianity transforms it into an eschatology centered upon a paradox: "self-realization as a legitimate, though unintended consequence of self-abnegation" (Niebuhr, 1934a:211). The depth of this paradox will be explored in his later works; at the moment, however, he invokes it as an indication of the practical superiority of Christianity over Marxism. While both qualify as "adequate mythologies," since both seem " to do justice to the suggestion of meaning in momentary chaos," the Christian eschatology has greater political relevance because it assures "the inspiration of a high morality and a consolation for the frustrations which moral purpose faces in history" (Niebuhr, 1934a:280). In other words, the Christian myth imaginatively portrays a spirit of religious disinterestedness that is not possible in Marxism. Thus the substantive insights that emerged from Niebuhr's experience of the political frustrations of the mid-1930s here are expressed in the categories of paradox and myth, which in turn will form the basis for the method of Christian realism.

The "Mythical Method" of Interpretation

Niebuhr's next book, *An Interpretation of Christian Ethics,* is a first attempt to reflect systematically on the transcendent perspective that he found in Christian myth. It is organized around the central figure in that myth, Jesus of Nazareth, and the understanding that the myth affords of what has come down to us as Jesus' moral teaching. The connection between the myth and the moral teaching needed clarification because, in Niebuhr's view, it has been obscured in the ethics of both Christian liberalism and orthodoxy. Since neither of them can recognize the myth as myth, neither understands the ethic of Jesus. By making the connection plain, Niebuhr hopes to formulate the ground rules for an "independent Christian ethic," one that will transform the aesthetic motif in religion into a coherent program for personal and social morality. Although the tone of this book is somewhat detached from the pressing political and spiritual concerns of *Reflections on the End of an Era,* it does not represent a new departure in Niebuhr's thought. While the comparison between Marxism and Christianity fades in importance, Niebuhr now concentrates upon the internal logic of the Christian myth and its constructive implications for religion and morality. For the issue at stake in that comparison by now had been resolved. With the abandonment of "political religion" and the rediscovery of Christianity as a "high religion" mediating the "assurance of grace" in the worship of a holy God, Niebuhr felt called upon to clarify theologically the meaning of his paradoxical vision.

Niebuhr's proposal for an "independent Christian ethic" is based on a recognition of the fact that both the liberals and the orthodox have failed to measure up to "the absolute and transcendent ethic of Jesus" (Niebuhr,

1935:5). Liberal Christianity fails because it is "unduly dependent upon the culture of modernity" (Niebuhr, 1935:1). The reason this dependence is wrong is not simply because bourgeois society faces the end of an era, but because an undue dependence on any culture compromises the ethic of Jesus. Orthodox Christianity has the opposite problem. In refusing to give even due recognition to modernity, it attains independence at the price of irrelevance: "Its religious truths are still imbedded in an outmoded science and . . . its morality is expressed in dogmatic and authoritarian moral codes" (Niebuhr, 1935:2). Since on both accounts the ethic of Jesus is taken literally—but not seriously—as a "possible and prudential ethic," Niebuhr in rejecting them wishes to take it seriously—but not literally—as a "relevant but impossible ethical ideal." How he proposes to do this becomes clear as he spells out the implications of his "mythical approach" to Christianity.

Understanding Christianity as a "mythical religion" allows Niebuhr to introduce the "mythical method" of interpretation. Religion in general discloses a "dimension of depth in life" by providing life with "a unity and coherence of meaning" (Niebuhr, 1935:3). Religion seeks to "trace every force with which it deals to some ultimate origin and to relate every purpose to some ultimate end." Its visions of an ultimate coherence beyond all conflicting experiences, not surprisingly, hinge upon "the relation between the finite and the eternal" (Niebuhr, 1935:8). Typically, there are two strategies for comprehending this relation: mystical religion and mythical religion. While both represent transcendence, they do so as polar opposites.

In Niebuhr's view, "mystical religion" affirms transcendence by denying immanence:

> The mystical carries the rational passion for unity and coherence to the point where the eye turns from the outward scene, with its recalcitrant facts and stubborn variety, to the inner world of spirit, where the unity of self-consciousness becomes the symbol of, and the means of reaching, the Absolute, a type of reality which is "beyond existence," "a mysterious silent stillness which dissolves consciousness and form" (Hierotheus). Thus religion, seeking after the final source of life's meaning and its organizing center, ends by destroying the meaning of life. Historic and concrete existence is robbed of its meaning because its temporal and relative forms are believed not worthy to be compared to the Absolute; but the Absolute is also bereft of meaning because it transcends every form and category of concrete existence. Mysticism is really a self-devouring rationalism which begins by abstracting rational forms from concrete reality and ends by positing an ultimate reality beyond all rational forms. [Niebuhr, 1935:14–15]

Niebuhr's reasons for rejecting mystical religion are both theoretical and practical. Theoretically, mysticism allows "the eternal forms which give body to temporal reality" to become "dissociated from it." Thus "the eternal becomes an undifferentiated transcendence." In other words, since mystical religion accomplishes the disembodiment of the Infinite, it represents a form of "bad" transcendence. Its practical inadequacies are a result of this badness. If history is "robbed of its meaning," then politics becomes impossible. More specifically, Niebuhr argues that both the "optimism of philosophical monism" and the "pessimism of dualistic mysticism" stem from this disembodiment of the Infinite. Since both perspectives fail to understand the "tragic realities of existence" and therefore are psychologically "detrimental to high moral passion" (Niebuhr, 1935:15), neither provides the adequate spiritual guidance necessary for sustaining a radical political commitment.

"Mythical religion" avoids condemnation by being paradoxical, insisting that the eternal is embodied through the finite, and cannot be grasped apart from it:

Myths are not peculiar to Hebrew religion. They are to be found in the childhood of every culture when the human imagination plays freely upon the rich variety of facts and events in life and history, and seeks to discover their relation to basic causes and ultimate meanings without a careful examination of their relation to each other in the realm of natural causation. In this sense mythical thinking is simply pre-scientific thinking, which has not learned to analyze the relation of things to each other before fitting them into its picture of the whole. Perhaps the simplest mythical thought is the animistic thought of the primitives in which each phenomenon of the natural world is related to a quasi-conscious or quasi-spiritual force with little or no understanding of the web of cause-effect relationships in the natural world itself. But mythical thought is not only pre-scientific; it is also supra-scientific. It deals with vertical aspects of reality which transcend the horizontal relationships which science analyzes, charts, and records. The classical myth refers to the transcendent source and end of existence without abstracting it from existence.

In this sense the myth alone is capable of picturing the world as a realm of coherence and meaning without defying the facts of incoherence. Its world is coherent because all facts in it are related to some central source of meaning; but is not rationally coherent because the myth is not under the abortive necessity of relating all things to each other in terms of immediate rational unity. The God of mythical religion is, significantly, the Creator and not the First Cause. [Niebuhr, 1935:15–16]

Mythical religion, in other words, is "good" transcendence because it "refers to the trancendent source and end of existence without abstracting it from existence." The eternal remains embodied and therefore both immanence and transcendence are taken seriously. Given mythical religion's origin in the free play of the human imagination, almost by definition it involves a problem of interpretation. The "supra-scientific" must be distinguished from the "pre-scientific" aspect of mythical thought so that the genuinely paradoxical attitude will not be confused with that which is merely "animistic." Unless this distinction can be made, there is no basis for appreciating myth's abiding truth while criticizing its vain imaginings. Niebuhr's "mythical approach" therefore concentrates on the "supra-scientific" truth in Christian myth.

Instead of developing this theory of mythical religion systematically, Niebuhr illustrates it primarily through an analysis of Christianity. Although the Christian religion throughout its history displays certain affinities to the mystical type, it has never abandoned the central thrust of Hebrew spirituality derived from the myth of a creator God. Consequently, Christianity affirms the world as "a realm of meaning and coherence without insisting that the world is totally good or that the totality of things must be identified with the Sacred" (Niebuhr, 1935:16). Viewing the world in this way means emphasizing God's transcendence without diminishing his immanence. It means understanding God as the Hidden God, "a God that *hidest thyself*, O God of Israel the Savior *(Isaiah xlv)*" (Niebuhr, 1935:17). In light of the myth of a creator God, the problem of accounting for evil in the world and human responsibility for it becomes acute. Monotheistic faith in a Hidden God promotes an "ethico-religious passion" in which "the whole of existence" becomes an object of moral concern. In theory there are several inadequate responses to this concern within the framework of mythical religion, each of which unduly relaxes tensions between transcendence and immanence. Not surprisingly, Niebuhr mentions Manichaeism and Gnosticism, which tend once more toward the disembodiment of the Infinite; but he also includes the "sacramentalism of Christian orthodoxy" where embodiment tends toward idolatry: "The natural world (including unfortunately the social orders of human history) is celebrated as the handiwork of God; and every natural fact is rightly seen as an image of the transcendent, but wrongly covered so completely with the aura of sanctity as to obscure its imperfections" (Niebuhr, 1935: 20). In contrast to this "constitutional disease" of mythical religion, the Hebrew prophetic movement fosters a spirituality capable of enjoying "the pleasures of this life without becoming engrossed in them," and affirming "the significance of human history without undue reverence for the merely human." Here the tensions generated by the paradoxes of mythical religion are sustained by affirming even more emphatically the worship of a holy God, the Judge and Redeemer of the world. The figure of Jesus, for Niebuhr, is the perfect expression of this prophetic insight.

At the heart of this "prophetic Christianity" Niebuhr finds the ethic of Jesus. Even while celebrating the goodness of his Father's creation, Jesus taught a love that judges and redeems the natural loves of human persons. In this sense, the ethic of Jesus "proceeds logically from the presuppositions of prophetic religion" (Niebuhr, 1935:22). As an absolute ideal, Jesus' "love ethic" judges every expression of human egoism, both individual and collective, by showing up the inevitable corruption involved in every form of self-realization. But it also promises to redeem human love by embodying an invitation to self-sacrifice: "He that findeth his life shall lose it; and he that loseth his life for my sake, shall find it" (Matt. 10:39). Faced with this invitation, however, Niebuhr insists that "the ethical demands made by Jesus are incapable of fulfillment in the present existence of man" (Niebuhr, 1935:35). If so, then what good are they? He argues that they are a relevant but impossible ethical ideal. But how the ideal of love can be both impossible and yet relevant is understood only against the background provided by the Christian cycle of myths.

The Christian Cycle of Myths

In applying the "mythical method" to the Christian myths of Creation, the Fall, and Atonement, Niebuhr interprets them for the "supra-scientific" truth of the human situation before a Hidden God, while ignoring the "pre-scientific" cosmogonies in which these truths are framed. His purpose throughout this exercise is to allow the paradoxical vision that he discerns in Christian myth to provide an ultimate coherence of meaning in which the ethical demands of Jesus may be taken seriously, but not literally. In this way, Christianity will continue to be a source of adequate spiritual guidance for social activists, without succumbing to the temptations represented by either "fanaticism" or "inertia."

The myth of Creation provides a context for understanding the totality of human aspiration and achievement. In Niebuhr's view, it discloses human nature's true bearing as the "image of God." Thus the "dimension of depth in life" is recognized as having ultimate religious significance. But since the creator is understood paradoxically as a Hidden God, the "image of God" is also paradoxical. Niebuhr describes it as follows:

This paradoxical relation of finitude and infinity, and consequently of freedom and necessity, is the mark of the uniqueness of the human spirit in the creaturely world. Man is the only mortal animal who knows that he is mortal, a fact which proves that in some sense he is not mortal. Man is the only creature imbedded in the flux of finitude who knows that this is his fate; which proves that in some sense this is not his fate. Thus when life is seen in its total dimension the sense of God and the sense of sin are involved in the same act of consciousness; for to be self-conscious is to see the self as a finite object separated from essential reality; but also related to it, or there could be no knowledge of separation. If this religious feeling is translated into moral terms it becomes the tension between the principle of love and the impulse to egoism, between the obligation to affirm the ultimate unity of life, and the urge to establish the ego against all competing forms of life. [Niebuhr, 1935:40]

When juxtaposed in this way, finiteness and freedom suggest both limits to human resources but also indeterminate possibilities within those limits. Somehow the recognition of limits suggests the imaginative possibility of limitlessness. Thus, for example, human persons aspire to perfection but never attain it. We thirst for omniscience, yet forget most of what we once knew. The pieces of proverbial wisdom—both trivial and profound—indicative of this paradox could be extended indefinitely; the point, however, is that they evoke a mood which Niebuhr identifies as religious, which he accounts for by recalling the "supra-scientific" truth in the myth of Creation. Made "to the image and likeness of God," we feel a constant tension between our aspirations and achievements because God created us that way, and we are encouraged to believe that he did so lovingly. We are charged with the task of living within limits, and not using them as an excuse either for aggression against others or for escape from common responsibilities. The myth of Creation, when interpreted according to the "mythical method," provides a "unity and coherence of meaning" along these lines.

The second movement of the cycle, the myth of the Fall, accounts for the fact that inevitably human persons refuse to live within limits. The paradox of finiteness and freedom becomes the source of evil as well as good. Niebuhr interprets the myth for the "pyschological and moral" truth it contains about human evil:

It is in its interpretation of the facts of human nature, rather than in its oblique insights into the relation of order and chaos as such, that the myth of the Fall makes its profoundest contribution to moral and religious theory. The most basic and fruitful conception flowing from this ancient myth is the idea that evil lies at the juncture of nature and spirit. Evil is conceived as not simply the consequence of temporality or the fruit of nature's necessities. Sin can be understood neither in terms of the freedom of human reason alone, nor yet in terms of the circumscribed harmonies in which the human body is bound. Sin lies at the juncture of spirit and nature, in the sense that the peculiar and unique characteristics of human spirituality, in both its good and evil tendencies, can be understood only by analyzing the paradoxical relation of freedom and necessity, of finiteness and the yearning for the eternal in human life. [Niebuhr, 1935:46–47]

The myth of the Fall, therefore, defines as "sin" the typical pattern of human response to the anxieties generated by the paradox of finiteness and freedom. In the complicated relationship between Adam and Eve and the Serpent, Niebuhr would have us discover the "supra-scientific" truth that sin both is and is not the ultimate source of moral evil in the world, and that sin is inevitable but not necessary. Immersed in a situation of "sin," human persons experience a sense of guilt along with the worship of a holy God. This sense of guilt—a recognition of the alien, the demonic, the unholy in ourselves—is explained in the myth of the Fall by linking it symbolically to an original rebellion against God.

Niebuhr's emphasis on the myth of the Fall and insistence on the truth of human sin has troubled many of his readers, both admirers and critics; nevertheless, the insights thus afforded are essential to his understanding of human nature. Perhaps no other aspect of his "more classical and historical interpretation" of Christianity was so controversial at the time he first proposed it. Religious liberals and secular intellectuals saw no meaning in this myth other than "the expression of a primitive fear of the higher powers"; for them it could not be taken seriously. Orthodox Christians took it literally as "an account of the origin of evil, when it is really a description of its nature." Thus Niebuhr's interpretation was attacked from both the left and the right by those who had a special interest in the traditional doctrine of original sin, either to affirm its view of "inherited corruption" as God's revelation or to dismiss it as indicative of "a darkly unconscious human fear of the very adventure of human existence." In contrast to both, Niebuhr hoped to interpret the myth as the embodiment of an abiding truth about "the dimension of depth in life." By insisting on the reality of the evil "that lies at the juncture of nature and spirit," he proposed to define the limits of human aspiration and achievement and thereby to overcome the superficialities of both optimism and pessimism regarding them.

Niebuhr interprets the final movement of the cycle, the myth of the Atonement, in terms of the situation disclosed in the myths of Creation and the Fall. The myth of the Atonement provides a model for living the paradox of finiteness and freedom with a renewed sense of humility. While the figure of Jesus[4] embodies an ethic of "sacrificial love" that promises to overcome the sense of guilt experienced as "sin," the human paradox finds an echo in the fact that the love that Jesus commands is as necessary as it is impossible. The myth of the Atonement illumines the religious purpose of this moral paradox by teaching human persons to utter a "cry of distress and contrition." Typically Niebuhr finds this paradox no more surprising than the fact that "every high mountain has a 'timber line' above which life cannot maintain itself" (Niebuhr, 1935:62). Just as the "majesties and tragedies" symbolized by the timber line should not be the occasion for "indifference" to the tasks of sustaining human life in the wilderness, so the "impossibile possibility" that marks the summit of Christian ethics is neither a "pure negation" of "natural morality" nor an expression of the futility of human endeavor. On the contrary, in Niebuhr's view it enhances them by giving coherent definition to the limits of human possibility.

The myth of the Atonement and the ethic of Jesus thus together symbolize a reconciliation that is an imaginative possibility for those willing to enter the circle of Christian faith and experience. But just as "sin" is recognized in a personal "dimension of depth," so the reconciliation afforded by the Atonement remains personal as well. Niebuhr explains:

> It is possible for individuals to be saved from this sinful pretension, not by achieving an absolute perspective upon life, but by their recognition of their inability to do so. Individuals may be saved by repentance, which is the gateway to grace. The recognition of creatureliness and finiteness, in other words, may become the basis for man's reconciliation to God through his resignation to his finite condition. But the collective life of mankind promises no such hope of salvation, for the very reason that it offers men the very symbols of pseudo-universality which tempt them to glorify and worship themselves as God. [Niebuhr, 1935:55]

The lack of symmetry here distinguishing individual from collective hopes for salvation underscores the paradoxical quality of Niebuhr's "assurance of grace." Because it is not supernatural in any objective sense, this assurance can be effective only when persons open themselves to it. This is what Niebuhr means by the "aesthetic motif in religion." Transforming the religious "social imagination" with a "cry of distress and contrition" necessarily is a personal movement of spirit; it may have an impact on social action, but only as it shapes the political commitments of individuals. To allow any broader interpretation of the myth of the Atonement, for Niebuhr, would be to fall into the idolatrous "sacramentalism" that stands opposed to "prophetic Christianity" as its inevitable temptation.

Thus the "independent Christian ethic" is understood against the background provided by the myths of Creation, the Fall, and Atonement. The myths describe human nature in such a way that it stands in irreducible tension to the command of Jesus. Instead of rejecting the command because of its impossibility, Niebuhr proposes to retrieve it as an ideal that both judges our achievements and yet lures us on to imagine possibilities that otherwise might never be attempted. Such an ideal, to be morally effective, is based upon two difficult truths: an unflinching realism about human nature ultimately inspired by a religious awareness of its limits and possibilities, and an uncompromising loyalty to the absolute moral demands of Jesus qualified by a humble recognition of our inability to fulfill them. When placed in creative tension these two truths represent Christian realism, both as a way of life embodying a rediscovery of one authentic form of Christian spirituality and as a method of interpreting the truth in the myths that underlie this spirituality.

The Truth in Myth

Granted that Niebuhr's "independent Christian ethic" is based on a mythical approach to Christianity, is there any evidence that he used it as a method in his later works? In fact there is: the pattern of thought outlined in the mythical method of *An Interpretation of Christian Ethics* is present with little modification throughout his later writings. Moreover, in at least four essays written at various times throughout this period, he either elaborates on this method or reformulates it, using different theological vocabularies.[5] These essays are as close as Niebuhr ever comes to methodological reflection on the basic categories of his thought.

If the method itself is paradoxical, so is Niebuhr's defense of it. He chooses perhaps the most obscure of Pauline metaphors to convey the sense of his approach. Among other things, St. Paul declares that "the ministers of God" must proceed "as deceivers yet true" (2 Cor. 6:8). Niebuhr takes this to mean that "what is true in the Christian religion can be expressed only in symbols which contain a certain degree of provisional and superficial deception" (Niebuhr, 1937b:3). Deception is risked because Christian truth cannot be expressed in straightforwardly rational ways. Christianity must bear witness to the fact that "the ground and fulfillment of existence lie outside of existence, in an eternal and divine will," while recognizing that it is impossible to give rational expression to an eternal and divine will. The existence in which and for which the divine will is revealed is historical and finite, as is all language used to interpret it, while the divine will itself is infinite and eternal:

> The relation between the temporal and the eternal is dialectical. The eternal is revealed and expressed in the temporal but not exhausted in it. God is not the sum total of finite occasions and relationships. He is their ground and they are the creation of His will. But, on the other hand, the finite world is not merely a corrupt emanation from the ideal and eternal. Consequently the relation of time and eternity cannot be expressed in simple rational terms. It can be expressed only in symbolic terms. [Niebuhr, 1937b:4]

Rather than accept this situation as an insoluble contradiction reducing theologians to silence, Niebuhr embraces it as a paradox calling them to be "as deceivers yet true."

Niebuhr recognizes that the task of communicating the truth of this paradoxical vision puts the theologian in a difficult position. His every attempt to speak of God necessarily will fail to embody the truth. Since human nature created to the image of God is no less paradoxical than the language used to describe it, the Christian theologian must deal "in mysteries without which man remains a mystery to himself." How, then, is the theologian's task to be understood? Ever faithful to the "aesthetic motif in religion," Niebuhr draws an analogy between the theologian and the portrait artist. An artist, he says,

> falsifies some of the physical details in order to arrive at a symbolic expression of the total character of his subject, this total character being a transcendent fact which is never completely embodied in any given moment of the subject's existence. A really great portrait goes beyond this and not only symbolizes the transcendent personality of the subject, but contains suggestions of a universal mood. The artistic license of the artist belongs in the same category as the artistic license of religion. In both cases it is subject to abuses. The artist may falsify reality and produce a caricature of his subject rather than a true portrait; and religious myths may falsify the facts of history and experience. But at their best, both artist and prophet reveal the heights and depths of human experience by picturing the surface with something more and less than scientific exactness. [Niebuhr, 1937a:27; cf. 1937b:4–6]

Embodying the Infinite in the finite, in other words, is a task that proceeds by way of indirection. "The heights and depths" cannot be reduced to the formulae of rational coherence, but they can be portrayed in a way that will evoke an imaginative response of self-recognition.

Admittedly, these reflections while suggestive, are vague; Niebuhr, however, occasionally was able to be more specific. In another of these essays on method, "The Truth in Myths," he considers the question, "What are the aspects of reality which can be stated only in mythical terms?" and answers with "the aspect of value" and "the dimension of depth in existence" (Niebuhr, 1937a:16–17). This response involves him in a complicated argument, for here he must defend myth against the competing claims of poetry, science, mysticism, and philosophy.

Given his fondness for the "aesthetic motif in religion," Niebuhr not surprisingly has a difficult time distinguishing religious myth from poetry. Borrowing a line from George Santayana, he observes that "poetry is religion which is no longer believed." From this he infers that poetry—at least in modern times—is tacitly skeptical about the representation of ultimate value. It "merely asserts values in terms of the goods and purposes of an individual in a given instance." By contrast, religious myth "seeks to comprehend facts and occurrences in terms of their organic relation to the whole conceived in teleological terms." Thus, while poetry is restricted to a private quest for personal meaning, religious myth has a public and social dimension. Consequently, it may conflict with science in a way that is foreign to poetry.

Both science and religious myth have reference to coherences found in the real world. But, while science investigates sequences observed in nature and history, "these sequences," according to Niebuhr, "reveal nothing of the internal unity in all organic growth." Since science thus is restricted to the field of "mechanistic interpretation," there can be no scientific analysis of "the aspect of value."[6] Religious myth, by contrast, embodies that aspect because it is not reducible to a primitive form of science. Echoing his previous remarks about "pre-scientific" and "supra-scientific" dimensions of myth, Niebuhr bases this claim on a distinction between "primitive myth" and "permanent myth." Insofar as the speculations of primitive myth conflict with the findings of modern science, they are abandoned as obsolete. These are what most people have in mind when they equate science with truth and myth with falsehood. Permanent myth, however, is the dimension of myth that discloses "abiding truths" about the human situation, thus conveying a sense of the meaning and value of human life as a whole. Since these "abiding truths" are "organic" and cannot be fully rationalized, in principle there can be no conflict between permanent myth and science.

The differences among myth, mysticism, and philosophy have another basis: each represents an alternative interpretation of the "dimension of depth" in existence. Both mysticism and philosophy are inadequate, says Niebuhr, because both presuppose a purely rational approach to myth. Mysticism's mistake is to bypass myth in its search for abiding truth. The result is a disembodied transcendence: "The God it found was emptiness and void" (Niebuhr, 1937a:28). Philosophy, in both its idealistic and its materialistic forms, seeks to interpret the meaningful in terms of the rational. Since, as Niebuhr contends, reason itself is only an instrument for drawing logical conclusions and not a substantive vision of reality, philosophy cannot attain to either the aspect of value or the dimension of depth through reason alone. To the extent that philosophers in their wisdom actually do succeed in illuminating these things, they do so by presupposing what Niebuhr calls "covert myth," an unacknowledged dependence on "abiding truth" orginally disclosed in religious myth (Niebuhr, 1937a:20). Niebuhr argues that what philosophers now and then do covertly should be done deliberately and openly; but this would mean "a return to a purer mythical approach," which entails the recognition of a distinctive role for theology.

Niebuhr is well aware that a return to theology and myth brings with it the risk of dogmatism. Yet he asserts that the mythical approach is just as far from dogmatism as it is from skepticism. In minimizing the risk of dogmatism, he hopes to justify his approach by appealing to experience. Other theologies—notably that of Karl Barth—are inadequate because "there is no effort to validate Christianity in experience against competition with other religions." Niebuhr elaborates:

How is it possible to avoid this dogmatism? It is possible only if it is realized that though human knowledge and experience always point to a source of meaning in life which transcends knowledge and experience, there are nevertheless suggestions of the character of this transcendence in experience. Great myths have actually been born out of profound experience and are constantly subject to verification by experience. [Niebuhr, 1937a:30]

Niebuhr's strategy for validating the truth in myths thus is certainly consistent with his insight into the circular relation of faith and experience. Furthermore, it promises to place a certain kind of critical check upon Niebuhr's theology and ethics, thus confirming their tendency toward Christian realism. Nevertheless, this suggestion of "transcendence in experience" needs further clarification.

Metaphysics and Myth

Although Niebuhr previously had suggested some sort of metaphysical understanding of the truth in myths—asserting, for example, that "these mythical terms are the most adequate symbols of reality because the reality which we experience constantly suggests a center and source of reality, which not only transcends immediate experience, but also finally transcends the rational forms and categories by which we seek to apprehend and describe it" (Niebuhr, 1937a:31)—a clarification was actually attempted in the essay "Coherence, Incoherence, and Christian Faith," first published in 1951. Unlike his previous efforts, which usually reasserted the reality of the circle of faith and experience while insisting on the paradoxical vision that he found there, this essay outlines a metaphysical strategy for showing the reasonableness of this perspective.

Niebuhr's strategy is based on certain generalizations about the nature of human experience and the limits of interpretability: "The whole of reality is characterized by a basic coherence. . . . The whole world is organized or it could not exist; if it is to be known, it must be known through its sequences, coherences, causalities, and essences" (Niebuhr, 1953:175). Thus "we instinctively assume that there is only one world and that it is a cosmos." This assumption stands behind every philosophical attempt to do metaphysics. Nevertheless, inevitably these attempts fail because "in the one world there are many worlds, realms of meaning and coherence; and these are not easily brought into a single system." Thus rational coherence cannot be made "the basic test of truth"; in fact, the incoherences introduced by the existence of "genuine freedom" suggest that a paradoxical vision of God, humanity, and the world may be the ultimate in human understanding (Niebuhr, 1953:178). Thus Niebuhr proposes to use a philosophical analysis of experience to reject all possible metaphysical systems based on principles of rational coherence. In the theoretical space created by this move, he hopes to introduce a "consideration of the relation of the supra-rational affirmations of the Christian faith to the antinomies, contradictions, and mysteries of human existence" (Niebuhr, 1953:179). Furthermore, the appeal to experience is not exhausted by the deconstruction of metaphysics; it also is used to reconstruct a "Christian doctrine of selfhood," which in the name of "biblical realism" provides a perspective for "interpreting the drama of human history as an engagement between man and God" (Niebuhr, 1953:197).

The resort to the perspective afforded by permanent myth, therefore, is justified in light of the rationally determined limits of all other interpretations of the world:

> There is, in short, no possibility of fully validating the truth of the Gospel if every cultural discipline is not taken seriously up to the point where it becomes conscious of its own limits and the point where the insights of various disciplines stand in contradiction to each other, signifying that the total of reality is more complex than any scheme of rational meaning which may be invented to comprehend it. [Niebuhr, 1953:196]

Given the metaphysical fact that experience is characterized by both "coherence" and "incoherence," rational systems of metaphysical belief are impossible. Since some sense of the ultimate coherence of things is necessary for decisive historical action, the search for abiding truth in myth thereby becomes reasonable. This search can be conducted critically if its metaphysical limits are respected. Dogmatism can be avoided if the "mythical method" continues to take its truth seriously but not literally. Despite the theoretical importance of this strategy, Niebuhr never pursued it with any rigor. Christian realism was born out of practical conflicts over the shape of "adequate spiritual guidance" for politicians and Christian social activists. His methodological reflections were to remain ad hoc, even though promising.

Method and Theology

While the categories of the "mythical method" of interpretation are characteristic only of Niebuhr's work of the late 1930s and early 1940s, the pattern of his later thought follows the same approach even as his theological vocabulary continues to change. Thus his discussions of the relationship of "mystery and meaning" (Niebuhr, 1946:152–73) and the dialectic of "coherence, incoherence, and Christian faith" (Niebuhr, 1953:175–203), bear a different relationship to Christian realism than do the earlier proposals couched in terms of religious "idealisms," "passions," and "illusions," as well as the various forms of "astute intelligence" needed to make them politically relevant. The difference consists in his rediscovery of one form of authentically Christian spirituality, the paradoxical vision that emerged from the political and spiritual turmoil of 1934. The proposals sketched out prior to that moment of truth and the semantic shifts implicit in them are interesting for their formal characteristics, but for the most part they remain rooted in the perspective that Niebuhr identified with Social Gospel liberalism. Nevertheless, their formality should not be despised: although the paradoxical vision had yet to emerge with full clarity, in these earlier efforts a significant trend can be discerned. Consistently, Niebuhr seeks to represent the truth of religion, not as an abstract value amenable to one form of reductive analysis or another, but as a substantive reality known only by way of "aesthetic" indirection. Even before the paradoxical vision emerged, Niebuhr recognized the nonstraightforward character of the truth in religious "passions" and "illusions." Even as it emerged and afterward, he insisted that the paradoxical vision was available only as myth.

The question of a "mythical method" of interpretation, therefore, was always premised on this concern for religious "truth" and its availability. If "the aesthetic motif in religion" were to have political relevance, it could not remain encapsulated in Niebuhr's personal sensibilities. Some way had to be found to dramatize its meaning and give it theological plausibility. This is what Niebuhr intended by the "mythical method." Since he was not inclined to pursue its implications in a general theory of what Paul Ricoeur has labeled a "poetics of the will," the method remained sketchy and tentative. But following Niebuhr's own sense of the issue, its validity may be assessed in terms of the theology that it actually made possible.

NOTES

1. It is a mistake to identify Niebuhr's theology too closely with the "dialectical theology" then making headway in Europe, as Paul Merkley does in *Reinhold Niebuhr: A Political Account*. While Niebuhr's thinking was enriched by his reading of theologians like Karl Barth and Emil Brunner, the major developments in his thought occurred independent of their influence. In fact, he is consistently critical of the political thinking of these theologians (cf. his remarks on Brunner in Niebuhr, 1935:95), and regarding Barth especially, he insisted on the epistemological differences separating "Barthian dogmatism" from Christian realism. In particular, he criticized Barth for failing to admit "a point of contact between the Gospel and the religious yearnings of mankind," which rendered his interpretation of the Bible at once "more literalistic and allegorical" than a genuinely mythical approach (Niebuhr, 1953:193–96). As the Preface to *An Interpretation of Christian Ethics* makes clear, the one theologian who did influence Niebuhr's formulation of the circle of faith and experience was his new colleague, the émigré Paul Tillich.

2. In discussing *Reflections on the End of an Era* after the article in *The World Tomorrow*, I am reversing the historical sequence, since *Reflections* was written earlier, during the winter of 1933–34. I take it up after the article on "The Problem of Communist Religion" because the latter serves to dramatize the question which is central to that book.

3. The terms "millennial hope," "apocalyptic," "eschatology," and "utopia" need to be clarified, since Niebuhr does not always distinguish their meanings in these early writings. A "millennial hope" literally refers to the expectation of a thousand-year reign of the saints with

Jesus Christ on earth upon his return in glory. Its meaning, however, has been extended to include any sort of vision of the perfect society, such as the political visions found in apocalyptic and utopian literature. An "apocalypse" literally is a revelation of God's ultimate plan for the world, usually including a catastrophic transformation of the world as we know it and the institution of a genuine kingdom of God, characterized by perfect justice and peace. A "utopia," for Niebuhr, at least, is a vision of the perfect society minus the ,theological trappings. Utopias are secular versions of the millennial hope of the kingdom of God. For Niebuhr they are not objects for humanistic speculation, but blueprints for revolution. Thus he can speak of a Marxist utopia. "Eschatology," finally, means Christian teaching concerning the last things on earth or the final end of humankind. It is a technical term in Christian theology. Niebuhr, however, uses it rather indiscriminately in his early writings to designate any vision of the final goal of history. In the later writings characteristic of Christian realism, he will draw a sharp and polemical distinction between utopia and eschatology. Utopias will refer to visions promoting the hope for a fulfillment of history in history, while Christian eschatology will refer to the paradoxical vision of a fulfillment of history beyond history. The term "utopian" will take on pejorative connotations because of Niebuhr's belief that such hopes make for political irresponsibility.

4. Niebuhr's Christology places primary emphasis on the cognitive significance of redemption. Redemption consists more in learning to see things in a new way than in possessing some sort of supernatural power. The figure of Jesus, of course, is the historic source of this new way of looking at things. For a helpful interpretation of the development of Niebuhr's Christology, see the essay by Paul Lehmann, "The Christology of Reinhold Niebuhr," in Lehmann, 1956:252–80.

5. The following are the four essays representative of Niebuhr's methodological reflection: "As Deceivers Yet True," in *Beyond Tragedy* (Niebuhr, 1937b:3–24); "The Truth in Myths," in *Faith and Politics: A Commentary on Religious, Social and Political Thought in a Technological Age*, ed. Ronald M. Stone (Niebuhr, 1937a:15–32); "Mystery and Meaning," in *Discerning the Signs of the Times* (Niebuhr, 1946:152–73); and "Coherence, Incoherence and Christian Faith," in *Christian Realism and Political Problems* (Niebuhr, 1953:175–203).

6. Besides the immediate polemical advantage of Niebuhr's instrumentalist view of science, it is significant as a piece of evidence relevant to Rubem Alves's accusation concerning the "silent agreements" between Christian realism and pragmatism and positivism. But while Niebuhr's view of science may be broadly "positivistic," it certainly does not imply that he is committed to what Alves calls the "revolt against transcendence." On the contrary, precisely because scientific reason is limited to "mechanistic interpretation," the possibility of religious transcendence remains open. While this way of understanding the relationship of science and religion has both its critics and its supporters, it is not clear that the strategy itself is indicative of spiritual bankruptcy.

3

Christian Realism as Theology

If I believe that the Christian understanding of man could help solve some of these crucial issues and could conserve the best achievements of liberalism better than traditional liberalism can conserve them, I do not for that reason wish merely to hitch Christian faith to this or to that political task. Christianity faces ultimate issues of life which transcend all political vicissitudes and achievements. But the answer which Christian faith gives to man's ultimate perplexities and the hope which it makes possible in the very abyss of his despair, also throw light upon the immediate historical issues which he faces. Christianity is not a flight into eternity from the tasks and decisions of history. It is rather the power and the wisdom of God which makes decisions in history possible and which points to proximate goals in history which are usually obscured either by optimistic illusions or by the despair which followed upon the dissipation of these illusions. Christianity must therefore wage constant war, on the one hand against political religions which imagine some proximate goal and some conditioned good as man's final good, and on the other hand against an otherworldliness which by contrast gives these political religions a seeming validity.

—Reinhold Niebuhr, "Ten Years That Shook My World,"
The Christian Century, *April 26, 1939*

Lively religious sentiments don't necessarily make a theologian. Nor is effective preaching synonymous with theology; still less is religious journalism. Theology is a form of theoretical reflection that seeks to give conceptual expression to the religious vision that inspires it. In short, theology is an intellectual exercise in the construction and criticism of religious doctrines, what traditionally has been defined as "faith seeking understanding." Despite the theological promise of Niebuhr's early writings, the perspective of Christian realism did not receive systematic exposition until a chance occasion forced him to project his major work, *The Nature and Destiny of Man.* Invited in 1939 to deliver the prestigious Gifford Lectures at Edinburgh University, Niebuhr seized the opportunity to elaborate, if not the most important, certainly the most ambitious work in American theology in this century.

Niebuhr's Gifford Lectures, *The Nature and Destiny of Man*, will thus be discussed here to see how well he succeeded in translating his religious vision into coherent and persuasive theology. From the previous chapters we have learned that his theology grew out of his understanding of the circular relationship of faith and experience. This circle and the paradoxical vision that emerged from it place a distinctive burden upon the theologian, calling not only for prophetic insight into the vicissitudes, the ironies, even the paradoxes of historical experience, but also for an aesthetic capacity for dramatizing this sensibility so that others might share in it. In addition to these capacities, so admirably displayed in his shorter works, especially his sermonic essays, the task of practical theology—at least as Niebuhr proposed it—also required the analytic rigor and synthetic power appropriate to serious theoretical reflection. To make the "abiding truth" of Christian myth available as theology, Niebuhr therefore had to address the concerns of the human sciences, in particular—given his emphases— therapeutic psychology and critical social theory.[1] While this agenda is obviously demanding, it is not so obvious that Niebuhr completely succeeded in measuring up to it. For if it is difficult to maintain "cooperation between the naturally incompatible factors of reason and imagination," it is almost impossible to wed "prophetic" sensibilities to the capacities necessary for constructing a good theory.

In what follows, Niebuhr's achievement in *The Nature and Destiny of Man* will be judged according to the demands that he placed upon himself. Leaving aside his major apologetic claim, namely, that "the faith of the Bible" has a more adequate interpretation of the human person in history than either a "consistent idealism" or a "consistent naturalism,"[2] I shall seek to show that the "mythical approach" to Christianity allowed Niebuhr to focus on two areas of interpretation, which may be designated as "theological anthropology" and "theology of history." I shall argue that, consistent with his paradoxical vision, the element of theological anthropology dominates the structure of Christian realism at the expense of its theology of history; and insofar as they are relevant to Christian realism's status as a model for practical theology, I shall note the strengths and weaknesses of this structure. While it is clear that Niebuhr intended to interrelate these elements in a comprehensive view of the human person situated in a meaningful history, the relation between the two is not worked out as carefully as it should be, if this theology is to be as theoretically rigorous as it is rhetorically persuasive.

"A Synthesis of Reformation and Renaissance"

From the beginning Niebuhr's theology was meant to contribute to "the ethical reconstruction of modern society" by sustaining a religious "social imagination," which itself was to guide a radical political commitment. While this intention was first reflected in his early efforts to combine Marxism and Christianity in "a frank dualism in morals," its full realization in light of the paradoxical vision is evident in the "synthesis of Reformation and Renaissance" sketched out in *The Nature and Destiny of Man*. Niebuhr's "more conservative religious convictions" had culminated in a modern rediscovery of the spirituality of the Reformation, which now was to serve as the perspective for both criticizing the errors and fulfilling the promise of the Renaissance.

The significance of this new synthesis is apparent as soon as its context is recalled. *The Nature and Destiny of Man* is Niebuhr's response to World War II and the issues that finally led to America's participation in it, as well as his hopes and fears for the postwar world. While Niebuhr had delivered the second part of his Gifford Lectures in the fall of 1939 "with the sound of falling bombs literally accompanying his words at times" (Merkley, 1975: 158), he published the second volume of *The Nature and Destiny of Man* in 1943, when it had already become apparent that Western civilization was not destined to vanish into the darkness of Nazism. His synthesis of Reformation and Renaissance therefore represents a proposal for the reconstruction of postwar Western culture. The paradoxical vision is to overtake the eclipse that threatened the values of both the Reformation and the Renaissance by providing a profound interpretation of the painful lessons of the immediate past:

> If, however, the modern generation is to be helped to find life meaningful without placing an abortive confidence in the mere historical growth, it is incumbent upon those who mediate the truth of the gospel to this generation, to accept and not to reject whatever truth about life and history has been learned in these past centuries of partial apostasy. This is the more important because the lessons which have been learned are implied in the whole Biblical-prophetic view of history, which, in its pure form, has always regarded history in dynamic terms, that is, as moving towards an *end*.
>
> A new synthesis is therefore called for. It must be a synthesis which incorporates the twofold aspects of grace of Biblical religion, and adds the light which modern history, and the Renaissance and Reformation interpretations of history, have thrown upon the paradox of grace. Briefly this means that on the one hand life in history must be recognized as filled with indeterminate possibilities. There is no individual or interior spiritual situation, no cultural or scientific task, and no social or political problem in which men do not face new possibilities of the good and the obligation to realize them. It means on the other hand that every effort and pretension to complete life, whether in collective or individual terms, that every desire to stand beyond the contradictions of history, or to eliminate the final corruptions of history must be disavowed. [Niebuhr, 1943:207]

Christian realism, in other words, is to walk a fine line between the optimism generated by Renaissance utopias and the defeatism too often encouraged by Reformation eschatologies. By so doing, it will save the basic truth of both.

Whatever the merits of Niebuhr's proposal,[3] it is clear that he can make good on his intention only by objectifying the paradoxical vision into constructive theology. For if the basic truth of the Reformation is to be distinguished from "its obscurantism and defeatism on all immediate and intermediate issues of life" (Niebuhr, 1943:205), it will have to be identified and criticized in relation to the basic truth of the Renaissance, its "rediscovery of the sense of a meaningful history" (Niebuhr, 1943:160). Identifying these truths and defending a theoretically coherent synthesis of them means running a greater risk of "deception" than in any of Niebuhr's previous works. For it is precisely the suggestiveness of these paradoxes that will have to give way to more straightforward theological discourse. Niebuhr, in other words, will have to construct a theology that clearly designates the reference point of his "mythical" insights into a "dimension of depth in life."

Theological Anthropology

Assuming that Niebuhr's paradoxical vision has genuine insight into the riddles of human nature and history, how can it be made available so that others might come to recognize its truth? Niebuhr's Christian interpretation of human nature, his theological anthropology, was meant to answer this question. Beyond the suggestions of meaning given in *An Interpretation of Christian Ethics*, he had to show that his theological concepts actually refer to human moods and motivations, which can be verified in experience if persons learn to recognize them properly. In addition, he had to show that this reference point was the true meaning of the biblical myths and symbols. To accomplish this twofold task, he proposed to link the biblical metaphors of "sin" and "grace" with recent advances in modern psychology. Borrowing critically from Karen Horney's *The Neurotic Personality of Our Time*, Niebuhr accepted her conclusions that "both 'the will to power' which Alfred Adler regards as the basic impulse and the libidinal impulse in Freud must be regarded as derivatives from a more basic anxiety," qualifying it only by insisting that her "purely sociological explanation" must be complemented by Søren Kierkegaard's insights in *The Concept of Dread* (Niebuhr, 1941:44). The resulting existential psychology was to be placed into critical tension with certain theological models—notably those of Augustine, Calvin, Pascal, and that "greatest of Christian psychologists," Kierkegaard. A theological anthropology would emerge from this tension, capable not only of establishing a plausible reference point for the paradoxical vision but also of demonstrating its validity according to the relevant theological criteria.

Niebuhr's theological anthropology is based, in other words, on the assumption that the problem of anxiety is not exhausted simply in consultation with one's physician. By anxiety he meant something more profound in its implications, a universal mood that lies at the heart of most human spiritual and physical disorders, a pervasive insecurity in the face of our own limits and possibilities, including finally the awareness of human mortality. Anxiety, for Niebuhr, represents the ultimate dimension of human nature, "the basis of all human creativity as well as the precondition of sin" (Niebuhr, 1941:183). While the forms it takes and its intensity may vary, every human person is driven by it. There is no final cure; for to eliminate anxiety would be to eliminate humanity itself. Thus, while the therapies proposed by modern psychology may treat successfully its neurotic manifestations, the meaning of anxiety requires deeper understanding than scientific explanations can provide.

Far from repudiating modern psychology's insights into this pervasive human phenomenon, Niebuhr uses them to objectify the "abiding truth" in Christian myth. As we have seen, his interpretation of the myth of Creation maintains that the image of God defines human nature as a paradoxical structure of finiteness and freedom. In affirming this paradox as "good," the myth reassures us that it is to be trusted as the basis of human life. But how is the phenomenon of anxiety to be reconciled with this paradox? Is it a reflection of the image of God, or does it have some other source? Does it represent a God-given limit to human nature, or is it an obstacle to the fulfillment of human possibility? Taking his cues from Kierkegaard, he redefines anxiety as the problem of meaning raised by a human nature at once both finite and free:

> Man is anxious not only because his life is limited and dependent and yet not so limited that he does not know his limitations. He is also anxious because he does not know the limits of his possibilities. He can do nothing and regard it as perfectly done, because higher possibilities are revealed in each achievement. All human actions stand under seemingly limitless possibilities. There are, of course, limits but it is difficult to gauge them from any immediate perspective. There is therefore no limit of achievement in any sphere of activity in which human history can rest with equanimity. [Niebuhr, 1941: 183]

The image of God, in other words, turns out to be an anxiety-provoking paradox of limits and seeming limitlessness. But how is it to be accounted for?

The myth of the Fall yields further insight. By misrepresenting God's purpose in creating this human paradox, the Serpent plants a suspicion. Once Eve's childlike trust is dispelled, human nature becomes a question mark. The Serpent's suggestion triggers an anxious response, which in turn provides the occasion for an original sin in the form of Adam and Eve's withdrawal from the primordial relationship of trust with God. The myth of the Fall thus becomes a disclosure of the obscure origins of anxiety and sin:

> The devil fell before man fell, which is to say that man's rebellion against God is not an act of sheer perversity, nor does it follow inevitably from the situation in which he stands. The situation of finiteness and freedom in which man stands becomes a source of temptation only when it is falsely interpreted. This false interpretation is not purely the product of human imagination. It is suggested to man by a force of evil that precedes his own sin. Perhaps the best description of this situation is the statement that sin posits itself, that there is no situation in which it is possible to say that sin is either an inevitable consequence of the situation nor yet that it is an act of sheer and perverse individual defiance of God. [Niebuhr, 1941:181]

Anxiety represents a "false interpretation" of the paradox of human nature. Since humanity both is and is not responsible for its anxiety, our inevitable response to it in an "original sin" makes each person both infinitely more and infinitely less than a tragic hero.[4]

Despite its obscure origins, original sin symbolizes the actual situation of human nature throughout history. Pictured in the myth as an act of infidelity born of distrust, original sin lends a peculiar quality to the aggressive and evasive patterns of human behavior. While these patterns are interpreted in terms of the traditional theological vocabulary of "pride" and "sensuality," it is clear that the phenomena referred to are none other than the "will to power" and the "libidinal impulse" described by Adler and Freud. Just as Karen Horney redefined both of these as manifestations of anxiety, so Niebuhr identifies "pride" and "sensuality" as consequences of original sin. As such, pride and sensuality are not meant to condemn all human aspirations and achievements, but to describe our inordinate responses to the inevitable insecurity of human life. In order to provide a comprehensive map of the disorders symptomatic of original sin, Niebuhr's theological anthropology includes a diagnosis of the forms of pride and sensuality. The forms of pride are distinguished according to the different ways that the will to power is exercised: pride of power, pride of knowledge, moral pride, and spiritual pride; while the forms of sensuality are as various as the objects of libidinal impulse.

"Pride of power" describes the disordered responses of those who seek to overcome their physical insecurity at the expense of others (Niebuhr, 1941:188). Singled out for particular emphasis are the illusions of self-sufficiency, and the various forms of greed and exploitation that inevitably make for injustice. By understanding these evils as a consequence of original sin, Niebuhr rejects the psychological explanations offered by Adler and Horney. Neither Adler's prescriptions for overcoming "specific forms of the sense of inferiority" nor Horney's diagnosis linking them to "the general insecurities of a competitive civilization" is perceptive enough. Consequently, the psychologists' "hope for their elimination in a cooperative society" is "still far short of the real truth" (Niebuhr, 1941: 192). If the disordered will to power is a consequence of original sin, then no form of human society in history will ever be able to eliminate it entirely. A more realistic goal would be to organize a system of restraints designed to stabilize a balance of power in the hopes of minimizing the inordinate expressions of "pride of power."[5]

"Pride of knowledge," or intellectual pride, describes human nature's anxious response to the inevitable limitations of the will to truth:

> All human knowledge is tainted with an "ideological" taint. It pretends to be more true than it is. It is finite knowledge, gained from a particular perspective; but it pretends to be final and ultimate knowledge. Exactly analogous to the crude pride of power, the pride of the intellect is derived on the one hand from ignorance of the finiteness of the human mind and on the other hand from an attempt to obscure the known conditioned character of human knowledge and the taint of self-interest in human truth. [Niebuhr, 1941:195]

Although pride of knowledge is ludicrous in those philosophers who vainly imagine themselves "the final thinker," it is no laughing matter when it informs the pretensions of modern ideologies. Marxism, for Niebuhr, is the most glaring example of this dangerous folly: it has unmasked the "ideological taint in the thought of all bourgeois culture" but remains blind to "the conditioned character of its own viewpoints" (Niebuhr, 1941:196). Pride of knowledge heightens the problem of power by sponsoring a host of rationalizations which seek to justify the inequities produced by a disordered will to power.

Moral pride inevitably follows intellectual pride. Just as the latter makes a spurious claim to absolute truth, so the former pretends to absolute goodness. "Moral pride is the pretension of finite man that his highly conditioned virtue is the final righteousness and that his very relative moral standards are absolute. Moral pride thus makes virtue the very vehicle of sin, a fact which explains why the New Testament is so critical of the righteous in comparison with publicans and sinners" (Niebuhr, 1941:199). The sin of self-righteousness, for Niebuhr, is most serious because of the "cruelties, injustices, and defamations against our fellowmen" that it has generated.

Spiritual pride is the ultimate sin insofar as it makes explicit the "self-deification" implicit in the previous forms. The religious aspirations of the human race represent the last stronghold of original sin. "For this reason religion is not simply as is generally supposed an inherently virtuous human quest for God" (Niebuhr, 1941: 200). On the contrary, religion "is to a great extent unbridled human self-assertion in religious disguise." Niebuhr does not shrink back from the implications of this theological critique of religion. Christianity, despite the fact that its myths disclose the true depths of human sinfulness, is just as liable to the corruption of spiritual pride as any other religion. Catholicism, for example, sins by identifying "the church too simply with the Kingdom of God," while Protestantism often turns its own religious protest against spiritual pride into "the instrument of an arrogant will-to-power against theological opponents" (Niebuhr, 1941: 202). Nor is this disorder limited only to the traditional forms of religion. The secular ideologies of the modern world, in turn, "can be as explicit in making unconditioned claims as the pope." Niebuhr concludes that "religion, by whatever name, is the inevitable fruit of the spiritual stature of man; and religious intolerance and pride is the final expression of his sinfulness" (Niebuhr, 1941:203). Paradox persists even at the pinnacle of spirit.

The forms of sensuality also stem from original sin. If pride is defined as an excessively self-centered response to anxiety, how is sensuality to be understood? Consistent with the confrontation between Christian tradition and modern psychology informing his theological anthropology, Niebuhr criticizes both "Christian puritanism" and "Freudian psychology" for having "too superficial a view of the complexities of the relationship of spirit to nature" (Niebuhr, 1941:234). Their identification of sensuality with sexual activity, as well as their diametrically opposed strategies for either repressing or expressing libidinal impulses are symptomatic of this error. As an alternative, he favors reinterpreting the Augustinian notion of "concupiscence" for its insight into the connection between pride and sensuality. Instead of understanding sensuality as "self-love," Niebuhr sees it as "the destruction of harmony within the self, by the self's undue identification with and devotion to particular desires and impulses within itself" (Niebuhr, 1941:228). In other words, the "sin" of sensuality is fragmentation, a dissolution of the centered self, an evasiveness that seeks escape from the burden of human paradox. Thus pride and sensuality constitute a polarity: pride describes humanity's inordinate aggressions as we seek security for the self at the expense of others; sensuality describes our inordinate evasions as we seek to escape from the burden of self-consciousness. While the forms of sensuality are as various as the possible objects of libidinal impulse, in Niebuhr's view they are one in manifesting the paradoxical consequence of original sin: the unrestrained pursuit of self-realization is self-defeating.

Niebuhr's anthropological mapping of humanity's response to anxiety culminates in a discussion of the futility of self-deception. That the excesses of proud self-assertion and sensual escapism ultimately do not satisfy human yearnings for fulfillment should come as no surprise. In the long run no one is fooled by our pretensions, least of all ourselves.[6] Hypocrisy may be the tribute that vice pays to virtue, but in the end the tribute is recognized as counterfeit. For self-deception is never so complete that we do not anxiously cling to our illusions whenever they are threatened. Indeed, with so little success in deceiving ourselves we seek all the more earnestly to persuade others of the truth of our pretensions. The paradoxical consequences of "self-deception," in other words, epitomize the unhappy situation of the sinful "self":

> If others will only accept what the self cannot quite accept, the self as deceiver is given an ally against the self as deceived. All efforts to impress our fellowmen, our vanity, our displays of power or of goodness must, therefore, be regarded as revelations of the fact that sin increases the insecurity of the self by veiling its weakness with veils which may be torn aside. The self is afraid of being discovered in its nakedness behind these veils and of being recognized as the author of the veiling deceptions. Thus sin compounds the insecurity of nature with a fresh insecurity of spirit. [Niebuhr, 1941:207]

As this passage makes clear, the psychological phenomena of anxiety and theological discourse on the topic of sin, pride, sensuality, and self-deception together form a coherent and plausible frame of reference for interpreting the "abiding truth" of the myth of the Fall. But while they substantively qualify the formal paradox of finiteness and freedom disclosed in the myth of Creation, they do not exhaust Niebuhr's view of human nature. Just as the Christian cycle of myths reaches its climax only in the myth of the Atonement, so Christian realism's theological anthropology remains incomplete without an interpretation of the "grace and truth" of Jesus Christ.

While the New Testament proclaims a reconciliation to God in Christ, the meaning of that reconciliation remains paradoxical. Inspired by certain themes in St. Paul's Letter to the Romans, Niebuhr interprets "Christ the Second Adam" as a figure revealing the full extent of the grandeur and misery of human nature. The myth of the Atonement completes the meaning of Creation and Fall, in the sense that the "dimension of depth in life" is never fully appreciated apart from this figure. At the same time, the despair attendant upon an unflinching recognition of the true situation of human nature is dispelled immediately by the reassurance of God's love symbolized by the cross of Christ. Recognizing both aspects of this "truth" is an invitation to accept "the grace of Christ." The myth of the Atonement, in other words, is the occasion for an imaginative act of repentance and faith.

While Niebuhr does not regard "grace" as a supernatural entity, he does speak of it as "the power not our own" and as "the forgiveness of sins" (Niebuhr, 1943:107–26). As "power in, and mercy toward, men," it promises genuine spiritual renewal. In short, if the Christian myths are embraced as abiding truth, they have the power to shatter the pretensions of the sinful self and to restore trust in God. This trust, or "justification by faith," renews a willingness to live the human paradox in an attitude of humility. Insofar as the believer accepts the myths as the "revelation" of a Hidden God and his mysterious but loving disposition toward humanity, they are apprehended as a "power not our own." "Forgiveness of sins" refers to a shattering of the self and its reconstruction, which follow as a consequence of this apprehension. The process of reconstruction is what is meant by "repentance" (Niebuhr, 1943:114). Niebuhr is convinced that his interpretation not only corresponds to "the moral and spiritual experience of men" but also represents the meaning of St. Paul's words in the Letter to the Galatians: "I am crucified with Christ: nevertheless I live; yet not I, but Christ liveth in me: and the life which I now live in the flesh I live by the faith of the Son of God who loved me, and gave himself for me (Galatians 2:20)" (Niebuhr, 1943:107). In other words, without the figure of Christ presented in the myth of the Atonement the human paradox remains opaque, and human life is chained to the treadmill of anxiety. With the figure of Christ, however, the paradox is illuminated in such a way that it may be lived in faith and humility.

The anthropological meaning of the "grace and truth" of Christ is worked out in a manner consistent with Niebuhr's interpretation of the myths of Creation and Fall. Consequently, grace is not some supernatural substitute for therapeutic psychology. It cannot eliminate anxiety and sin so much as offer a way of coping with them. Just as sin, in Niebuhr's view, is overcome "in principle but not in fact," so grace does not miraculously transform human nature. Thus while Niebuhr insists that repentance is genuinely possible, he also contends that all pretensions to sinlessness are suspect as evidence of spiritual pride. His reasons for this interpretation are at once theoretical and practical. Theoretically, he assumes that the "grace and truth" of Christ must be understood in a manner consistent with the paradoxical vision of a Hidden God. Since the Hidden God cannot abrogate the created order of things and their actual historical development, the Atonement must represent a redemptive strategy of divine powerlessness. The figure of the suffering Messiah given in the myth thus fittingly symbolizes the limits and possibilities of grace. Practically, however, Niebuhr's view is linked to his suspicions regarding the spiritual pride of Christianity. The mistaken assumption that grace is a supernatural entity at the disposal of the churches and objectively communicated in the sacraments, in his opinion, led historically to certain pernicious forms of religious self-righteousness, engendering both fanaticism and cruelty.[7] Whatever the justice of this suspicion, it is clear that while Niebuhr's understanding of grace is fairly unorthodox, it is perhaps the only one coherent with the basic structure of his theology.[8]

Finiteness and freedom, anxiety, sin and grace, thus together form the structure of Niebuhr's Christian interpretation of human nature, his theological anthropology. As a theological project this structure must provide coherent answers to questions of reference and meaning. In other words, it must allow the meaning he discovered in the Christian cycle of myths to become intelligible, if not acceptable, to anyone capable of serious reflection—such public availability being the price of practical relevance. His strategy, in short, was to correlate this meaning with the reference points mapped out in modern psychological studies of anxiety. The myths were interpreted as presenting a coherent picture of the usual range of human response to anxiety, and a promising way of coping with these responses. Given "the basic facts of experience," they are used to define the possibilities for a renewal of religious faith, hope, and love. Nevertheless, this theological anthropology appears to be restricted to affairs of the heart, matters likely to be pondered in private. Since Niebuhr's motive in formulating this perspective is ultimately to provide guidance in public affairs, his theology of history will try to bridge the gap between private meaning and public relevance.

Self and Society: Bridging the Gap

Niebuhr's theology of history is meant as a Christian interpretation of human destiny. But when Niebuhr speaks of human destiny, no longer is he concerned primarily with the "heights and depths" of the human self as such but with the relationship between this self and modern societies engaged in the processes of historical development. Since in Niebuhr's opinion, the paradoxical vision provides an ultimate meaning not only for the self but also for history as a whole, this claim must be clarified in his theology of history.

The link between human nature and destiny as Niebuhr understands them is not self-evident. It is possible to dismiss his theological anthropology as ahistorical, as so restricted to the inner world of private religious experience that it provides no adequate perspective for interpreting either society or history. As we shall see, liberation theologians make this kind of claim against both progressive Catholic and liberal Protestant theologies: abstract generalizations about human nature represent an obstacle to critical historical consciousness.[9] Their anthropologies, in other words, inhibit an awareness of the dialectical patterns of social development—the role of political, economic, and social structures, technological advances, as well as geographic, ethnic, and linguistic differences—and their significance for interpreting historical change. If this objection is valid, it also holds for Christian realism. While Niebuhr was not unaware of the significance of these structures, he insisted that they cannot illuminate the ultimate context of human action in history, that "total environment . . . which includes both eternity and time." In short, only a "Christian interpretation of human nature" can clarify that context. Nevertheless, by itself Niebuhr's theological anthropology is incomplete. For it neither elaborates the relation between his view of the self and the moral situation of society, nor makes explicit the meaning of history as a whole. Both these issues, in turn, suggest a more fundamental problem: the relationship between Christian myth and history must be clarified—not just the biblical history that culminates in the cross of Christ but also the history of Christianity's continuing impact on Western civilization. Because of their indispensable role in establishing the practical relevance of the paradoxical vision, each of these issues is taken up in the theology of history that Niebuhr outlines in the second half of *The Nature and Destiny of Man*.

Before turning to this theology of history, let us examine the way in which Niebuhr establishes a theological perspective comprehending both self and society. Throughout his career he was concerned to relate the two, although his understanding of them fluctuated significantly. While his works consistently call for the "ethical reconstruction of modern society," in the beginning he posed the problem facing society in terms of a contrast between "personal religion" and "impersonal civilization." This contrast is indicative of a polarity between self and society that Niebuhr tried to overcome in various ways. *Moral Man and Immoral Society*, for example, introduced consideration of the symbolic power of religion in order to emphasize the social implications of its "illusions." But the "frank dualism in morals" that he advocated there suggests that just as society is more than an aggregate of selves, so the problems of social ethics are of a different order from those of personal morality. Nevertheless, Niebuhr did not rest content with the uneasy juxtaposition of idealism regarding selves and cynicism regarding society implied by this dualism. His rediscovery of an authentically Christian spirituality meant that the abiding truth in myth provides guidance for public affairs as well as personal meaning. Inspired by this rediscovery, *The Nature and Destiny of Man* is meant to show how finiteness and freedom, anxiety, and sin and grace are the key to understanding the moral and religious situation of human societies. Just as individuals may interpret their actions in terms of these categories, so patterns of social and institutional behavior may similarly be illuminated. For in Niebuhr's view, the problem of anxiety is just as fundamental to the soul of society as to an individual self.

All the same, there are certain important restrictions on this use of these categories. Niebuhr's political experience suggested that human groups and institutions possess a power that is more than a magnification of the individual "will to power." Collective power possesses an aura of authority and seems to follow a logic of its own. Consequently, as Niebuhr often points out, "reasons of state" may be invoked to justify policies that are morally objectionable when considered as the actions of individuals (Niebuhr, 1941:209). While he hopes to exorcise the demonic side of collective power—for example, "the temptation to idolatry . . . implicit in the state's majesty"—he does not reject its responsible exercise. Instead, he notes that the "inevitable moral tension between individual and group morality" constitutes a crucial challenge for Christian realism, both practically and theoretically.[10]

Niebuhr's theoretical response to this challenge begins to emerge in his analysis of sin in the first half of *The Nature and Destiny of Man*. The behavior of human groups and institutions exhibits "the conflict of grace and pride" no less than do the private moods of the individual self. But the disorders identified as "pride" and "sensuality" are complicated by society's inability to recognize them. While "repentance" is always a possibility for an individual thanks to the inevitable failure of "self-deception," there is little likelihood that a group will renounce its illusions and voluntarily change its policies. "Collective egotism" in all its forms is much more persistent, and the rationalizations that justify it are much more plausible, than the shaky defenses of personal selfishness. Niebuhr cites racism, nationalism, and class prejudice as examples of collective egotism, in which disordered social relationships are legitimated by a host of ideological rationalizations (Niebuhr, 1941:209–13). The point is not that human association as such is evil, but that it is more prone to sin and less amenable to grace than is an individual self. While an individual is never quite able to silence the gnawing awareness of personal pretense, the idols manufactured in the course of our associations often do succeed in masking the naked truth of collective egotism.

As Niebuhr's analysis suggests, the pervasiveness of sin in society is clarified by linking the religious problem of idolatry with the modern social problem of ideology. By a certain metaphorical extension, the public life of society is redefined in terms of the paradoxes and temptations characteristic of the private life of the self. The link between idolatry and ideology presupposes that there is an analogy between the structures of personal existence and the structures of social life, one that makes it possible to speak simultaneously of both. When describing the perplexities of the self, for example, Niebuhr denounces the "tyranny" of pride and the "anarchy" of sensuality, categories that are central to his analysis of political disorder. Even the term "collective egotism" as a framework for analyzing the problem of power and ideology presupposes this dual reference. While there is nothing new about this analogy—it being at least as old as Plato's attempt to envision a model city-state mirroring the well-ordered soul—in Niebuhr's hands it provides the formal basis for extending the meaning of his theological categories from human nature to human destiny.

This formal analogy borrowed from the Greeks[11] is qualified, however, by a substantive example taken from the Hebrews—the legacy of Hebrew "prophetic religion,"to be exact. In general, Niebuhr uses this term to designate his understanding of the Christian cycle of myths, its continuity with a biblical perspective, and its relevance for effective social action now and in the future. But here "prophetic religion" refers specifically to the decisive chapter in the history of Israelite religion, in which the struggle over "collective egotism" within the nation reached its climax. The prophet Amos stands at the head of a tradition that illuminates the political import of the conflict of holiness and sin disclosed in the myths of Creation and the Fall. Rebellion against God is not simply an affair of the heart, but a corrupting force in society which results in gross injustice. The alienation experienced as sin is not simply a sense of unworthiness accompanying the dramatic encounter of the human and the divine, but an objective condition threatening the integrity of the nation's covenant with God, and thus its political well-being. To capture the meaning of the example of prophetic religion, Niebuhr offers the rather cryptic formula, "Equality of sin, inequality of guilt" (Niebuhr, 1941:219).

Both parts of the formula are necessary, if the example is to be appreciated fully. "Equality of sin" refers not only to the universality of human involvement in anxiety and its consequences, but also to the objective situation of injustice characteristic of all human institutions. The formula reflects the prophets' penchant for indiscriminate criticism of the just and the unjust alike, which Niebuhr finds epitomized in the Pauline assertion that "all men are equally sinners in the sight of God." "Inequality of guilt," however, represents "the prophetic note of moral discrimination between rich and poor, between the powerful and the weak, the proud and the meek" (Niebuhr, 1941:224). Niebuhr thus understands "guilt" as something determinable in the moral order of things, a failure to measure up to socially defined moral responsibilities. Here the prophets are seen as bridging the gap between the religious problem of sin and the moral problem of guilt. In their denunciations of the idolatrous corruptions of Israelite religion, they criticize the ruling classes, who bear direct responsibility for the breakdown of both piety and social justice (Niebuhr, 1941:223). "Collective egotism," as it turns out, is never anonymous for "prophetic religion." Those entrusted with a dominant share of the social power bear a dominant share of guilt for the sins of society. "Equality of sin, inequality of guilt" thus represents a formula seeking to do justice to both "ultimate religious perspectives and relative historical ones."

However faithful to the example of the prophets, the formula is not without its problems. Typically, it might be argued that capacities for moral discrimination are undermined by the indiscriminate nature of prophetic denunciations of sin. But Niebuhr disagrees. In his opinion, "the Biblical insight into the sinfulness of all human nature actually supports rather than contradicts the prophetic strictures against the wise, the mighty, the noble and the good. For without understanding the sinfulness of the human heart in general it is not possible to penetrate through the illusions and pretensions of the successful classes of every age" (Niebuhr, 1941:227). Nevertheless, the formula reflecting this prophetic perspective requires further clarification. How, for example, does it establish a reference point for Niebuhr's theology of history in critical social theory similar to the relationship between his theological anthropology and modern psychology? While the formula "agrees with the known facts of history," Niebuhr also adds the following by way of explanation:

Wherever the fortunes of nature, the accidents of history or even the virtues of the possessors of power, endow an individual or a group with power, social prestige, intellectual eminence or moral approval above their fellows, there an ego is allowed to expand. It expands both vertically and horizontally. Its vertical expansion, its pride, involves it in sin against God. Its horizontal expansion involves it in an unjust effort to gain security and prestige at the expense of its fellows. The two forms of expansion cannot be sharply distinguished because, as previously noted, spiritual pretension can be made an instrument of power in social conflict, and dominant power, measured socially, inevitably seeks to complete its structure by spiritual pretensions. [Niebuhr, 1941:226]

Even though this appeal to the anthropological fact that human nature must be understood "both vertically and horizontally" is suggestive of the way in which "equality of sin, inequality of guilt" might refer to social structures, the theoretical basis for this suggestion is never developed systematically.

Despite the ambiguities and theoretical difficulties of the transition from theological anthropology to theology of history, it is clear that Niebuhr uses the Greek analogy and the Hebrew example to do two things: (1) to establish a biblical warrant for his metaphorical extension of the meaning of the anxious self to society as a whole, and (2) to introduce the perspective from which he will present his understanding of the point where Christian myth and history intersect. The Hebrew prophets, in other words, are part of a historical sequence that has decisive importance for Niebuhr's interpretation of the myth of the Atonement. For the abiding truth in this myth is disclosed in a way that differs from the primordial character of the myths of Creation and the Fall: it is embodied in the historic figure of Jesus Christ. This difference means that in explicating the relevance of this abiding truth to the problem of social action in history, Niebuhr must also situate it in history as the decisive moment in the realization of history's meaning as a whole. Thus his theology of history inevitably becomes a "historical Christology."

Theology of History: Christology

The myth of the Atonement, unlike those of Creation and the Fall, is rooted in an event that itself is publicly available as part of world history. For in some sense its abiding truth is contingent upon the historical reality of its central character, Jesus of Nazareth, a human person who lived and died at a particular time, in a particular place, as a member of a particular society confronted by its own particular problems. By contrast, Creation and the Fall provide a primordial description of the human condition, claiming universal validity in its reference to perennial human moods and motivations. While these descriptions are dependent upon the myths of a particular religious tradition with its own historical development, their "truth" is independent of the historical origins of these myths. For the myth of the Atonement to work as myth, however, the life and teachings of the historical Jesus must correspond more or less reliably with the figure of Christ which it proclaims as the absolute center of religious devotion.[12]

This lack of symmetry between the primordial character of Creation and the Fall and the historicity of the Atonement presents a problem for all Christian theologies that try to interpret the religious meaning of biblical narratives. While the problem may in fact be ignored both by orthodox Christians who regard these stories as divinely inspired witnesses to supernatural events in history and by those liberals who regard them all indifferently as "ciphers" encoded with a timeless moral truth, in principle it cannot be evaded by theologians who insist on taking them seriously but not literally as symbols of religious transcendence in history. Beyond the inadequacies of language for expressing the truth of the paradoxical vision generally, the problem of the historicity of the myth of the Atonement is twofold. Not only does it concern the epistemological difficulty of correlating the historical Jesus with the claims raised by faith in him as the Christ; more important for practical theology, it concerns the existential difficulty of establishing the moral relevance—the "absoluteness" or "universality" —of this one person's life for history as a whole. While the two aspects of the problem are distinct, insofar as the latter presupposes an adequate solution to the former, Niebuhr did not separate them in this historical Christology. As we shall see, his failure to do so further weakens his theology of history.

Assuming that the Christian cycle of myths discloses universal truths regarding human nature, Niebuhr sought to elaborate their meaning for "human destiny" by interpreting them in the context of Judeo-Christian religious history. By reading the lesson of this particular history in terms of the universal problem of meaning in history, Niebuhr hoped to show its relevance for social action. Specifically, the myth of the Atonement embodied in the figure of Jesus Christ is understood primarily in relation to the ways in which the myths of Creation and the Fall helped to shape and were shaped by Jewish religious history.[13] Central to this strategy is an account of the historic vicissitudes of prophetic religion. In Niebuhr's view it culminates in an "unexpected reinterpretation of prophetic Messianism" which corresponds in its essential meaning to the paradoxical vision. By working out these ideal correspondences, Niebuhr intends to do justice to the existential paradox of moral "absoluteness" in the relativities of history, as well as the epistemological problem of myth in history.

The appropriate religious response to the situation depicted by the myths of Creation and the Fall, of course, is "repentance," an effort to seek a reconciliation that overcomes alienation and restores an authentic relationship with God. This response, implicit in the myths themselves, is made explicit in the biblical stories that follow them, stories of typical human efforts at reconciliation, which usually turn out to be idolatrous. Accordingly, Niebuhr interprets the history of biblical religion in general as a never completely successful search for salvation, one governed by the inevitable logic of Creation and the Fall. Furthermore, the particularities of biblical history take on universal significance when they are interpreted in terms of the ideal types Niebuhr uses to categorize the world's religious history: "Where a Christ is not expected" and "Where a Christ is expected" (Niebuhr, 1943:1–31). The logic of these categories reflects his concern to emphasize both the universality of the quest for reconciliation and the distinctiveness of the biblical response to it.[14]

The category "Where a Christ is not expected" covers those religions that Niebuhr previously discussed as "mystical religions." Here he identifies them as "classical materialism from Democritus to Lucretius," "classical idealism and mysticism" from Plato to Plotinus, as well as "Taoism, Hinduism, and Buddhism." Reflecting the yearning for salvation from history, they propose either to reduce history to nature or to escape from history into eternity. Such efforts in evasion, for Niebuhr, are refuted by the paradox of human finiteness and freedom. The anxieties generated by this paradox will not be silenced either by a naturalism that simply ignores the questions raised by human awareness of mortality, or by an idealism that ignores the human person's "organic relation to the temporal process" (Niebuhr, 1943:11). The other category, "Where a Christ is expected," comprehends those religions previously discussed as "mythical religions." Later on, Niebuhr will list "Christianity and Judaism . . . possibly Zoroastrianism, . . . perhaps Mohammedanism" as "historical religions" (Niebuhr, 1953: 179), as well as various religious heresies and political ideologies inspired by them. Characteristic of this type is a desire to take historical existence seriously, and to include it in the hope for salvation.

Subtle distinctions are required to understand the differences among historical religions. Implicit in all of them is the question of a Christ, since their hope for salvation tends to be embodied in some specific redeemer figure, a Messiah. Thus the problem of Messianism becomes as complex as the historical religions themselves, and so it requires an additional set of ideal types to comprehend it. Accordingly, Niebuhr identifies "three elements or levels of Messianism: (a) the egoistic-nationalistic element, (b) the ethical-universalistic element, and (c) a supra-ethical religious element as expressed in Prophetism." Although these types may exist independently of one another, all three are manifest in Hebrew religion. Niebuhr therefore uses it to map the logic of historical religions in general and Messianism in particular.

By explaining these "three elements or levels of Messianism" in terms of the history of Israel, Niebuhr is able to show how they historically interact.

The first type, egoistic-nationalistic Messianism, identifies salvation with the "triumph of nation, empire, or culture" (Niebuhr, 1943:18). It is most prone to the corruptions of collective egotism, and most vulnerable to historical collapse because of them. This type is exhibited not just in the Israel of the Judges and Kings, but also in the various Christian nationalisms of Europe, as well as in Nazism. The second type, an ethical-universalistic Messianism, implies a rejection of the first by projecting the hope for a "shepherd-king" bringing universal justice and peace (Niebuhr, 1943:19). Here the corruption is more subtle, as power and goodness must be identified either through ideological rationalization or through a utopian expectation that cannot be realized in history. Examples of the second type are the universalistic theologies of kingship in Israel, Egypt, Babylonia, and Persia, the pious hope for a "good Caesar" characteristic of the history of Christian Europe, and contemporary aspirations for the triumph of a revolutionary vanguard, such as the role of the "proletariat" in Marxism. The third type, prophetic Messianism in its "supra-ethical religious dimension," is painfully aware of the ambiguity of ethical-universalism. Since power and goodness cannot be perfectly reconciled in history, to claim that they have been or that they will be so reconciled is to invite both historical and spiritual disaster. The prophet Amos unmasked the moral pretense of such hopes, declaring in the name of Yahweh, "Are ye not as children of the Ethiopians unto me, O children of Israel? (Amos 9:7)" (Niebuhr, 1943:23). Niebuhr takes this to mean that the "Holy One of Israel" is "a God who transcended the interests of Israel." Indeed, "Amos' predictions of judgment upon Israel are really only incidental to a more far reaching criticism of all forms of optimistic Messianism." The "supra-ethical religious dimension" of Messianism at its pinnacle thus "apprehends a divine word of judgment, spoken against the whole human enterprise by faith" (Niebuhr, 1943:25). Prophetic Messianism, it seems, culminates in a deeply religious awareness of the transcendent justice and holiness of a Hidden God.

But this level of prophetic insight, far from resolving the problem of meaning in history, actually sharpens it. Although prophetic Messianism interprets history, its word of judgment rings out in harshly negative tones: "The problem of meaning in history is how history can be anything more than judgment, which is to say, whether the promise of history can be fulfilled at all" (Niebuhr, 1943:27). Niebuhr thus describes the impasse reached by prophetism:

> The assurance that God will complete history by overcoming the ambiguity of the momentary triumph of evil yields to the question of how God will complete history by overcoming the perennial evil in every human good. The "hidden" sovereignty of God, which demands a fuller disclosure in the Messianic reign, is hidden, not be-

cause the divine power is not fully disclosed but because the relation
of divine mercy to divine wrath remains a mystery. [Niebuhr, 1943:
30–31]

After the prophets there are various attempts to break this impasse, notably
in the apocalyptic writings, for example, the book of Enoch (Niebuhr, 1943:
33). Niebuhr interprets these as the "logical culmination" of Messianism
rather than its corruption, because "they look forward to the final disclosure of the 'hidden' Messiah, which is to say that the Messianic reign is
regarded as the final revelation of the obscured sovereignty of God and the
confused meaning of history." But they also dramatize the "failure" of
prophetic Messianism, since, in the face of the incongruous triumph of the
enemies of Yahweh, the reassertion of God's sovereignty too often is
accompanied by "a veritable orgy of vindictive triumph" (Niebuhr, 1943:
33). Thus the apocalyptic writings represent for Niebuhr "invariably right
questions" and "usually wrong answers" (Niebuhr, 1943:34). Despite the
promise of these writings, the impasse reached by prophetic Messianism is
never quite resolved.

Against this background Niebuhr interprets the meaning of Jesus Christ.
In his teaching Jesus repudiates the lesser forms of Messianism and transforms the higher with the "outrageous idea of a suffering Messiah." Thus,
according to Niebuhr, Jesus fulfills the legacy of prophetism by rejecting
both the "Hebraic legalism" that had overcome the spirit of the Deu-
teronomic Code (Niebuhr, 1943:39) and the "nationalistic particularism"
of the sons of Abraham. Furthermore, Jesus' teaching clarifies the supra-
ethical religious dimension of prophetic Messianism by shifting emphasis
away from the problem of "separating the sheep from the goats" to "the
final enigma" concerning "the evil in every good and the unrighteousness
of the righteous" (Niebuhr, 1943:43). Jesus, in other words, overcomes the
impasse of prophetic Messianism by embodying the idea of "vicarious
suffering." Niebuhr explains:

He takes the sins of the world upon and into Himself. This is to say
that the contradictions of history are not resolved in history; but they
are only ultimately resolved on the level of the eternal and the divine.
However, the eternal and the divine that destroys evil is not some
undifferentiated eternity which effaces both the good and the evil of
history by destroying history itself. God's mercy must make itself
known in history, so that man in history may become fully conscious
of his guilt and redemption. The Messiah must give his life as "a
ransom for many." [Niebuhr, 1943:46]

This "unexpected reinterpretation of prophetic Messianism," in short,
carries an assurance of "divine mercy" in the paradoxical notion that
"God suffers in history."

But this unexpected reinterpretation is based not only on the teachings of Jesus but also on the quality of his life and death. The crucifixion becomes the climax of Jesus' history and the symbol of humanity's final reconciliation with a Hidden God. "Understood by Christ as a necessary 'ransom for many,' " the crucifixion becomes a "sacrificial death upon the Cross" (Niebuhr, 1943:53). Thus, for Niebuhr, myth and history converge in the cross of Jesus Christ. As a symbol the cross becomes the center of the Christian myth of the Atonement, clarifying the teachings of Jesus whose meaning it perfectly embodies. The "final enigma," in short, yields to the paradoxical vision of humanity reconciled to God through the sufferings of Christ. Thus the Atonement is disclosed in history, but salvation is not possessed in history. The power and goodness of God are disclosed in the powerlessness of Christ, and the wisdom of God is disclosed in the folly of a suffering Messiah. As Niebuhr contends, "it is by the contemplation of the whole of this history in terms of expectation and fulfillment that Christian faith arrives at the confession, 'Surely this was the Son of God' " (Niebuhr, 1943:53).

Before turning to the way in which Niebuhr explicates the practical relevance of this historical Christology, we must note its strengths and weaknesses. Its purpose is to anchor the myth of the Atonement in the history of Jesus of Nazareth, and thereby to ensure that the meaning of the Christian cycle of myths remains paradoxical, not just in the general sense of conveying the truth of the paradoxical vision but specifically by disclosing this vision as embodied in the destiny of a particular historical figure. Thus although the myth of the Atonement responds to the situation represented primordially by the Creation and the Fall, its "abiding truth" is not a timeless universal whose meaning can be expressed simply in anthropological terms. While Niebuhr uses the Pauline idea of "Christ the Second Adam" to explicate the myth's anthropological significance, this does not mean that Jesus Christ is merely a symbol of human nature's perfection. As a person with his own historic destiny, Jesus Christ may be that, but he is so much more besides: he is, Niebuhr claims, the embodiment of history's paradoxical fulfillment insofar as his life actually represents "a ransom for many." The strength of this claim should now be obvious. It ensures that the paradoxical vision really is public in its reference and historic in its meaning.

The weakness, however, stems from the burden of proof that this claim entails. By insisting on a historical Christology, Niebuhr assumes the closest possible correspondence between the Jesus of history and the Christ of faith, a convergence between the events of this particular person's life and death and the religious meaning that Christianity has discovered in them. The argument for this convergence is a standard one: the facts of Jesus' life and death, what he taught and what he accomplished, are verifiable historically, and their meaning is confirmed in Christian faith and experience. But what if the critical study of history will not verify these facts? What if the relationship between Jesus' teaching and the religious history of Israel raises as many historical questions as it answers? What if, for example, the historical Jesus never formulated "the idea that God suffers in history"? What if his relationship to Jewish apocalypticism is not quite as clearly critical as Niebuhr makes it out to be? The list of historical problems could be extended indefinitely; the point, however, is not that this Christology is without justification, but rather, that it is vulnerable to historical criticism.[15] For if the verifiable facts do not converge as neatly with the narrative's religious meaning as Niebuhr would have it, then the delicate balance between myth and history is jeopardized. The historical Jesus, in that case, would become more an occasion for myth-making than the person in which it is actually embodied. Yet it is clear that Niebuhr needs the historical Jesus for Christianity's promise of meaning in history to be real. If the cross of Christ—however paradoxical—remains the definitive expression of the Hidden God's grace and truth, it must be more than a religio-poetic symbol of Niebuhr's own religious sensibility—however profound. To the extent, therefore, that this convergence is assumed rather than demonstrated, Niebuhr's historical Christology remains disturbingly tentative.

Theology of History: Eschatology

Despite its epistemological difficulties, the role played by Niebuhr's Christology in his theology of history should be apparent. As the embodiment of the myth of the Atonement, the figure of Jesus Christ is the definitive expression of the paradoxical vision, the guarantee that its assurance of grace is both religiously meaningful and historically true. Concern over the problems of historical verification entailed by this claim should not, however, distract attention from the fact that the meaning of this Christology remains mythical in Niebuhr's sense. In short, it discloses the "dimension of depth in life" and an "abiding truth" about it. It illuminates human nature and thus provides an orientation for historical action. Niebuhr summarizes this orientation by characterizing history as "the conflict between grace and pride."

The meaning of this conflict is a reflection of Jesus' paradoxical teaching about the kingdom of God. In reinterpreting the *eschata*, that is, "prophetic and apocalyptic hopes" regarding history's end, Jesus taught "the double affirmation that on the one hand the 'Kingdom of God has come' and on the other hand that 'the Kingdom of God will come' " (Niebuhr, 1943:47). Transferred to the stage of history, these affirmations mean that history after Christ is "an interim between the disclosure of its true meaning and the fulfillment of that meaning" at the end of history (Niebuhr, 1943:49). In other words, "a continued element of inner contradiction is accepted as its perennial characteristic":

Thus reconstructed, the idea that history is an "interim" between the first and second coming of Christ has a meaning which illumines all the facts of human existence. History, after Christ's first coming, has the quality of partly knowing its true meaning. Insofar as man can never be completely in contradiction to his own true nature, history also reveals significant realizations of that meaning. Nevertheless history continues to stand in real contradiction to its true meaning, so that pure love in history must always be suffering love. But the contradictions of history cannot become man's norms, if history is viewed from the perspective of Christ. [Niebuhr, 1943:51]

Just as anxiety is not eliminated from human nature, so "contradiction" is not eliminated from human history. This understanding of history as an "interim" is consistent with Niebuhr's paradoxical interpretation of salvation as realizable "in principle but not in fact." Implied by it is Niebuhr's "religious reservation" about collective human endeavors: no human association, Christian or otherwise, can claim to have established a perfect society—a kingdom of God—on earth. All such assertions are rejected as either "ideological" pretensions or "utopian" projections. In either case, they are emphatically not the meaning of Christian eschatology. This reservation necessarily entails a critical attitude toward the claims of public institutions and religious groups, including the Christian churches. Insofar as they identify themselves with the kingdom of God, they furnish additional evidence of the persistence of "the conflict of grace and pride."

Having formulated the abiding truth of Christian eschatology, Niebuhr tries to show how it is illustrated in the historic vicissitudes of Western civilization. While the teachings of Jesus proclaimed this eschatological principle, St. Paul actually formulated its theological meaning in a doctrine of grace (Niebuhr, 1943:100–126). Nevertheless, Christian history after them for the most part not only failed to understand this doctrine, it also exhibited the practical consequences of such a failure. The life and thought of St. Augustine of Hippo represent an exception to some extent, since his work gives "the first clear and explicit expression" to the fact "that the primary issue of life and history is the relation of grace to sin, rather than the subordinate problem of eternity to time" (Niebuhr, 1943:134). Even so, in Niebuhr's opinion, the great African bishop of the early fifth century—at once the father of both Catholic and Protestant theology—settled into a "qualified perfectionism," which provided the intellectual foundations for the medieval church. Only with the Reformation were the pretensions of the "Catholic synthesis" exposed, and an eschatological understanding of "the conflict of grace and pride" restored. Its doctrine of justification by faith "represents the final renunciation in the heart of Christianity of the human effort to complete life and history, whether with or without divine grace" (Niebuhr, 1943:148). But while the Reformation thus is a religious event of central importance to Christianity, the churches inspired by it went on to betray in practice the abiding truth they had grasped in faith. Even in failure, however, the Reformation helped to shape "the debate on human destiny in modern culture."

Niebuhr locates this debate in terms of its origins in "the destruction of the Catholic synthesis." Since not only the Reformation but also the Renaissance emerged from that event, they represent the historic forces that succeeded in giving modern culture its characteristic insights into "the possibilities and limits of man's historic existence" (Niebuhr, 1943:147). In analyzing these forces, Niebuhr's purpose, of course, is to lay the foundations for his proposed "synthesis of Reformation and Renaissance." Consequently, his strategy is to point out the inadequacy of their responses to "the conflict of grace and pride" while also clarifying what "truth" they might still contribute to the "ethical reconstruction of modern society." His argument, in essence, is that while both movements emerge from the same legacy of "classical" and "Biblical-Christian" impulses that previously had shaped the "Catholic synthesis," their responses to these impulses differ not only from medieval Christianity but also from each other.

The Renaissance blended "the classical confidence in human capacities" with "the Biblical-Christian impulse toward sanctification and the fulfillment of life" including "history itself" in a "rediscovery of the sense of a meaningful history" (Niebuhr, 1943:160). The Reformation, on the other hand, "was the historical *locus* where Christian conscience became most fully aware of the persistence of sin in the life of the redeemed" (Niebuhr, 1943:184). The tension between the two is evident from the fact that the logic of Renaissance thought tends toward "utopian" conceptions culminating in "the modern idea of progress" (Niebuhr, 1943:164), while the focus of the Reformation becomes so fixed on the "one central paradox of the Gospel to history" that it tends "to disavow all intermediate cultural tasks on the ground that the final wisdom is not to be found there" (Niebuhr, 1943:210). By placing the two in tension, Niebuhr hopes that the errors of each will be checked by the opposing tendency in the other. The projected "synthesis between culture and Christian faith" to emerge from this tension will recognize that "the Reformation has rediscovered the final truth about life and history," while the Renaissance will continue to provide orientation to "the pursuit of proximate answers and solutions" to "intermediate cultural tasks" (Niebuhr, 1943:210–11).

Christian Realism as Theology

The way in which Niebuhr uses this synthesis to provide practical orientation to the tasks at hand in reconstructing the postwar world will be discussed in the following chapter. For the moment, a brief summary and analysis of the theological achievement of *The Nature and Destiny of Man* is in order.

The theological structure articulated in that book remains impressive for its coherence. Given Niebuhr's paradoxical vision and the mythical approach by which he continually rediscovered its meaning in biblical narrative, it is clear that the central tasks of this theology were to distinguish its theoretical reference and to clarify its practical relevance. Since the vision emerged from his private experience as a religiously sensitive social activist, the task, in other words, was to secure its public availability so that others might also accept it as a perspective for action. Niebuhr fulfilled this requirement by constructing a theological anthropology, which located the meaning of this vision in terms of the common human phenomena of anxiety. Using recent studies in modern psychology to map systematically the substantive insights generated by his mythical approach to the Bible, Niebuhr constructed a Christian interpretation of human nature. The other dimension of the task, clarifying the practical relevance of this theory, was taken up in a theology of history.

Here Niebuhr's achievement must be regarded as less than completely successful. For, given the polarity between personal religion/impersonal civilization, human nature/human destiny, self/society, characteristic of Niebuhr's thinking throughout, it is not clear that *The Nature and Destiny of Man* theoretically reconciles these poles, as it must if this theology is to have the practical impact claimed for it. No doubt the classical analogy between the structures of the "self" and those of "society" is suggestive, as is the example of biblical prophetism's insight into the connection between personal faith and social justice. But theoretically these strategies cannot offer much more than a metaphorical extension of Niebuhr's interpretation of human nature to history as a whole. The other elements of his "theology of history" are equally suggestive, but also equally tentative. While his reading of the history of Western civilization as a "conflict of grace and pride" serves to illustrate the meaning of his theological anthropology, it does not specify theoretically the ways in which human groups and institutions actually manifest this conflict. In other words, the connection between the history of theological concepts and the processes of social development remains for the most part unanalyzed. Thus instead of correlating his religious insights into the paradox of sin and grace with some form of critical social theory, he restricts the reference of his theology of history to the history of ideas.

If Niebuhr's theology of history is to be more than a metaphorical extension of his anthropology, these theoretical relationships will have to be made explicit. But instead of pursuing that point, Niebuhr's theology of history bases its historic reference on that unique convergence of Christian myth and history represented in the figure of Jesus Christ. While it is only to be expected that his theology of history would be founded on a historical Christology, it is also clear that this foundation is not as solid as it must be if the conflict of grace and pride is to be more than a religious symbol still in need of theoretical clarification.

Thus despite the impression of coherence, the weakness in Christian realism as theology must be recognized. If, as I have argued, its theoretical reference to both human nature and history must be adequately established for it to have the practical relevance that Niebuhr claims for it, then it seems fair to say that although Christian realism does provide a plausible theory of human nature, its theoretical understanding of history remains relatively sketchy. The practical consequences of this weakness will become apparent as we proceed. At the moment, they may be anticipated by calling attention once more to Niebuhr's proposed "synthesis of Renaissance and Reformation." The "truth" of both is preserved by acknowledging the Reformation's insight into matters of ultimate concern and the Renaissance's competence in "proximate," or less than ultimate, matters. While this division of labor is consistent with Niebuhr's theology as a whole, the question is whether it unwittingly restricts the critical potential of Christianity's "abiding truth." Does it not, for example, restrict the relevance of this truth to those moments of self-recognition in which individuals actually confront their personal dimension of depth in life? Obviously such moments necessarily have practical relevance, especially when the individuals in question are engaged in a common search for "proximate solutions" to social problems. But in what way do these moments actually provide theoretical perspective on that search? What we've seen so far of Christian realism is both suggestive and promising; Niebuhr's effort to make its practical meaning more explicit will now be examined as we retrace the outlines of his ethics.

NOTES

1. As we shall see in this chapter and the next, Niebuhr tried to establish the theoretical meaning of his insights in a critical correlation with Karen Horney's psychological account of anxiety and Karl Mannheim's sociology of knowledge. His strategy in each case is different: Horney's psychology is used to clarify the cognitive claims made in Niebuhr's theological anthropology, while Mannheim's critical social theory is used to develop a "middle axiom" for linking theology and ethics. This difference results in a theoretical weakness: although the sociology of knowledge is used to clarify the role of an eschatological perspective in criticizing the "idolatrous" pretensions of both ideologies and utopias, it does not thereby yield criteria for identifying their inadequacies on anything other than a religious basis. This theoretical weakness has practical significance for Christian social activists, since they need guidance not only concerning the religious pretensions of ideologies and utopias, but also concerning the economic and social interests that they represent. If this theoretical weakness is appreciated, then the ideological drift often detected in Niebuhr's later works becomes intelligible.

2. I propose to ignore the apologetic claim for two reasons: (1) since this analysis focuses on the systematic coherence and adequacy of Christian realism as a model for practical theology, its apologetic stance is not directly relevant; (2) in any case, the validity of the apologetic claim is much more difficult to establish than the systematic issues under discussion here.

3. To be appreciated properly, Niebuhr's proposal deserves to be compared with other efforts of similar scope, which have proved to be significant in shaping the intellectual and moral agenda for the postwar West. Karl Popper's *The Open Society and Its Enemies*, and *The Dialectic of Enlightenment* written by the founders of the Frankfurt School of Social Re-

search, Max Horkheimer and Theodor W. Adorno, immediately come to mind as a useful basis for comparison. While neither of these represents the crudely consistent "idealism" and "materialism" that Niebuhr places in opposition to his own perspective, they do attempt a reassessment of the foundations of Western culture in light of the events culminating in World War II. Their views diverge systematically from each other, and they offer substantively different diagnoses of the relationship of reason and passion, of alienation, and of history, myth, and society, from those outlined in *The Nature and Destiny of Man*.

4. Throughout the period of his mature work, Niebuhr insisted that a Christian interpretation of human nature is "beyond tragedy." In short, neither Adam and Eve nor the Serpent share the fate of Prometheus, and Yahweh's jealousy is not that of Zeus. Christian myth is not meant to evoke a response of terror and pity; still less, in Niebuhr's view, does it promote a spirit of resignation to one's "fate." Instead, its purpose is ironic, in the sense that it provides a sobering perspective from which the paradox of "finiteness and freedom" can once more be lived as a creative possibility. This point is developed in "The Significance of Irony" (Niebuhr, 1952:151–74).

5. The practical consequences of the "pride of power" serve as the point of departure for Niebuhr's reflection on "the balance of power" principle within his "theological framework for social ethics." This principle is discussed in Chapter 4, below.

6. Niebuhr's discussion of the futility of self-deception is an anthropological reflection of his theological understanding of the Hidden God. Though "hidden," God's presence is emphatically providential in the sense that the structures of both human nature and history reflect his "mercy," and their violation sooner or later evokes his "wrath." The mercy and wrath of a Hidden God, in other words, are intrinsic to the structure of human action and thus may be recognized in the experienced futility of self-deception.

7. This is Niebuhr's prophetic view of the historic meaning of Roman Catholicism. His polemical stance did not change until his later years when his growing appreciation for the social philosophy of Jacques Maritain and the promise of Vatican Council II caused him to revise it. The later, more irenic mood is reflected in an interview with Niebuhr published in Patrick Granfield's *Theologians at Work* (1967: 51–68).

8. The unorthodox tendencies of Niebuhr's understanding of grace have been noted by critics and sympathizers alike. Rachel Hadley King's *The Omission of the Holy Spirit from Reinhold Niebuhr's Theology*, for example, accuses Niebuhr of adhering to a scientific worldview that precludes belief in "miracles," that is, the direct intervention of God in human affairs suspending the natural laws of cause and effect. King sees Niebuhr's inability to understand grace as "sanctification" as entirely consistent with his refusal "to question science's assumptions that nature's cause and effect sequences are unbroken": "My contention is that Niebuhr is searching desperately for some middle ground that will allow him to keep Biblical Christianity while denying that the supernatural God ever intervenes directly in the affairs of men, and that Niebuhr fails, because this denial eventually undercuts his claim that God is righteously loving" (King, 1964:101). For King, Christian realism thus is nothing more than "a kind of prophetic Deism." Paul Lehmann, in a more sympathetic manner, shares a similar uneasiness about Niebuhr's understanding of grace. After working out the relationships between the *Christus pro nobis* and *Christus in nobis* dimensions to Niebuhr's theology, Lehmann questions why the Christological element of Christian realism is so obscure and "so tardily drawn to the attention of his contemporaries" (Lehmann, 1956:277). His answer is that Niebuhr's failure to understand grace, or the *"Christus in nobis"* as *"operative* wisdom and power" is due to his neglect of the theology of the Holy Trinity. Seizing upon Niebuhr's apparent disregard of the *filioque* controversy in the development of the orthodox understanding of grace (Lehmann, 1956:278), Lehmann claims that "unless the Spirit proceeds from the Father and from the Son there is no way of guaranteeing either the Christological substance of the apprehensions of faith or the personal character of the fulfillment of the self and history symbolized in and by the Cross." Applied to Christian realism this claim makes for the following criticism: "Despite its insistence upon the Cross as the standpoint from which it is possible to make sense out of the manifold and complex dynamic of history, Niebuhr's Christological thinking does not sufficiently stress 'the mighty acts of God' as transforming events which, having actually occurred, serve as beacon lights in a sea of historical relativity whereby the channel to the fulfillment of human destiny is charted." In terms of the theology of grace, Lehmann's criticism means a significant revision of Niebuhr's formula on salvation: "Sin is overcome not merely 'in principle' but also 'in fact.' Justification is not only a principle of meaning and a historical possibility. People are 'in fact'

justified and the fruits of faith in sanctification, however tenuous, are actual human and historical realities." This revision, obviously, would fundamentally alter Niebuhr's understanding of Christian eschatology, and with it the basic perspective of Christian realism.

9. The link between this suspicion against theological anthropology and a substantively different notion of the relationship between Marxism and Christianity is discussed in Chapter 7, below.

10. Niebuhr's practical response to the challenge is worked out in his argument that the moral teachings of Jesus constitute an "impossible but relevant ethical ideal." While this ideal is meant to illuminate the difficult choices facing social activists, it is not to be interpreted as a command requiring unthinking obedience. The problem, however, for Niebuhr is to specify any situations where the ideal embodied in the ethic of Jesus clearly overrides considerations of political realism. If no such situations can be defined, then the relevance of this "impossible possibility" may be restricted to the private affairs of the self, a conclusion at odds with Niebuhr's intentions at least. This strategy and its difficulties are discussed in Chapter 4, below.

11. Not surprisingly, even in making use of this analogy, Niebuhr remains critical of Greek social philosophy. Specifically, he denounces "the simple identification of morals and politics in the thought of Plato and Aristotle, and their inability to find any perspective from which to judge the relative character and contingent achievement of their Greek city-state" (Niebuhr, 1941:214). This assessment is consistent with a critical awareness of the idealizing tendency built into the analogy between self and society, which would warrant qualifying it with insights taken from other sources, for example, the social realism of the biblical tradition.

12. The relationship between myth and history characteristic of the New Testament narratives is admirably summarized in Perrin, 1974:17–37. The problems that this relationship creates for modern theologians are carefully analyzed in Harvey, 1966.

13. Niebuhr's approach to the myth of the Atonement is not the only plausible one in Christian theology. His interpretation reflects certain fundamental choices that must remain controversial. By emphasizing the relationship to Jewish religious history, for example, Niebuhr tends to neglect the impact of Hellenism on New Testament Christologies. Furthermore, the designation of these narratives as a myth of Atonement itself reflects Niebuhr's judgment on the subordinate role of the theme of Incarnation in constructing a historical Christology. While these choices may be recognized as broadly Protestant in perspective, in my opinion they reflect rather than define the basic differences between Christian realism and liberation theology.

14. These categories, no doubt, also reflect the apologetic purpose of Niebuhr's philosophy of religion. Since, in Niebuhr's view, "nothing is so incredible as an answer to an unasked question" (Niebuhr, 1943:6), these categories thus identify the world's religions in order to engage them in theological polemics.

15. Christian realism's vulnerability here is of a different order from that of either liberation theology or the so-called dialectical theology with which it is often associated (Harvey, 1966: 132). In comparison with dialectical theology, Niebuhr's difficulties are implicit rather than explicit, because he is less precise in making and using the standard distinctions between *Historie* and *Geschichte* characteristic of this school. Nevertheless, the problems involved in dialectical theology which Van Harvey has identified are also typical of Niebuhr's work, especially, for example, in his discussion of the resurrection of Christ in *Faith and History*. Unlike the interpretation given in *The Nature and Destiny of Man*, where the resurrection is taken as an eschatological symbol of human fulfillment transcending history, here the historicity of the resurrection does have a bearing on "the recognition of the true Christ" (Niebuhr, 1949:145–50). On the whole, however, these difficulties weaken rather than completely overturn Niebuhr's theology of history, since it is clear that his focus remains fixed on the existential meaning of the myth, and his interpretations consistently refrain from making supernatural claims. The differences between Christian realism and liberation theology on this point are discussed in the final section of Chapter 8, below.

4

Christian Realism:
A Theological Framework for Social Ethics

To understand that the Christ in us is not a possession but a hope, that perfection is not a reality but an intention; that such peace as we know in this life is never purely the peace of achievement but the serenity of being "completely known and all forgiven"; all this does not destroy moral ardour or responsibility. On the contrary, it is the only way of preventing premature completions of life, or arresting the new and more terrible pride which may find its roots in the soil of humility, and of saving the Christian life from the intolerable pretension of saints who have forgotten that they are sinners.
—*Reinhold Niebuhr*, The Nature and Destiny of Man, *volume 2, 1943*

His colleague and friend John C. Bennett once characterized Niebuhr's contribution to Christian ethics as making "way for such solutions to our problems as are possible by clearing away the idealistic and utopian illusions which have flourished among religious liberals and secular intellectuals" (Bennett, 1956:50). In light of the previous analysis of Christian realism as theology, this description is helpful as a point of departure for appreciating the limits and possibilities of what Niebuhr referred to as his "theological framework for social ethics." For as we have seen, Niebuhr responded to the challenge provided by the "inevitable moral tension between individual and group morality" by scrutinizing precisely those illusions that tended to obscure this tension in a cloud of utopian expectation.

Yet as the analysis just presented also suggests, Christian realism may have succeeded better in addressing the problems that this tension creates for individuals than it did for groups. Although Niebuhr intended Christian realism as a perspective offering moral guidance on how to act responsibly in a political situation defined by "the conflict of grace and pride," it is not clear that he established this conflict's reference to history in such a way as to be anything more than metaphorically suggestive. Granted that his theological anthropology does represent the outline of a theoretically coherent Christian moral psychology, his theology of history does not achieve a similar theoretical status. Instead of clarifying the conflict of grace and pride in terms of the structural tensions and contradictions characteristic of the history of society, Niebuhr's theology of history becomes a history of theological ideas whose relationship to the processes of social development remains unanalyzed. Yet if Niebuhr were right in calling initially for a synthesis of "vital religious idealism" and "astute intelligence," Christian realism's theology of history should be more explicit in its theoretical assumptions regarding these processes.

In moving now from theology to ethics, we shall begin to see the practical consequences of this theoretical weakness. While Niebuhr's efforts at "clearing away the idealistic and utopian illusions" did bear fruit in an "independent Christian ethic," his proposal—I shall argue—represents not much more than a "dispositional ethic" for politicians and social activists. Even though this dispositional ethic must be recognized as a major contribution in its own right, it does not exhaust the promise of Christian realism as a model for practical theology.

"An Independent Christian Ethic"

The very existence of Christian ethics is a disputed question today. This is true not simply because the moral teachings of the New Testament seem so often to fly in the face of common sense, but more importantly because it is doubtful that there is any strictly logical connection between religion and morality. Rigorous philosophical analysis shows that the range of meanings ordinarily assigned to moral terms like "good" and "right" cannot be deduced from religious descriptions of human action, for example, "holy and pleasing to God" (Frankena, 1973:295–317). Furthermore, such logical analyses merely confirm what has already occurred in the processes of modernization. The pluralism of moral beliefs and practices in our society testifies to the fact that no one religious absolute serves as the logical presupposition of whatever standards of morality we hold in common. As a consequence, Christian ethics is problematic not only in its logical status but also in its practical relevance to the public world where political choices are made.

These problems have led some to conclude that Christian ethics is superfluous, that any attempt to make a connection between religion and morality is simply a matter of personal taste, and not worth discussing in public. Recent anthropological studies, however, continue to emphasize the pervasive relationship between them. Clifford Geertz's analysis of religion as a cultural system, for example, describes the ways in which religious beliefs and moral practices mutually reinforce each other (Geertz, 1973:87–125). The "powerful, pervasive, and long lasting moods and motivations" sustained by religion represent an integral system defined as both "world-view" and "ethos." Any given religion's success in seeming "uniquely realistic" is contingent upon the degree to which its correlation between religious vision and moral choices actually works. The more intimate the unity of theory and practice, the more plausible and vital the religion. Geertz's observations suggest that despite the theoretical difficulties much remains to be said about the practical relevance of religious ethics.

In order to grasp the situation of Christian ethics in particular, it is necessary to distinguish ethics and morality. A moment's reflection should convince us that there's more to ethics than the logical analysis of moral terms. Ethics is a means to an end; it is the theory of a particular human practice, the practice of morality. Morality is almost impossible to define, but it is instantly recognized as human action consciously directed according to some standard of goodness or rightness. It is characteristic of human persons, and has everything to do with the way we respond to our limits and possibilities. Indeed, ethics itself is based on a moral imperative, the moral imperative of "fairness." It tries to achieve a rational consistency in human action, since inconsistency seems not only irrational but also unfair. Such consistency is sought by using various strategies to clarify the values we profess and their practical consequences. Ethics therefore is concerned to articulate our moral ideals, our notions of vice and virtue, of duties responsibly discharged or irresponsibly evaded; and it tries to assess what reasons may be given for them. It also prescribes rules for moral conduct and provides models for interpreting the circumstances in which the rules may apply. All of these theoretical strategies are means directed to an end, to promote the use of reason in the practice of morality so that human beings might become more fully human. Christian ethics is just one way of organizing these strategies. It proceeds from an explicit awareness of the religious basis of its moral point of view. While it need not claim that Christianity is the exclusive source of moral wisdom, it is dedicated to clarifying the moral implications of its distinctive religious vision.

Niebuhr's proposal for an "independent Christian ethic" serves to illustrate this point. In it he argues that "the distinctive contribution of religion to morality lies in its comprehension of the dimension of depth in life" (Niebuhr, 1935:2–3). This assertion, of course, is the major premise of his "mythical approach" to Christianity. But he also uses it to develop a contrast between "secular" and "religious" morality. Secular moralities, according to Niebuhr, are based on rational considerations of self-interest, and therefore the ethics based on them tend to be "purely prudential." Prudence, however, is not the focus of concern in religious moralities:

A religious morality is constrained by its sense of dimension of depth to trace every force with which it deals to some ultimate origin and to relate every purpose to some ultimate end. It is concerned not only with immediate values and disvalues, but with the problem of good and evil, not only with immediate objectives, but with ultimate hopes.

It is troubled by the question of the primal "whence" and the final "wherefore." It is troubled by these questions because religion is concerned with life and existence as a unity and coherence of meaning. [Niebuhr, 1935:3]

Since, in his view, it is "impossible to live at all without presupposing a meaningful existence," religion's contribution to morality is indispensable.

All the same, Niebuhr does not argue that "morality is logically dependent on religion" in the sense previously mentioned. In fact, the strategy of his "independent Christian ethic" presupposes just the opposite, since a "natural morality" must be rationally valid for his proposals to make sense at all. Thus his concern is not with the logical status but with the practical relevance of Christian ethics, which he tries to defend as an "impossible possibility."

This deliberately paradoxical term signals Niebuhr's intention of construing Christian ethics in a manner consistent with his "mythical approach" to Christianity. The "ethic of Jesus" presents an "impossible possibility" insofar as it commands a love that is beyond human capacity. Jesus' command to love—love of God above all things, love of neighbor as ourselves, even love of enemies—is absolute and uncompromising. But it is also paradoxical in view of the abiding truths of Christian myth: it is "possible" because human persons are free to aspire to it; it is "impossible" because our anxious responses to human finiteness preclude its perfect realization. Nevertheless, the "impossible possibility" remains relevant because it provides a critical perspective on human thinking and acting. The ideal of "sacrificial love," in other words, is relevant as a lure to ever higher levels of moral aspiration and as a judgment on the inadequacy of every moral achievement. The "impossible possibility" thus realizes Niebuhr's notion of a "religious morality" by relating "the dimension of depth in life" (the human paradox of finiteness and freedom as symbolized in Christian myth) to some ultimate end (Jesus' command to love). His claim is that this "independent Christian ethic" not only comprehends "existence as a unity and coherence of meaning" but thereby also provides critical perspective on the limits and possibilities of purely "natural morality." In that sense, for Niebuhr at least, Christian ethics is neither superfluous nor merely a matter of personal taste.

Religious Pacifism: An Example

Niebuhr's way of establishing the relevance of his "framework for social ethics" may be appreciated by seeing how it is used to resolve a complex moral issue. It may also help to illustrate the peculiar difficulties of his understanding of Christian ethics. His writings on pacifism, especially those published just prior to America's entry into World War II when many Christian groups in the country sympathized with the isolationism of the

America First Committee, provide an illuminating example. The essay, "Why the Christian Church Is Not Pacifist" (Niebuhr, 1940:1–32) is especially helpful because it presents Niebuhr's position in the theological categories which he was developing at that time for *The Nature and Destiny of Man.*

Niebuhr's discussion of pacifism is a complicated one, not simply because he interpreted the ethic of Jesus as an "impossible possibility," but also because he was himself a pacifist during the 1920s and early 1930s. Although his later position diverged from this commitment, there is one unchanging center in his approach to the question: his steady recognition that the ethic of Jesus, or "the law of love," in fact is "absolute and uncompromising" in commanding "non-resistance to evil" (Niebuhr, 1940:10). But from the beginning he also insisted that "the gospel is something more than the law of love." The question throughout his career, then, was: How should a Christian respond to the ethic of Jesus? Indeed, it is important to note that Niebuhr never considered this to be a pointless question. The ethic of Jesus had to be interpreted in light of the religious meaning of Christianity as a whole.

Over the years Niebuhr's view of pacifism changed as his interpretation of Christianity developed. During World War I he supported Woodrow Wilson's effort to "make the world safe for democracy," only to become a pacifist in disgust over the vindictiveness of the Peace of Versailles. Continued experience as a Christian social activist, however, qualified his commitment to pacifism in significant ways. In light of the realities of the class struggle, he eventually recognized that some form of coercion is necessary to restrain the institutionalized violence of capitalism. Generalizing the point, he concluded that the exercise of political responsibility was impossible without using the instruments of coercion, violent or otherwise. While he admired Mahatma Gandhi as a moral and political leader, he was not about to equate his strategy of "nonviolent resistance" with Jesus' moral absolute of "nonresistance to evil" (Niebuhr, 1932b: 243). On the other hand, he recognized the spiritual dimensions of "nonviolent resistance," its educational appeal to the residues of moral goodwill and self-discipline. All the same, nonviolence was still a form of coercion, a subtle and at times very effective tactic in the struggle for social justice (Niebuhr, 1932b:240–42). Thus when he resigned from the Fellowship of Reconciliation in 1934, he conceded that he was among those "who are pacifists only in the sense that they will refuse to participate in an international armed conflict" (Niebuhr, 1934c:256). But in that case, he added, perhaps they were not pacifists at all. Niebuhr's lingering reservation against "international armed conflict" broke down during the late 1930s. He emphatically rejected the policy of appeasing Hitler and reluctantly came to the conclusion that moral resistance to fascism inevitably would lead to war. Even so, his realistic assessment of these difficult political choices continued to be tempered by a sense of fidelity to the ethic of Jesus.

Accordingly, he sought to minimize conflict and violence wherever possible. Such was his record as a moralist on the issue of pacifism. The question is: How did he justify his changing views as a Christian ethicist?

Despite the intensely polemical tone of his essay "Why the Christian Church Is Not Pacifist," Niebuhr did not want to rule out the possibility of a genuinely Christian pacifism. His purpose was limited to defending Christian realists against the charge of apostasy, and to exposing the pretensions—intellectual as well as moral—of the kind of pacifism then fashionable among liberal Protestants. In working out his ethical perspective, Niebuhr accepts the thesis of Meno Simons that the ethic of Jesus represents an absolute ideal of nonresistance. He even admits that the "Christian perfectionism" of authentic "sectarians" is "a valuable asset for the Christian faith" (Niebuhr, 1940:5) as a necessary witness to the law of love. Nevertheless, this witness is incompatible with the exercise of political responsibility:

> This perfectionism did not give itself to the illusion that it had discovered a method for eliminating the element of conflict from political strategies. On the contrary, it regarded the mystery of evil as beyond its power of solution. It was content to set up the most perfect and unselfish individual life as a symbol of the Kingdom of God. It knew that this could only be done by disavowing the political task and by freeing the individual of all responsibility for social justice. [Niebuhr, 1940:5]

By contrast, the more common pacifism could be judged heretical because it fostered the illusion that it is a fairly easy thing to reconcile political involvement with "the simple gospel of Jesus."

At this point the peculiar emphases of Niebuhr's Christian ethics, his concern with the interpretation of moral character and circumstances in light of the "total Gospel" of sin and grace, come into play. Modern pacifism is wrong because it is based on a view of human nature that cherishes "the belief that man is essentially good at some level of his being":

> They believe that if you can abstract the rational-universal man from what is finite and contingent in human nature, or if you can only cultivate some mystic universal element in the deeper levels of man's consciousness, you will be able to eliminate human selfishness and the consequent conflict of life with life. These rational or mystical views of man conform neither to the New Testament's view of human nature nor yet to the complex facts of human experience. [Niebuhr, 1940:7–8]

Consequently, the law of love cannot be interpreted as "just another law, but a law which transcends all law." The issue for Christian ethics, then, is not precisely what Jesus taught and commanded, but how those teachings are to be applied in light of the total gospel.

As a framework for ethics, Niebuhr's interpretation of the total gospel does two things. First, it emphasizes the absoluteness of the ethic of Jesus; second, it argues that this ethic cannot be realized in history as a simple possibility. Niebuhr's insistence that the commands of Jesus must be understood in light of "the New Testament's view of human nature" actually leads him to reject any rationalization of those commands in the hope of making them more acceptable. Commonly, pacifists have rationalized Jesus' "ethic of nonresistance" as allowing for "nonviolent resistance" in order to justify their engagement in certain political actions. Niebuhr contends that it is more accurate to admit that "the ethic of non-resistance can have no immediate relevance to any political situation" (Niebuhr, 1940:10).

But if the ideal of nonresistance has no immediate relevance, of what use is it? Do Christians merely pay lip-service to it, and then go on to think and act like everyone else? Obviously, this is not what Niebuhr means by fidelity to the ethic of Jesus. The law of love "remains a principle of criticism over all forms of community in which elements of coercion and conflict destroy the highest type of fellowship." Furthermore, this principle itself represents a twofold strategy: (1) "Indiscriminate criticism," in other words, the attempt to view all human endeavors from the perspective of the kingdom of God, illuminates the sinful elements common to all political relationships. Such criticism, it is hoped, will help "to mitigate self-righteousness," and foster "the spirit of contrition" necessary "to restrain the impulse of vengeance sufficiently to allow a decent justice to emerge" (Niebuhr, 1940:23). Thus the awareness of the absolute ethic of Jesus should have a significant impact on the character and dispositions of Christians engaged in politics. (2) "Discriminate criticism" means that the ethic of Jesus serves as an ideal standard of approximation. If Christians cannot hope to fulfill this ideal in a perfect society, at least they can try to do what is possible. This is the difficult path of accepting a share of public responsibility. As a standard of approximation, "the law of love" therefore provides a benchmark for judging between greater goods and lesser evils.

In justifying his support for the war effort of the Allies, Niebuhr appeals to both principles. A realistic assessment of the situation reveals that a choice lies between the tyranny of Nazism and the terrible but temporary anarchy of war. Tyranny may mean peace, "but it is a peace which has nothing to do with the peace of the Kingdom of God" (Niebuhr, 1940:16). Thus the religious pacifist's claims are suspect according to the principle of indiscriminate criticism. But what about the option for war? Here Niebuhr uses the principle of discriminate criticism to force a fateful choice:

One of the most terrible consequences of a confused religious absolutism is that it is forced to condone such tyranny as that of Germany in the nations which it has conquered and now cruelly oppresses. It usually does this by insisting that the tyranny is no worse than that which is practised in the so-called democratic nations. Whatever may be the moral ambiguities of the so-called democratic nations, and however serious may be their failure to conform perfectly to their democratic ideals, it is sheer moral perversity to equate the inconsistencies of a democratic civilization with the brutalities which modern tyrannical States practise. If we cannot make a distinction here, there are no historical distinctions which have any value. All the distinctions upon which the fate of civilization has turned in the history of mankind have been just such relative distinctions. [Niebuhr, 1940: 16–17]

While this interplay between the strategies of discriminate and indiscriminate criticism is faithful to the example of the Hebrew prophets,[1] Niebuhr never really clarifies the ethical reasons justifying the "relative distinction" that is based upon it. Although he assumes that it is consistent with the law of love, his warrants seem to stem from another source as well. Thus he "is persuaded to thank God in such times as these that the common people maintain a degree of 'common sense' " which "has been lost among Christian idealists." In other words, since common sense, or natural morality, retains a capacity to identify and resist injustices, it must provide a basis for discriminate criticism, along with Christian prophecy.

But instead of clarifying the relationship between the two, Niebuhr once more describes the general features of Christian prophecy:

The overt conflicts of human history are periods of judgment when what has been hidden becomes revealed. It is the business of Christian prophecy to anticipate these judgments to some degree at least, to call attention to the fact that when men say "peace and quiet" "destruction will come upon them unaware," and reveal to what degree this overt destruction is a vivid portrayal of the constant factor of sin in human life. A theology which fails to come to grips with this tragic factor of sin is heretical, both from the standpoint of the gospel and in terms of its blindness to the obvious facts of human experience in every realm and on every level of moral goodness. [Niebuhr, 1940: 17–18]

Just as Niebuhr's mythical approach to Christianity appeals to experience in order to validate its insights, so his "theological framework for social ethics" must appeal to both "natural" and "religious" morality to establish its principles of criticism. Despite the ambiguity of their relationship, it is clear that maintaining a creative tension between them is the characteristic task of Christian realism.[2]

Out of his struggle with the question of pacifism, then, the distinctive agenda of Niebuhr's Christian ethics becomes apparent. It emphasizes

A THEOLOGICAL FRAMEWORK FOR SOCIAL ETHICS 87

questions of interpretation, and tends to illustrate—even while neglecting
theoretically—the complexities of moral choices. Niebuhr is clearly more
interested in understanding the religious vision and its immediate practical
consequences than in formulating the series of inferences that reflective
analysis discovers linking the two. Christian realism thus is an ethic that
stresses the cultivation of proper dispositions on the part of individual
moral agents. It also relies heavily on the moral intuitions of common sense
informed by a biblical view of human nature. Niebuhr claims that this
agenda is a faithful rendering of the substantive meaning of Christianity:

> In its profoundest insights the Christian faith sees the whole of human
> history as involved in guilt, and finds no release from guilt except in
> the grace of God. The Christian is freed by that grace to act in history;
> to give his devotion to the highest values he knows; to defend those
> citadels of civilization of which necessity and historic destiny have
> made him the defender; and he is persuaded by that grace to re-
> member the ambiguity of even his best actions. If the providence of
> God does not enter the affairs of men to bring good out of evil, the evil
> in our good may easily destroy our most ambitious efforts and frus-
> trate our highest hopes. [Niebuhr, 1940:30]

But Niebuhr's reflections on religious pacifism not only introduce the
typical agenda for his ethics; they also raise certain critical expectations
about it. His "theological framework for social ethics" takes up the challenge of defending the practical relevance of Christianity. Furthermore, as
the example suggests, that defense is based on showing how the tension
between the principles of indiscriminate and discriminate criticism may be
maintained creatively. In other words, the burden of proof for Christian
realism as an ethic is to clarify the relationship between religious devotion
to an "impossible possibility" and a moral commitment to "the nicely
calculated less and more" that gives ethical consistency to political
choices. In what follows, this tension will be reflected in Niebuhr's clarification of love and justice as moral dispositions entailed by his "Christian
interpretation of human nature," and in his recommendations concerning
ideological conflict and political organization consistent with his "Christian interpretation of human destiny." In each case, in order to establish
the practical relevance of Christian ethics, Niebuhr must show how his
proposals offer a substantive orientation to the public world where political
choices are made. Let us begin with love and justice.

Love and Justice: An Ethic for Politicians

In keeping with his original intention of wedding a vital religious idealism
to an astute social intelligence, Niebuhr made the ideals of love and justice
central to his ethics from the beginning. *Moral Man and Immoral Society,*

for example, juxtaposes them as two indispensable moral absolutes: "A rational ethic aims at justice, and a religious ethic makes love the ideal," the distinction being that "love meets the needs of the neighbor, without carefully weighing and comparing his needs with those of the self" (Niebuhr, 1932b:57). Justice, at this stage in his thinking, represented a rational ideal demanding an equal distribution of goods and services. Love, on the other hand, represented a passionate concern for "the transcendent and absolute worth" of "the neighbor, and thus encourages sympathy toward him." Both were considered necessary for social action, even though neither would find perfect realization in society. The frank dualism in morals that Niebuhr counseled at this time suggested that the ideal of love was more likely to govern personal relationships; and justice, the actual strategy and tactics of social change. Thus Niebuhr initially conceived the relation between the two as one of coordination.

After the political crisis of the mid-1930s, Niebuhr revised his understanding of love and justice. In *An Interpretation of Christian Ethics* love is now regarded as "the crown of Christian ethics . . . the most difficult and impossible of moral achievements" (Niebuhr, 1935:137). This new estimation is based on insights into "love as forgiveness" inspired by both his experience of the crisis and his reflections on Christian myth. Experience suggested that love is profoundly relevant to the pursuit of justice, since "no system of justice established by the political, economic, and social coercion in the political order is perfect enough to dispense with the refinements which voluntary and uncoerced human kindness and tenderness between individuals add to it" (Niebuhr, 1935:123). Furthermore, the pinnacle of love represented by "self-sacrifice" has special relevance to the problems created by cynicism and fanaticism in politics. Although some form of religious myth always provides the moral basis for social action, the Christian ethic of love enables a person "to engage in social struggle with a religious reservation" (Niebuhr, 1935:141). Niebuhr commends this reservation as the fruit of religious disinterestedness; its root is "love as forgiveness." This pinnacle of love, of course, is the "impossible possibility" disclosed by reflection on Jesus' ethic in light of Christian myth. At this stage love and justice are linked in a relationship of subordination: love is seen as both more comprehensive and more ultimate than justice.

The full implications of this view of love and justice become explicit in *The Nature and Destiny of Man*, which systematically elaborates Niebuhr's theological interpretation of the myths of Creation, the Fall, and Atonement. The theological anthropology presented there thus provides a framework in which love and justice are analyzed as moral dispositions. Grounded in the paradoxical phenomena of anxiety, the complexity of their relationship is mapped out according to a dialectic of original sin and original righteousness.

"Original righteousness" is a term used to describe Adam and Eve's mythical condition before the Fall. Its reference is given in the experience of absence, in the yearning for wholeness and harmony implicit in the universal mood of anxiety. Niebuhr interprets this dimension of depth as "the law of love" embedded in human nature by its creator:

> The specific content of this higher law, which is more than law, this law which transcends all law, this original righteousness which even sinful man has, not as a possession but in his sense of something lacking, has been tentatively defined, and this definition must now be further explicated. It contains three terms: (a) The perfect relation of the soul to God in which obedience is transcended by love, trust and confidence ("Thou shalt love the Lord thy God"); (b) the perfect internal harmony of the soul with itself in all of its desires and impulses: "With all thy heart and all thy soul and all thy mind"; and (c) the perfect harmony of life with life: "Thou shalt love thy neighbor as thyself." [Niebuhr, 1941:288–89]

Original righteousness, therefore, is the knowledge of what ought to be, the law of human freedom (Niebuhr, 1941: 280). It is an ultimate norm for the human self, comprehending both the "natural law . . . derived from man's essential nature" and the "theological virtues, that is, the virtues of faith, hope, and love" understood as "ultimate possibilities over the requirements of natural law"[3] (Niebuhr, 1941:285).

These distinctions within the one ideal condition of original righteousness correspond to the paradox of human nature, at once both finite and free, and to the mythical disclosure that Adam is both a "creature" and made to the "image of God." This paradox describes that elusive dimension of self-consciousness in which human persons accept responsibility for their freedom. That act, which Niebuhr designates as "self-transcendence," is the center of the moral conscience, the interiority upon which the dispositions of the moral life are built.

"Original sin" means that this essential perfection and harmony is yearned for and recognized in the imperfection and disharmonies of our actual life. Thus our actual experience of original righteousness is more accurately described and interpreted as follows:

> Real love between person and person is therefore a relationship in which spirit meets spirit in a dimension in which both the uniformities and the differences of nature, which bind men together and separate them, are transcended. This is no simple possibility. Each soul remains, in a sense, inscrutable to its fellows. It is a possibility only by way of the love of God. All human love between person and person is frustrated by inscrutable mysteries in the heart of each person and by opaque "walls of partition" between man and man. Inasfar as human love is a possibility, therefore, it is always partly a relation between

the soul and soul via their common relation to God. Inasfar as it is not a possibility it points to God as the final realization of the possibility. Where the love of God does not undergird and complete the relation of man to man, the differences which nature creates and sin accentuates, differences of geography, race, time, place and history, separate men from one another; and the similarities of nature and of reason may indeed unite men but not on the level of spirit and freedom. [Niebuhr, 1941:294–95]

Thus just as the myth of the Fall substantially qualifies the paradox of finiteness and freedom, so original sin qualifies original righteousness. It is never known directly but is glimpsed as "the consciousness and memory of an original perfection in the self-as-transcendent."

Niebuhr's moral dialectic of original righteousness and original sin modifies the picture of love and justice in significant ways. On the one hand, if original righteousness described our nature as it exists in history, then the relation of love and justice would unfold as the interplay between an ideal of perfect mutuality and the principles and structures of maximal equality. Under such circumstances mutual love and justice among equals would constitute a harmony in which love transcended justice as a symbol of the highest aspirations of human freedom. But original righteousness does not describe the actual situation of persons in history. In light of original sin's response to anxiety, the facts of disharmony as actually experienced mean that mutual love pursued for its own sake becomes a self-defeating egotism, while single-minded dedication to the principle of equal justice more often than not provides an occasion for either cynicism or fanaticism. Thus the moral dispositions of love and justice are placed in the context defined by the "abiding truth" of Christian myth.

Since Niebuhr believes that the moral impasse symbolized by original sin can only be overcome religiously, he returns to Christian myth for illumination. In keeping with his interpretation of the myth of Atonement, he takes the cross of Christ as the disclosure of "sacrificial love." The impossible possibility symbolized by the cross is related to mutual love as the real to the ideal. Since of itself mutual love tends to generate responses that are neither mutual nor loving, sacrificial love seeks to realize the ideal, but with a different strategy. Perfect mutuality, in other words, can be approximated only if the element of self-interest is checked by a willingness to self-sacrifice. Despite the fact that this "pinnacle of love" is the norm for all Christian moral dispositions, it can be realized fully in this life only in rare circumstances. Ordinarily it means a willingness to forgive and forget, a disposition to accommodate oneself to the interests of others more than is morally required.

Sacrificial love has a subtle relationship to the principles of justice. Since such love is always a spiritual adventure involving the personal decisions of individual moral agents, there may be certain circumstances in which it is inappropriate. Usually political questions fall into this category, since inevitably they involve the interests of others for whom the agent bears some responsibility. In such a situation "the sacrifice of those interests ceases to be 'self-sacrifice.' It may be the unjust betrayal of those interests" (Niebuhr, 1943:88). Thus in circumstances dominated by original sin, by spiritual disharmony and social conflict, sacrificial love is a realistic option only when individuals are free to dispose of themselves without regard for the interests of others. In all other situations, sacrificial love serves to symbolize undefined higher possibilities that might shatter our self-satisfaction with any partial realization of justice.

As interpreted by Niebuhr, sacrificial love cannot be understood apart from its concrete embodiment in the myth of the Atonement. He summarizes his view by enumerating three ways in which the sacrificial love of the cross transcends the standards of mutuality characteristic of natural morality: *(a)* "Sacrificial love *(agape)* completes the incompleteness of mutual love *(eros)*, for the latter is always arrested by reason of the fact that it . . . is obviously not sufficiently free of preoccupation with self to lose itself in the life of another" (Niebuhr, 1943:82). Mutual love, in other words, must be "the unintended rather than the purposed consequence of the action" (Niebuhr, 1943:84). Thus Niebuhr postulates a dialectical relationship between religious and natural morality in his ethics. *(b)* "The Cross represents a transcendent perfection which clarifies obscurities of history and defines what is possible in historic development" (Niebuhr, 1943:86). Specifically, Niebuhr insists that "the Christian faith in its profoundest versions has never believed that the Cross would so change the very nature of historical existence that a more and more universal achievement of sacrificial love would finally transmute sacrificial love into successful mutual love, perfectly validated and by historical consequences." This second point locates the principle of discriminate criticism by ruling out those misinterpretations that confuse sacrificial love with Christian perfectionism. *(c)* "The Cross represents a perfection which contradicts the false pretensions of virtue in history and which reveals the contrast between man's sinful self-assertion and the divine *agape*" (Niebuhr, 1943: 89). This final point emphasizes the fact that sacrificial love should give birth to a religious sense of repentance. Thus Niebuhr derives the principle of indiscriminate criticism. Taken together, these three points suggest that in light of the cross of Christ the ideal of sacrificial love paradoxically defines the ultimate end of Christian morality. Without the ultimate paradox embodied in the cross, sacrificial love—in Niebuhr's opinion—would be a meaningless betrayal of the hard-won common sense of moral responsibility.

In Niebuhr's theological framework for social ethics, then, love and justice designate certain "powerful, pervasive and long-lasting moods and motivations" that provide orientation for Christian social action. They not only describe the basic dispositions of Christian moral character, but also provide a critical perspective on human aspirations and achievements. The practical relevance of these dispositions is based on Niebuhr's hope that a willingness to risk self-sacrifice in the interests of mutuality will enhance the human capacity to act for social justice. At the very least, Christians may learn compassion and humility in an attempt to live the paradox of love and justice.

Niebuhr's discussion of love and justice thus helps to make explicit the connection between his theology and his ethics. In fact, that is their chief strength: by translating the substantive insights of his theological anthropology into a dispositional ethic, they confirm the internal coherence of Christian realism. That very strength, however, is complemented by a weakness. The problem involves the adequacy of this dispositional ethic, its apparent lack of criteria of applicability. How does this discussion of love and justice illuminate the difficult tactical decisions that social activists must actually make?

Consider the following example. In what way does the disposition of sacrificial love substantively inform the actions of those involved in the realities of social conflict? Niebuhr remarks:

> The victim of injustice cannot cease from contending against his oppressors, even if he has a religious sense of the relativity of all social positions and a contrite recognition of the sin in his own heart. Only a religion full of romantic illusions could seek to persuade the Negro to gain justice from the white man merely by forgiving him. As long as men are involved in the conflicts of nature and sin they must seek according to the best available moral insights to contend for what they believe to be right. And that will mean that they will contend against other men. Short of the transmutation of the world into the Kingdom of God, men will always confront enemies. [Niebuhr, 1935: 140–41]

These observations, of course, reflect that mixture of Christian prophecy and common sense characteristic of Niebuhr's principle of discriminate criticism. But any action based directly on the ideal of sacrificial love apparently is overruled by it. In fact, his whole point is to criticize the "romantic illusions" of those who would act solely on the basis of "love as forgiveness." In this case, love's impact seems restricted to the inner recesses of the "heart."

Nevertheless, Niebuhr recommends the religious reservation for its help in exorcising the demonic pretensions that inevitably accompany social conflict. Thus, although the dispositions in question do not translate directly into behavioral rules, they are supposed to exert a subtle yet pervasive pressure on the moral sensibilities of Christian activists. But beyond their illuminative use in scrutinizing political "illusions," it remains difficult to pin down the practical difference that these dispositions actually make in any given case. This difficulty, however, should not lead us to dismiss them. It may simply reflect the fact that Niebuhr's dialectic of love and justice is restricted to a dispositional ethic, meant to provide orientation for the consciences of social activists, especially those faced with the realities of political responsibility in any meaningful way. Nothing more and nothing less.

Niebuhr's formulation of criteria of applicability—his behavioral tests for these dispositions—is presented elsewhere in his recommendations concerning ideological conflict and political organization. Nevertheless, the difficulty in establishing the practical consequences of this dispositional ethic continues to reflect the problem that first emerged in trying to understand his principles of indiscriminate and discriminate criticism. What is the nature of the tension between the ideal of "sacrificial love" and "the best available moral insights"? How is it to be resolved both in theory and in practice? The strategies of his Christian ethic so far discussed may plausibly be counted as an ethic for politicians, but they do not yet constitute a genuinely social ethic. The difference will become apparent as we proceed.

Political Ethics: "The Test of Tolerance"

What extends Niebuhr's theological framework for social ethics beyond the limits of this dispositional ethic is his attempt to develop certain middle axioms. The term "middle axiom," once a commonplace in American Christian ethics, refers to "attempts to define the directions in which, in a particular state of society, Christian faith must express itself." These "provisional definitions" are precisely "middle" axioms because they seek to make the connection "between purely general statements of the ethical demands of the Gospel and the decisions that have to be made in concrete situations" (Long, 1967:108). They are "provisional" because they are derived from the Christian ethicist's historical consciousness, his or her analysis of contemporary society and its problems. If the practical relevance of Niebuhr's "independent Christian ethic" is to be appreciated, an analysis of his middle axioms should be useful.

In *The Nature and Destiny of Man* Niebuhr offers two theoretical strategies that qualify as middle axioms: (1) "the test of tolerance" as an orientation to problems of ideological conflict, and (2) "the balance of power" as an orientation to problems of political organization. Significantly, both of these are presented as applications of his theology of history. They are designed to relate his interpretation of history as "a conflict of grace and pride" and his proposal for "a synthesis of Reformation and Renaissance" to the task of ethical reconstruction in the postwar Western world. Thus they do not simply apply his anthropological categories to the perennial "quest for truth and the achievement of just and brotherly relations with our fellowmen" (Niebuhr, 1943:213). In addition, they reflect the ways in which these "forms of historical activity" have been approached in the modern world. Not surprisingly, therefore, Niebuhr's middle axioms are a result of a theologically motivated reading of history and the social sciences. His test of tolerance is informed by the sociology of knowledge; and his understanding of the balance of power, by modern political philosophies. In either case, of course, Niebuhr uses the social sciences as resources for Christian ethics, and not as a method for theology.

Niebuhr's awareness of the problem of ideological conflict goes all the way back to his initial search for a successful synthesis of "religious idealism" and "social intelligence." Eventually he came to realize that these two elements could not be isolated, that there were cognitive dimensions to religious idealism and moral passions involved in social intelligence. The semantic shifts that occurred in his categories, from "religious idealism" to "religious passion" to "illusion" to religious and political "mythology," indicate a deepening theological awareness of the problem. Thus when he formulated his appreciation of Christianity as a form of prophetic religion, inevitably the prophets' denunciation of idolatry became increasingly important in his attempt to criticize conflicting mythologies and their impact on contemporary politics. While Niebuhr was developing his theological perspective, certain social theorists, notably Karl Mannheim, were also analyzing the political crisis of the 1930s as a problem of ideological conflict. In *The Nature and Destiny of Man* and in some of the works that followed it Niebuhr, noting the parallels linking his concern with Mannheim's, offered a "Christian interpretation" of the problem of ideology and criticized the inadequacies of alternative analyses. But before examining his proposal, let us review the state of the question in the social sciences at that time.

Soon after the term "ideology" was minted, it became an accusation, a weapon in the class struggle. Karl Marx used it in this sense to define the false-consciousness by which the gross inequities of the political economy of capitalism were either justified or ignored. Somewhat sarcastically, Marx described ideologies as "the ideas of the ruling classes" or "ruling ideas." As a weapon in the struggle, ideological criticism meant unmasking false-consciousness, by analyzing its "truth" in terms of the structure of society and its contradictions. For Marx, Christianity was the classic example of an ideology. It provided the rulers with a religious legitimation of their dominant position in society while it mesmerized the ruled with the divine inevitability of their condition. When Marx declared that the "critique of religion is the beginning of all critique," he meant that the class struggle must begin by dispelling the illusions of ideology. His own general theory, a critique of the capitalist political economy as a whole, promised to provide the standard of interpretation for this therapeutic exercise.

Over the years the specific meaning that Marx attached to "ideology" within the class struggle tended to disappear. The meaning of the term was generalized so that it included the ideas of social movements inspired by

Marx himself. Marxism came to be viewed as a part of the problem of ideology rather than its solution. Mannheim's *Ideology and Utopia* assumes this development and seeks to redefine it in terms of a sociology of knowledge. The result is an analysis in which all social theories involved in the class struggle are relativized. Both ideologies and utopias are defined as situationally related interpretations of society. Neither entirely corresponds to reality as such, but the lack of correspondence distinctive of either may be understood functionally: "Ideologies" are "situationally transcendent ideas" whose projected contents are never realized, while "utopias" may "succeed through counter-activity in transforming the existing historical reality into one more in accord with their own conceptions" (Mannheim, 1936: 195–96). In other words, "ideology" defends the status quo by fostering inaction, while "utopia" may inspire action to overcome it. Given the fact that the political crisis was characterized by a stalemate between "dominant groups" and "ascendant groups," Mannheim hoped that ideological conflicts might be transcended if both groups submitted to arbitration by a third group identified with neither, a class of "free-floating intellectuals" (Mannheim, 1936:156–64).

Whatever the merits of this proposal, it is clear that Mannheim's analysis helped to relativize the problem of ideology. To unmask the ideology of the ruling class, Marxism assumed the standpoint of the proletariat as some sort of absolute standard of truth and tried to give it scientific expression. But, Mannheim argued, since this standpoint is not absolute, it cannot provide the scientific validity claimed for it by some Marxists. It, too, is vulnerable to ideological criticism: "Socialist thought, which hitherto has unmasked all its adversaries' utopias as ideologies, never raised the problem of determinateness about its own position. It never applied this method to itself and checked its own desire to be absolute" (Mannheim, 1936:225). By contrast, "free-floating intellectuals," while not possessing an absolute standpoint, do represent a new kind of science, the "sociology of knowledge." Mannheim thus hopes that they will minimize ideological conflict by showing all parties how to become critically aware of the limits of their perspectives.

Niebuhr's position is critical of both Marx and Mannheim. Accusing them of superficiality, he criticizes their approach to the problem for being confined to the cognitive level. Their theories of false-consciousness and their formulae for critical consciousness, in other words, assume that ideology is "the mere ignorance of ignorance" (Niebuhr, 1941:195), an inattention to the conditioned character of human knowledge. But in Niebuhr's view, this ignorance is not so innocent. Ever the moralist, he finds an element of pretense that he takes as evidence of the pervasiveness of intellectual pride:

> Knowledge of the truth is thus invariably tainted with an "ideological" taint of interest, which makes our apprehension of truth something less than knowledge of *the* truth and reduces it to *our* truth.

The cultural quest is furthermore confused by the premature claims of finality which men invariably make for their finite perspectives. This pretension is the sinful element in culture. It includes not merely the effort to deny the finiteness of our perspectives but to hide and obscure the taint of interest and passion in our knowledge. This pride is the real force of "ideology." [Niebuhr, 1943:214]

Niebuhr's point, of course, must be understood in the context provided by his theological anthropology. Ideological conflict ultimately is the problem of self-deception played out among human communities rather than within the hearts of individuals. The basic phenomena of human anxiety are common to both. Paradoxically created to the image of God, human persons aspire to absolute truth, yet can achieve it only partially, perspectivally. The very structures of human language, the limits and possibilities of discourse, suggest this rift between human aspiration and achievement in the pursuit of knowledge (Niebuhr, 1937a:41–46). Inevitably this paradox occasions anxious pretensions to knowledge of *the* truth. An ideological taint thus pervades all human thought and action. As evidence that the taint involves a moral as well as a cognitive dimension, Niebuhr cites the way in which ideological conflicts usually proceed. The mutual accusations of moral bankruptcy characteristic, for example, of the struggle between Stalinists and Trotskyites betray the fact that more is involved here than a mere ignorance of ignorance.

If the problem of ideological conflict is deeper than "false-consciousness," then its solution lies with neither the victory of the "proletariat" nor the verdict of a class of "free-floating intellectuals." If Niebuhr is right in his criticisms of Marx and Mannheim then, insofar as ideology pretends to an absoluteness that can only be understood as "idolatry," he has a good case for seeing it as a religious problem requiring a religious solution. Just as the prophets overcame idolatry with faith in the true God, so Niebuhr—consistent with his paradoxical vision of the Hidden God and his interpretation of the conflict of grace and pride in history—argues that the ideological taint may be overcome, in principle, "in moments of prayerful transcendence," which rely on the shattering power of the grace of Christ (Niebuhr, 1943:217). The qualification "in principle" means that prayer is no more capable of producing an "unconditioned mind" than is the sociology of knowledge. But it may occasion a religious disinterestedness that will carry over "into our interested thoughts and actions so that it creates some sense of pity and forgiveness for those who contend against our truth and oppose our action." A sense of pity and forgiveness—once again Niebuhr is commending the practical relevance of certain dispositions. Of themselves these do not resolve ideological conflicts; but they may serve to mitigate them by absorbing some of the bitterness and cruelty that all too often accompany the fanaticism of those convinced of their own truth and righteousness.

Niebuhr is realistic enough to know that this invitation to prayer will seem merely platitudinous unless it is backed up by some sort of behavioral test. While the dispositions of pity and forgiveness recommend themselves as a religious solution to the pathologies of human pride, where is the middle axiom that translates them into a perspective for addressing the problems of contemporary society? In Niebuhr's opinion, "the test of tolerance" provides such a perspective. An attempt to give a "Christian interpretation" to one of the central moral aspirations of modern Western humanism, this test spells out the meaning of the proposed "synthesis of Reformation and Renaissance" for society's "quest for the truth."

The test of tolerance is based on a typically modern awareness of the perspectival character of truth. Mannheim's sociology of knowledge asserts, and Niebuhr's paradox of finiteness and freedom confirms, that there is no absolute standard of truth capable of adjudicating ideological disputes. Even so, the "problem of truth," for Niebuhr, is not the epistemological puzzle generated by relativism, but its practical consequences. An awareness of the relativity of perspectives threatens to lock society into a cycle of cynicism and fanaticism: a cynicism born of despair over the limits of truth, matched by a fanaticism bent on denying those limits, both of which complicate the practical problem of ideological conflict. The test of tolerance, however, is meant to break this cycle: "The test is twofold and includes both the ability to hold vital convictions which lead to action; and also the capacity to preserve the spirit of forgiveness toward those who offend us by holding convictions which seem untrue to us" (Niebuhr, 1943:219). Both parts of the test are important. Neglect of the first part results once more in cynicism; neglect of the second, in fanaticism.

In explaining the relevance of this test, Niebuhr draws on his theology of history. The conflict of grace and pride is punctuated by the vicissitudes of tolerance in the history of Christianity. Niebuhr thus places the test in the context of Christian failures to grasp the paradox of sin and grace. Catholicism, for example, is described as "intolerant in principle." Its "peculiar doctrine of grace" leads it "to claim unconditioned possession of the truth" (Niebuhr, 1943:221), a claim that has entailed quite logically the policies represented by the Inquisition.[4] The Protestant Reformation, on the other hand, is "tolerant in principle, but not in fact." Niebuhr's mixed verdict here stems from his interpretation of "justification by faith" and Protestantism's failure "to apply this insight to the cultural problem so that it would mitigate the spiritual pride of man"[5] (Niebuhr, 1943:231). The historic realization of the principle of religious tolerance, in fact, was the achievement of the Renaissance and "Sectarian Christianity." Nevertheless, these movements also fail the test because each of them tended to restrict the principle to explicitly religious affairs, the latter out of indifference to nonreligious concerns, the former out of indifference to religion itself. The result was a withdrawal from social responsibility on the part of the children of the Reformation, and an inability to check "the implicitly religious fanaticism generated in ostensibly secular political and social movements" on the part of the children of the Renaissance.

In view of these historic failures, the test of tolerance reaffirms the aspirations of both the Renaissance and the Reformation, while offering a religious perspective from which they might be applied to the problems of contemporary society. This middle axiom, of course, reflects Niebuhr's view of the political crisis of the 1930s. Religious liberals and secular intellectuals had failed to understand the demonic aspects of the ideological conflict between democracy, socialism, and fascism. Thinking that a rational arbitration of differences might be possible, they had only managed to encourage even higher flights of fanaticism and cynicism. World War II was understood accordingly as a chastening lesson concerning the practical relevance of a religiously based test of tolerance. Nevertheless, the test itself remains inapplicable without a political structure oriented to it. This structure Niebuhr proposed in his other middle axiom, "the balance of power."

Political Ethics: "The Balance of Power"

Even if the problem of ideology can be mitigated as Niebuhr suggests, the conflict of social interests remains. Resolving such conflicts requires more than a sense of pity and forgiveness on the part of those involved in them. It requires a "structure of justice" capable of creating and sustaining human community, while successfully avoiding the twin perils of tyranny and anarchy. This is how Niebuhr conceived the problem of political organization in contemporary society. His middle axiom "the balance of power" proposes a solution to it.

Niebuhr's interpretation of the structures of justice is contingent upon his understanding of the nature of political power, which in turn is derived from his theological anthropology. Thus he locates the realities of power within a general interpretation of the human condition: human nature is a paradox of finiteness and freedom, and so human capacities to act are limited in various ways; the exercise of power therefore is always a synthesis of "vitality and reason" involving elements of both persuasion and coercion. This anthropological reflection suggests two things: first, since no one is omnipotent and no one is utterly powerless, the exercise of power inevitably occurs within human community; second, the kinds of power are as various as the forms of human activity, and likewise irreducible to one another.

However trivial in appearance, these insights do serve to define a context in which the limits and possibilities of human power may be recognized. Their practical relevance stems from the fact that they tend to highlight the distinctive character of political power: "Political power deserves to be placed in a special category, because it rests upon the ability to use and manipulate other forms of social power for the particular purpose of organizing and dominating the community" (Niebuhr, 1943:263). This insistence on the special character of political power comes in opposition to those theories that tend to reduce all forms of power to economics. In fact, such "economism" is the central theoretical error that Niebuhr's middle axiom is designed to combat.[6]

The balance of power thus assigns to politics the special task of creating and maintaining an "organizing center" capable of orchestrating the vitalities of the community without degenerating into tyranny or anarchy. The operation of this organizing center is described as follows:

> This centre must arbitrate conflicts from a more impartial perspective than is available to any party of a given conflict; it must manage and manipulate the processes of mutual support so that the tensions inherent in them will not erupt into conflict; it must coerce submission to the social process by superior power whenever the instruments of arbitrating and composing conflict do not suffice; and finally it must seek to redress the disproportions of power by conscious shifts of the balances whenever they make for injustice. [Niebuhr, 1943:266]

Niebuhr's notion of an organizing center thus represents an irreducibly political theory of government. In contrast to the perspectives of both liberals and Marxists, "government" is neither simply a reflection of class interests, nor merely an expression of rational consensus. As a "structure of justice" it seeks an "equilibrium" in which unjust disproportions of power may be overcome.

Once established, the organizing center, or government, must constantly readjust this equilibrium in the direction of social justice. Since government not only maintains the balance of power, but is itself a significant factor in it, Niebuhr favors those strategies that "embody the principle of resistance to government within the principle of government itself"[7] (Niebuhr, 1943:268). Thus the balance-of-power principle entails a new vindication of constitutional democracy. The point of Niebuhr's middle axiom is formulated most succinctly in *The Children of Light and the Children of Darkness:* "Man's capacity for justice makes democracy possible; but man's inclination to injustice makes democracy necessary" (Niebuhr, 1944:xiii). In other words, human nature being what it is, there will never come a time when society can do without democratic institutions designed to restrain the abuses of power.

Given the generally negative tone of Niebuhr's analysis of power, what purpose guides this structure of justice besides the restraint of evil? Must government be confined to maintaining order? Clearly, this is not Niebuhr's intention. An organizing center must be guided by the ideal of justice. Niebuhr's middle axiom thus must also define the direction in which justice is to be realized. Recall that, among other things, "original righteousness" symbolizes a brotherhood among all human persons insofar as they are "creatures" made to the "image of God." Niebuhr, in other words, understands justice as an ideal of equality. Nevertheless, this transcendent ideal is paradoxical, since our basic equality as persons embodying the image of God is accompanied by a host of inequalities that not only serve to differentiate us as individuals but also to promote the general welfare of the human community. Both equality and inequalities are believed to be the result of the Hidden God's love toward us. Consequently, brotherhood cannot mean a strategy bent on eliminating differences among human persons, but entails instead a communal sense of responsibility for others. Social justice means the extension of this sense of obligation from the immediacy of primary relationships, as in the family, to the more complex and abstract ties that bind society as a whole (Niebuhr, 1943:248). It proceeds through an open-ended commitment to expand the scope of "rational calculation of the needs of others as compared with our own interests," out of a common sense of human decency and fairness. Niebuhr believes that this ideal of social justice can be approximated most effectively by working within the structures of constitutional democracy. The balance of power must be directed to this end by politicians and social activists who have accepted the discipline of the test of tolerance.

More precise formulations of these principles are not pursued with much thoroughness. While Niebuhr is interested primarily in emphasizing their cultural relativity, he also rejects the attitudes taken toward such principles, represented by legalism and cynicism. An open-ended commitment to social justice cannot be discharged simply by fulfilling the law. Perhaps the law needs to be changed. On the other hand, the cynical view that rejects laws "merely as tools of egoistic interest" underestimates "the capacity of communities to synthesize divergent approaches to a common problem and to arrive at a tolerably just solution" (Niebuhr, 1943:249).

In explaining the relevance of this second middle axiom, Niebuhr interprets "the Christian attitude to government" in light of his theology of history. The Bible's "double approach of prophetic criticism and priestly sanctification," in tension with the political theories of classical Greece, has addressed the twin perils of tyranny and anarchy throughout Western history. The results, not surprisingly, manifest "the conflict of grace and pride": medieval Catholicism achieved "a synthesis in the realm of political theory," but its "prophetic Biblical criticism upon the injustice and pride of rulers" served as "the instrument of the papal-ecclesiastical claim of dominion" (Niebuhr, 1943:274). The political theories of both the Reformation and the Renaissance take up one and then another fragment of the synthesis. Thus both movements oscillated between extreme optimism and extreme pessimism regarding the "structures of justice," at one moment courting tyranny, at another, anarchy. Finally, a solution *in principle* did emerge among "those Protestant groups which came closest to an understanding of both the vice and the necessity of government and both the peril and the necessity of a free interplay of social forces": "moderate

Anglicans . . . ; semi-sectarian movements like English Independency; and finally the later Calvinists" (Niebuhr, 1943:278). Although "the vindication of the right of self-government and the elaboration of effective constitutional forms for the expression of the right, was the fruit of many secular as well as religious, movements," Niebuhr's own view of constitutional democracy is based on this Protestant perspective. Indeed, he summarizes the meaning of this second middle axiom as a witness to "justification by faith in the realm of justice":

> Whatever may be the source of our insights into the problems of the political order, it is important both to recognize the higher possibilities of justice in every historic situation, and to know that the twin perils of tyranny and anarchy can never be completely overcome in any political achievement. These perils are expressions of the sinful elements of conflict and dominion, standing in contradiction to the ideal of brotherhood on every level of communal organization. There is no possibility of making history completely safe against either occasional conflicts of vital interests (war) or against the misuse of the power which is intended to prevent such conflicts of interests (tyranny). To understand this is to labor for higher justice in terms of the experience of justification by faith. Justification by faith in the realm of justice means that we will not regard the pressures and counter pressures, the tensions, the overt and covert conflicts by which justice is achieved and maintained, as normative in the absolute sense; but neither will we ease our conscience by seeking to escape from involvement in them. We will know that we cannot purge ourselves of the sin and guilt in which we are involved by the moral ambiguities of politics without also disavowing responsibility for the creative possibilities of justice. [Niebuhr, 1943:284]

"A Theological Framework for Social Ethics"?

In light of this analysis, the strengths and weaknesses of Niebuhr's ethics may now be better appreciated. While his intention indeed was "to make way for such solutions to our problems as are possible by clearing away . . . illusions," it is not apparent that he succeeded in giving sufficiently precise definition to his proposed theological framework for social ethics. Despite its rhetorical impressiveness, even a sympathetic critic must admit that Christian realism has yet to measure up to its promise as a theoretical perspective.

In the course of this discussion enough of a pattern has emerged to warrant venturing a diagnosis of this weakness. Given the origins of this theology in Niebuhr's personal faith and experience, from the beginning the problem has been one of establishing Christian realism's availability as public discourse. While this is a difficult challenge for any modern theology, the strategy required by Niebuhr's paradoxical vision of humanity before a Hidden God makes the task especially difficult. Since the abiding truth of this vision cannot be expressed straightforwardly but only in the paradoxes yielded by a mythical approach to Christianity, the problem becomes one of establishing its reference to human nature and history in explicitly theoretical terms. Thus the metaphors of divine transcendence and immanence, which for Niebuhr constitute "the aesthetic motif in religion," had to be translated into theology and ethics. His theology partially succeeded in making these metaphors available by elaborating a theological anthropology, which interpreted the paradoxes in terms of modern psychology. But since his theology of history failed to become theoretically explicit in its reference to the structures and processes of historical development, its contribution is limited to illustrating the insights of his theological anthropology. In short, its theoretical possibilities are only partially realized.

The additional difficulties in Niebuhr's theological framework for social ethics may be understood as a consequence of this structural weakness in his theology. Just as from the beginning Christian realism as theology is faced with the problem of public availability, so from the beginning as ethics it is faced with the "inevitable moral tension between individual and group morality." Given the fact that Niebuhr's theological anthropology dominates his theology of history, it is not surprising that his theological framework for social ethics speaks more directly to the concerns of individuals than groups. Nevertheless, the individuals whom Niebuhr addresses are rarely anonymous; typically, they are politicians and Christian social activists. The strength of Christian realism as an ethic, in other words, is that it consistently makes the meaning of the paradoxical vision relevant to the "moods and motivations" characteristic of such individuals. Its "dialectic of love and justice," in short, adequately provides a dispositional ethic for politicians. Even so, Niebuhr's framework for social ethics hardly ignores the problems of group morality. By formulating certain middle axioms, he also meant to make the paradoxical vision relevant to the most pressing problems plaguing "the ethical reconstruction of modern society." But while these axioms are impressive for their consistency in representing his theological perspective, theirs may be only a limited usefulness as guidelines for social ethics.

The issues raised by Niebuhr with these middle axioms, obviously, are crucially important. Given even a minimal awareness of the history of the twentieth century, the need for some sort of critical perspective on ideological conflicts and some sort of structure of justice for resolving conflicts of social interest clearly represent items of the highest priority for any agenda in social ethics. The issues are not in doubt; but the adequacy of Niebuhr's solutions to them is. Thus the test of tolerance is proposed as a solution to the problem of ideological conflict. "Moments of prayerful transcendence," Niebuhr hopes, will provide critical perspective allowing conflicting groups to overcome the "pretense" tainting their claims to truth. While this test adequately diagnoses the "dimension of depth" to problems of ideological conflict, and proposes a remedy that at once reflects the insights of Christian prophecy and common sense, it may be inadequate because it provides no guidance for solving the conflict at any other level. Once "the taint of interest and passion" has been recognized, and the sinful "pretense" repented for, how does the test of tolerance help conflicting groups to understand—let alone to resolve—the social tensions and structural contradictions that their ideologies reflect?

In all fairness to Niebuhr, it must be recognized that his balance-of-power axiom is meant to provide guidance precisely at this point. Conflicts of social interest are to be "managed" by establishing an "organizing center" or "government" dedicated to the approximation of "justification by faith in the realm of justice." But while this axiom represents a Christian "vindication of constitutional democracy" and rightly recognizes the special character of political power, it lacks specific criteria for distinguishing the abuse of such power from its proper exercise. Niebuhr's middle axioms, in other words, remain intuitive precisely where they should be more explicit. As such they are too closely related to the dispositional ethic of love and justice to provide adequate theoretical perspective on the problems peculiar to social ethics.

While these middle axioms consistently express Christian realism's theological concerns as a whole, their inadequacy is a reflection of the weakness of its theology of history in particular. Since Niebuhr was unable to correlate this theology with critical social theory, the resulting ambiguity in its reference to the structures of historical development means that his middle axioms are strangely tentative in their approach to these structures. It is as if Niebuhr's insights into the "dimension of depth" to problems of ideological and social conflict were purchased at the price of critical perspective on their other dimensions. Thus despite their intuitive plausibility, the middle axioms in the end reflect the same weakness that has plagued Christian realism throughout. Just as Niebuhr's theology has difficulty comprehending self and society in a systematically coherent theory, so in his ethics the connection between principles of discriminate and indiscriminate criticism is not adequately clarified. Although such a weakness does not diminish the effectiveness of Christian realism as a dispositional ethic, which in any case must be appropriated imaginatively by individuals, it does count against middle axioms intended as a framework for social ethics.

The practical consequences of this theoretical weakness take on special urgency in this context where Christian realism has been denounced as an ideology of the Establishment. In order to assess the merits of this charge, let us examine the praxis of Christian realism—Niebuhr's use of his theological framework to interpret American society and politics after World War II. If there is any merit to the suspicion of weakness in Niebuhr's position, its consequences should be evident in praxis.

NOTES

1. This interplay between the strategies of discriminate and indiscriminate criticism was discussed in Chapter 3, above, in relation to Niebuhr's insight into the connection between religious faith and social justice, expressed in the formula "Equality of sin, inequality of guilt," which was based on the example of the Hebrew prophets.

2. The creative tension called for here is reflected in Niebuhr's proposal for "a synthesis of Reformation and Renaissance," in which he acknowledges the Reformation's insight into matters of ultimate concern and the Renaissance's competence in "proximate," or less than ultimate, matters. This synthesis, while not providing any greater precision in understanding the relationship between these principles of indiscriminate and discriminate criticism, does serve to locate their sources in Western intellectual history.

3. Niebuhr's appeal to the mythical state of original righteousness is meant to establish the anthropological basis for both natural and religious moralities. His understanding of these remains paradoxical because the basis of natural morality is recognized only in the experience of negativity, in the yearning for wholeness and harmony implicit in human anxiety. This experience, precisely in its negative relationship to what "is," becomes the key to what "ought" to be. It furnishes a moral imperative, a law encompassing both natural and religious moralities, with the latter representing higher possibilities for the fulfillment of the former. The logical puzzles involved in Niebuhr's appeal to original righteousness need not detain us here.

4. The fact that Niebuhr sees Catholicism failing the test is less important than the logic of his analysis. The tacit assumption is that certain complex institutional phenomena, such as the Inquisition, can be explained as consequences of certain alleged theoretical failures, such as the Catholic understanding of grace. Whatever the merits of this attempt to correlate theological theory with ecclesiastical practice, it is consistent with Niebuhr's theology of history, which presupposes that the fate of certain Christian theological doctrines holds the key to Western cultural history. In this context, it is interesting to note that Jacques Maritain's *Integral Humanism* offers a Catholic version of the same claim (1973:8–34). I have explored this parallel elsewhere (McCann, 1978:164–67).

5. Niebuhr attributes Protestantism's failure to its "Bibliolatry," an aberration that "implied 'sanctificationist' principles in the realm of culture and truth" (Niebuhr, 1943: 229). By way of clarification, Niebuhr says that "the authority of the Bible was used to break the proud authority of the church; whereupon the Bible became another instrument of human pride." This analysis is consistent with the tacit assumptions of Niebuhr's theology of history. Not only does it presuppose the priority of ideas over social structures in understanding historical change, but it sees this particular episode as an illustration of the anthropological truth about grace and pride.

6. Niebuhr's criticism of economism is directed against "both liberal and Marxist social interpretations." While this point is mentioned only in passing here, in *The Children of Light and the Children of Darkness* (Niebuhr, 1944) a systematic analysis of the relationship between politics and property is attempted.

7. This conclusion is consistent with the epistemological assumptions of the test of tolerance. Precisely because no ideology is privileged in its cognitive perspective, removing the ideological taint entails a willingness to submit to arbitration within a self-correcting governmental process, which institutionalizes a system of checks and balances. At this point the link between the two axioms is most explicit: the test provides a "dispositional" orientation, and the balance of power a political structure, for working out "proximate solutions" to common problems. Since no ideology is privileged, these solutions can be only "piecemeal." As the conclusion to this chapter suggests, what is questionable in Niebuhr's middle axioms is not their intuitive plausibility or their consistency with his theology as a whole, but their adequacy in providing theoretical orientation for social activists.

5

Christian Realism: A Critique of Its Praxis

*The new international community will be constructed neither by the
pessimists, who believe it impossible to go beyond the balance of
power principle in the relation of nations to each other; nor by the
cynics, who would organize the world by the imposition of imperial
authority without regard to the injustices which flow inevitably from
arbitrary and irresponsible power; nor yet by the idealists, who are
under the fond illusion that a new level of development will emanci-
pate history of these vexing problems.*

*The new world must be built by resolute men who "when hope is
dead will hope by faith"; who will neither seek premature escape from
the guilt of history, nor yet call the evil, which taints all their achievements, good. There is no escape from the paradoxical relation of
history to the Kingdom of God. History moves towards the realization
of the Kingdom but yet the judgment of God is upon every new
realization.*

—Reinhold Niebuhr, The Nature and Destiny of Man, *volume 2, 1943*

Christian realism's promise as a model for practical theology stems from
the fact that Niebuhr's rediscovery of an authentically Christian spirituality
occurred amid the frustrations of radical politics. The "adequate spiritual
guidance" that he found in the paradoxical vision of humanity before a
Hidden God he hoped would sustain a "more radical political orientation"
on the basis of "more conservative religious convictions." In the previous
chapters we have examined the theological strategy by which he tried to
make this guidance available to others. But as he was formulating and
explaining these more conservative religious convictions, Niebuhr was
also gradually abandoning his more radical political orientation in favor of
"piecemeal reformism." In view of this development, the question at stake
in a critique of Christian realism's praxis is whether the ideological drift
apparent in Niebuhr's later works logically follows from a theoretical
perspective inspired by the paradoxical vision; and if so, what are its
consequences in terms of the continued relevance of Christian realism as a
model for practical theology?

Ironically, while they differ regarding its consequences, both those who praise Niebuhr as "the Establishment theologian" and those who condemn Christian realism as "an ideology of the Establishment" tacitly presuppose an affirmative answer to this question. Together they can appeal to the fact that Niebuhr himself considered his later political moderation to be just as much a reflection of the "circular relationship between the presupposition of faith and the facts of experience" as his earlier political radicalism.

Another view, however, is possible and in fact is suggested by the previous analysis. In light of the theoretical weaknesses of Christian realism as theology and ethics, the ideological drift of the later years may be explained as a consequence of these weaknesses rather than as necessarily entailed by the paradoxical vision itself. If that is the case, then Christian realism's continued promise as a model for practical theology must rest on the merits of Niebuhr's religious vision rather than simply upon either his success or his failure as an interpreter of American society and politics after World War II.

In this chapter some of the evidence relevant for judging between these two views will be presented. In order to make this critique as sharply focused as possible, I shall restrict the discussion to Niebuhr's interpretation of the United States' role in the cold war, and his attitude toward the Third World in general and Latin America in particular. My purpose is twofold: first, to analyze the actual performance of Christian realism as a practical guide to politics, and second, to make explicit the connection between Christian realism and the issues central to its confrontation with liberation theology. In light of this discussion, the chapter will conclude with an assessment of the weaknesses of Christian realism.

The Cold War and the American Hegemony

World War II, obviously, did not result in an ethical reconstruction of modern society. While it did eliminate what had been perceived as the greatest immediate danger to Western civilization, the threat of Nazi tyranny, the outcome of the war was unexpected in many ways. In Europe it left a temporary power vacuum, which the United States and the Soviet Union were to fill as "organizing centers," with Soviet domination of Eastern Europe providing sufficient reason for the American domination of Western Europe. As a result, the two major wartime allies found themselves locked into a new kind of cold war, itself apparently the only alternative to the Armageddon now made possible by the development of nuclear weapons. Thus what Niebuhr had envisioned as a balance of power in international politics was to be guaranteed in fact by a new balance of terror. During this period, then, Christian realism presented itself as a way of understanding and coping with the unprecedented responsibilities and frustrations of the cold war.

Christian realism's balance-of-power principle was not designed originally to address the problems of international politics. It emerged instead from Niebuhr's reflections on the way in which the class struggle seemed to have been mitigated in the United States by the policies of Roosevelt's New Deal. In fact, Niebuhr had used the politics of unemployment as an èxample of how the organizing center responds to "the development of social conscience on any current issue" (Niebuhr, 1943:249). Consistent with his understanding of social conflict, Niebuhr argued that hardened ideological positions—for example, *laissez-faire* liberalism's picture of the unemployed as "victims of sloth rather than the caprices of an intricate industrial process"—usually are softened by an occasional feeling of pity for the "less fortunate" coupled by persistent fear of a "revolt of the poor." These responses, understandable as perhaps a residual reflection of love and justice among the "privileged classes," make possible a willingness to "compromise between conflicting viewpoints and interests." The organizing center therefore is able to act upon such sentiments to develop proximate solutions to domestic problems like unemployment. So impressed did Niebuhr become with the federal government's success as an organizing center that by the late 1940s he announced the achievement of "rough justice" in American domestic politics. The United States, he declared, "has achieved balances of power in the organization of social forces and a consequent justice which has robbed the Marxist challenge of its sting" (Niebuhr, 1952:91).

Nevertheless, this success did not mean that there was no further need of a prophetic perspective. As Niebuhr explained, it was one of the "ironies" of American history that this practical "triumph of experience over dogma" had not been matched by similar achievements in the realm of theory. He cites two examples: (1) "the debate in the western world on the institution of property was aborted in America" (Niebuhr, 1952:103); and (2) "the lip service which the whole culture pays to the principles of *laissez-faire* makes for tardiness in dealing with the instability of a free economy" (Niebuhr, 1952:105). But in these cases, the task is to bring American social theory into line with American political practice. Christian realism's agenda for domestic politics, therefore, was to focus increasingly on interpreting "the triumph of the vitality of our democratic institutions," and on extending "the triumph of 'common sense' in American history." With rough justice more or less assured at home, Niebuhr thus could concentrate on the intractable problems facing the United States abroad.

While Niebuhr's postwar concern for international politics represents no dramatic departure from his previous interests, there is a significant change in the way he approaches it. Recall that his concern can be traced all the way back to his experience during World War I as executive secretary for the War Welfare Commission of his denomination and his participation in Sherwood Eddy's American Seminars during the early 1920s. Prior to the outbreak of World War II he maintained this interest, interpreting foreign affairs primarily in relation to the vicissitudes of American domestic politics. His reflections on the conflict between fascism, Communism, and liberalism in the Europe of the 1930s, for example, were still informed by his practical concern to understand the Great Depression in the United States and to develop a strategy to overcome it. By hindsight, however, it is clear that his campaign against American isolationism on the eve of World War II helped to establish a new set of priorities in his thinking. From then on the international situation increasingly became the central, if not the exclusive, focus of Christian realism.

While the reasons for this shift in Niebuhr's thinking are complex, its result is fairly simple. Besides the overriding urgency of the effort to resist Nazism, and the broader horizons opened up by his new theological perspective, Niebuhr's increasing prominence as a national religious leader and political figure may also have had its part in it. But however this change is explained, its significance is evident from the fact that the American secretary of state, George C. Marshall, in 1947 invited him to join the U.S. State Department's Policy Planning Staff, along with such notables as George F. Kennan, Paul H. Nitze, Louis J. Halle, C. B. Marshall, Dorothy Fosdick, and Hans Morgenthau (Stone, 1972: 169–70). The group became known as the "realist school" of American foreign policy, and Niebuhr is commonly regarded as its intellectual father.

In analyzing the contribution made by Marshall's Policy Planning Staff, Kenneth W. Thompson identified five characteristics of the new "political realism," each of which corresponds to a significant element in Niebuhr's Christian realism:

> The common elements are: (1) the tendency to avoid moral absolutes in international politics; (2) a rejection of the escape from power politics attempted by writers on international relations in the 1920s and 1930s; (3) a distrust of concepts of human perfectibility and moral progress in human affairs; (4) a passion for the study and interpretation of history; and (5) the conviction that a rather explicit conception of man is helpful to political thought. [Stone, 1972:170]

Of the five, the most important is the "explicit conception of man," a more or less secularized version of Niebuhr's theological anthropology. Christian realism's view of "man" thus served as the framework for political analyses in which psychological reflections on "national character" (cf. Niebuhr and Heimert, 1963) were crucial for understanding the actions of other nations and America's response to them. The other points fall into line with this focus: the "interpretation of history" is guided by this "conception of man," and the substantive conclusions reached about "progress," "power politics," and "moral absolutes" all reflect Niebuhr's understanding of "justification by faith in the realm of justice." Christian realism's influence in shaping the mixed discourse of this group of political realists is a tribute to Niebuhr's success in making his paradoxical vision plausible to American common sense, whatever the verdict may be on its moral consequences or ideological implications.

To the moderately reformist policies emerging from this group, Niebuhr contributed his special sensibility to the ironies of history. In promoting a sense of irony, and the greater political maturity that he hoped it would inspire, Niebuhr saw the legacy of isolationism as the greatest single obstacle. Built upon the reality of the United States' geographical distance from Europe and the myth of American innocence and European corruption, isolationism represented a nostalgia for the imagined agrarian utopia of the early nineteenth century and a refusal to accept the responsibilities created by American economic and military power in the twentieth century. Although Niebuhr felt that a return to the isolationism of the prewar years was impossible, he feared that it might lead to "a policy of adventurism" in the face of the frustrations of the cold war (Niebuhr, 1953:54). In Niebuhr's diagnosis, the United States had to be educated to its global responsibilities and provided with a reasonable set of goals for its foreign policy.

The structures of international politics and the ironies of the cold war suggested to Niebuhr that the United States had no reasonable alternative to accepting its role as an organizing center. Twentieth-century hopes for world government, invested first in the League of Nations and then in the United Nations, were, if not an illusion, at least premature. The constitutional arrangements embodied in the United Nations would remain abstract, Niebuhr predicted, unless they were built upon cultural, political, and economic foundations, which simply did not yet exist. Nevertheless, the United Nations was useful as a "forum for international diplomacy" (Niebuhr, 1959: 16). Niebuhr hoped that it would provide some moral restraint upon the unrestricted pursuit of national self-interest.

In view of the realities of international conflict, the world thus had to be organized at some level higher than the nation but lower than world government, if anarchy were to be avoided. Niebuhr used the word "hegemony" to refer to this level of organization: it designates the relations between a dominant world power and the dependent states that it organizes. Although a hegemony is based primarily on political power, it clearly presupposes the exercise of all other forms of power as well. Empire is one form of hegemony; alliance is another. The term is deliberately neutral regarding the question of empire, so that it may include both the United States and the Soviet Union, world powers that are avowedly "anti-imperialist" in their ideologies. Given the unacceptable alternatives of tyranny and anarchy, hegemony promised more justice and peace than might otherwise be achieved.

In the perspective of world history, the United States' ascent to hegemonic power itself contained a note of irony. While the nation's birth in a revolutionary war against the British Empire made it a symbol for the ideals of the Enlightenment and the principle of national self-determination, later on it had flirted with imperialism under the guise of "manifest destiny." Even so, this ideology was not overtly imperialistic, but was meant to justify the creation of a continental autarky "from sea to shining sea." Thus even the Spanish-American War was undertaken with a "sense of mission" inspired by the Enlightenment's ideal of autonomy. Its declared purpose was to liberate Cuba and the Philippines from the decadent but still oppressive Spanish Empire.[1] America's expansionism from a loose federation of colonies on the Atlantic seaboard to a continental power with overseas interests, in other words, had taken place within an ideology of "anti-imperialism."

Now, Niebuhr felt, the irony needed to be recognized and the ideology revised. With the eclipse of the national empires of Spain, Portugal, Holland, England, and France, the United States had to step into the vacuum or risk seeing the world organized as one great Soviet tyranny. American hegemony was to be exercised primarily in relation to Europe, but it also included Latin America, the peripheries of Asia, and the Middle East, insofar as these were to mark the limits of Soviet expansion. Unlike the previous national empires, the American hegemony was to be organized as a series of alliances, such as the North Atlantic Treaty Organization (NATO) for the military defense and political stabilization of Western Europe, and the Southeast Asia Treaty Organization (SEATO), which intended similar goals for the periphery of Asia. Fully aware of the mixed motives behind it, Niebuhr commended the Marshall Plan as an example of what could be achieved through the exercise of hegemonic responsibility (Niebuhr and Heimert, 1963:143–44).

The Example of British Colonialism

Given the fact that the United States was relatively unprepared for this new role, it stood in need of a model. Not surprisingly, Niebuhr looked to the history of empires both ancient and modern to supply one. In defense of his thesis that hegemony could be the source of much good if exercised responsibly, Niebuhr cited the record of British colonialism. Despite its history of economic exploitation, British colonialism was impressive for its humanitarian achievements. The abolition of slavery in East Africa and the suppression of the custom of *suttee* in India, as well as advances throughout the empire in responsible government, education, and health standards, all counted in favor of the British. In particular, Niebuhr pointed to the example of "the large group of British proconsuls who combined the impulse of dominion with a strong impulse of responsibility toward subject peoples, and a passion for raising the cultural level of the colonies," men like Lord Cromer in Egypt, Kitchener and Gordon in the Sudan, and Lugard in Nigeria (Niebuhr, 1959:210–11). Their success in advancing the status of subject peoples eventually led to the transformation of the empire into the British Commonwealth of Nations, "one of the greatest political triumphs of the modern era" (Niebuhr, 1959:212). But above all, British colonialism had managed to preserve some semblance of world peace in the century separating the surrender of Napoleon at Waterloo and the assassination of Archduke Francis Ferdinand at Sarajevo.

Niebuhr concluded that these positive achievements were due to Britain's ability to exercise hegemony within a framework of "free parliamentary institutions" (Niebuhr, 1959:209). The gradual triumph of parliamentary democracy in Britain provided a forum for public debate regarding imperial policies. Thus the same forces promoting the reform of British political institutions gradually extended their concern to include the overseas dependencies. Reform movements in Britain, for example, strengthened the hand of those who favored "indirect rule" and the gradual development of indigenous legal systems guided by realistic standards of political justice. The enlightened imperial policies that emerged from this parliamentary system, in Niebuhr's view, "contributed to the final achievement of nationhood."

But there were also certain negative features of British colonialism. One of these is Anglo-Saxon racism. Despite its superior record in many other respects, "British dominion insisted on a separation of the dominant and the subject peoples." While Niebuhr was unable to provide much insight into the causes linking racism and colonialism, he did find the depth of the problem "sobering."[2] Another negative feature is the "resentment" of the colonial peoples, which surfaced in the wake of the empire. Whether justified or not, such resentment retards development because "it so obsesses the colonial peoples with the evils arising from imperialism that some time is required for the emancipated nations to come to terms with the economic and political problems, which are not derived from imperial dominion" (Niebuhr, 1959:211).

In view of these negative features, Niebuhr felt challenged to clarify his analysis of hegemony in light of Marxist theories of imperialism. Emphatically rejecting the Marxist thesis that imperialism is the necessary consequence of capitalism, he argued that although the economic motive—the drive to exploit the resources of subject peoples or to extend trade to them—"often plays a large part in imperial ventures, it is never the sole motive of imperial expansion" (Niebuhr, 1959:202). Equally important are what he calls the "missionary motive" and the "desire for power and glory." The first factor represents the zeal for spreading the benefits of one's own religion, culture, or way of life, and the second, the expression of "national vitality." Niebuhr does not define these motives further. His position is that they cannot be understood merely as the ideological reflection of economic interest, and therefore must be taken seriously on their own terms. Moreover, in his opinion, the modern national empires are a result of contact between "the highly integrated nations of Europe in juxtaposition to the politically less integrated nations of Asia and Africa" (Niebuhr, 1959:202). In other words, the contact occurred in a power vacuum in which the European hegemonies inevitably asserted themselves. On the whole, then, his theoretical criticisms of Marxism's analysis of imperialism are a reflection of his view of the irreducible complexity of the forms of power, and his emphasis on the distinctiveness of political power. They also reflect Christian realism's tendency to interpret collective social interests as manifestations of national character analogous to the paradoxical structure of human selfhood.

In addition to these theoretical differences, Niebuhr had practical reasons for rejecting Marxist theories of imperialism. Given the realities of the cold war, Marxism glosses over the fact of "communist imperialism" by equating imperialism with capitalism. Such obscurantism allows "the Russian empire" to "exploit the resentments of the colonial peoples who are or who were under the domination of the western nations" (Niebuhr, 1959:253–54). By contrast, Niebuhr argues that both "communist imperialism" and American hegemony manifest the basic pattern of imperialism: a power vacuum inevitably filled by an "organizing center." Thus the Marxist theory itself is a weapon in the cold war between the two hegemonies. However understandable the "resentments of the colonial peoples," the facts themselves require a more balanced interpretation.

With these reflections on imperialism in general and the legacy of British colonialism in particular, Niebuhr hoped to reassure his readers that the exercise of American hegemony not only could be morally responsible but also was morally necessary in the postwar world. There could be no question of the immorality of hegemonic domination as such, but only regarding the morality of its consequences in specific situations. Given the United States' traditional ideology of anti-imperialism, it was necessary to clarify the nature of its hegemonic responsibility, so that the nation might steer a course between isolationism and adventurism, between an appeasement of the "Russian empire" and a moral crusade culminating in a "preventive war." In light of the model provided by the achievements of British colonialism, the United States could reasonably hope to avoid both tyranny and anarchy if it continued to exercise its power within the system of checks and balances built into its democratic institutions. American hegemony, in short, was not a step on the way to utopia, but it might be preferable to the likely alternatives. In order to achieve even this limited goal, the nation would have to be educated to the political wisdom of humility and self-restraint, precisely those dispositions emphasized by Christian realism.

"The So-called 'Uncommitted' Nations": An Ironic View

Needless to say, Niebuhr understood the situation of the nations of Asia, Africa, and Latin America within the context of this struggle for hegemony. He was so impressed by the Soviet-American polarity that he readily discounted the claims of these nations to an independent perspective: "The so-called 'uncommitted' nations are, in fact, in various degrees either committed or partially committed either to the Russian or to the western power center" (Niebuhr, 1959:12). Thus it is clear that he would have had his doubts about the existence of an independent Third World. Nevertheless, since "the so-called 'uncommitted' nations" had become involved in the cold war, Niebuhr found it necessary to address their view of the situation. In a chapter of his book *The Irony of American History,* analyzing "The International Class Struggle," for example, Niebuhr tries to offer an explanation of Asian hostility to the American hegemony as symbolized by the Korean War. His purpose is to show why Marxism in particular is so plausible, yet so erroneous in its analysis of the situation of these nations. By so doing, he hopes to promote a more ironic view of the "so-called 'uncommitted,' " one that will provide no excuse for American policies of "adventurism."

The anti-Americanism of Asian intellectuals, in Niebuhr's opinion, must be viewed as a result of the success of the "revolutionary religion" of Marxism. While Marxism is no longer "a living creed" in Western Europe, it continues to have profound appeal "for the desperate peoples of impoverished agrarian-feudal economies in the whole non-industrial world" (Niebuhr, 1952:111). By successfully exploiting the lack of dynamism characteristic of Asian cultures, this revolutionary religion presents itself as "the harbinger of a great hope." It also poses as a "science" of historical development, and "thus comes to a world tired of defeatist religions, as an emancipatory force" (Niebuhr, 1952:122). But the basis of Marxism's appeal has little to do with the accuracy of its analyses of agrarian-feudal economies. Indeed, Niebuhr insists, the Marxist theory that "poverty is caused solely by exploitation . . . is no more true than the contrasting bourgeois belief that distinctions of poverty and wealth are due primarily to differences of skill, thrift, and industry." Consequently, when applied to international politics, "the Marxist interpretation of inequalities between nations is . . . more untrue than its interpretation of such inequalities within a particular nation" (Niebuhr, 1952:118). Marxism's success, therefore, is due to its emotional appeal. "It places the blame for an unfortunate situation entirely upon others," and thus satisfies "a deep instinct of the human heart" (Niebuhr, 1952:117).

Communist propaganda to the contrary, the problems of Asia are only in part caused by economic exploitation under Western imperialism. The serious differences between rich nations and poor nations are rooted first in the uneven distribution of the world's natural resources, and second, in the differences in standards of productivity (Niebuhr, 1952:110). These differences, however, have become even more serious as a result of "the impact of a technical society upon a non-technical one." Niebuhr elaborates:

Even the most grievous injustices of the feudal world are not as responsible for the abject poverty of its agrarian poor as the low efficiency of its economy. Moreover, when industry is introduced, its first effect is, as it was in Occidental nations, to heighten the injustices. Liberal opinion in the western world rightly stresses the necessity for technical assistance in raising the productivity of the whole non-industrial world. But it usually does not recognize that, even if every form of exploitation is avoided in this development, it is not possible to transmute an agrarian culture into a technical civilization without vast cultural and social dislocations. To counter the force of communism in the agrarian world we are under the necessity of telescoping developments which required four centuries of European history. [Niebuhr, 1952:116]

The problems of production and distribution, in other words, are not simply a consequence of imperial policies bent on securing the dependence of colonial peoples. The desperate situation of poverty, now exacerbated by the "impact of a technical society upon a non-technical one," simply will not disappear once the imperial yoke is broken.

Niebuhr's sobering assessment of the prospects for Asian development is based in part on a consideration of political and cultural factors often ignored by economic analyses. He notes, for example, that in most cases Western imperialism was preceded, accompanied, and superseded by corrupt and inefficient governments, themselves representative of unjust feudal aristocracies. But the behavior of these ruling elites, in turn, must be understood as a reflection of Asian cultural values. Consistent with his general assumption regarding the correlation between a society's religious and moral beliefs and its political institutions, Niebuhr asserts that the problems of Asian development are compounded by the inadequacies of Eastern religions. In short, since these "lack historical dynamism," Asian societies inevitably display "indifference toward problems of nature" (Niebuhr, 1952:119) and a lack of appreciation for the "dignity of the individual" (Niebuhr, 1952:125).[3] Inasmuch as a democratic society requires a foundation in both humanistic and scientific values—"as found in the Hebrew faith, in Greek humanism, and in the Christian religion"—the prospects for Asia are bleak indeed.

In view of this situation and the understandably emotional appeal of Marxism, it is very difficult for the American hegemony to be properly appreciated in Asia. The struggle with the Soviet Union requires that the United States be represented at least along Asia's periphery.[4] But in taking up this "defensive" position, Americans have been "held responsible for the post-imperial ills of the non-technical cultures far beyond [their] deserts" (Niebuhr, 1952:115). The United States' genuine achievements, such as an individual sense of responsibility and a stable pattern of free democratic institutions, are either ignored or viewed with contempt. The exercise of hegemonic power, therefore, must be viewed as a necessary but thankless task.

In the immediate context of the Korean War, Niebuhr's ironic view of "the so-called 'uncommitted' nations" was meant to foil the naiveté of some conservatives who saw "the vast revolutionary upheavals in Asia which resulted in the extension of communism there, as merely the consequences of mistakes on the part of our Department of State, and as capable of rectification by rigorous military action on our part" (Niebuhr, 1953:64). Christian realism's critical focus, in short, was directed against those who would involve the United States in a "preventive war" against China and the Soviet Union. By contrast, Niebuhr insisted that the very limited usefulness of coercive military power be recognized. America cannot allow itself to be tempted by the ultimate power of nuclear weapons into policies that promise "not only to put an end to the recalcitrance of our foes but to eliminate the equivocal attitudes of the Asian and other peoples, who are not as clearly our allies as we should like them to be" (Niebuhr, 1952:75). The greatest danger is that the frustrations of responsibility will trigger a "public temper of fear and hatred" that will lead to "a kind of apoplectic rigidity and inflexibility in American foreign policy." Nevertheless, Niebuhr's tone in presenting this warning was rarely strident, for he considered it unlikely that the partisans of "adventurism" would ever again be taken seriously. Even Eisenhower's election in 1952 found Niebuhr expressing a properly ironic hope that "the responsibilities of office" would disabuse the Republicans of their traditional illusions (Niebuhr, 1953:65). The American hegemony, in other words, was to be exercised on the basis of a bipartisan foreign policy. Consistent with the thrust of his counsels throughout the postwar period, Niebuhr's intention was to increase understanding and to reduce the hysteria attendant upon the cold war.

Niebuhr's attempt to maintain this perspective of irony is fairly consistent with his theological framework for social ethics. The counsels of patience and restraint are a timely application of his dispositional ethic and, under the circumstances, perhaps the best possible advice to give to those responsible for American foreign policy. Such counsels also reflect his middle axioms in various ways. Insofar as the test of tolerance addresses the problem of ideological conflict with an invitation to introspective prayer, it reinforces Niebuhr's emphasis on questions of moral psychology. The motives of those involved in such conflicts not only receive more attention than do the ideologies themselves, but also are judged in terms of Christian realism's anthropological categories. Thus, for example, Niebuhr's discussion of "the international class struggle" highlights the self-deception implicit in the attitudes of those Asian intellectuals who allow their resentments to blind themselves to their own exploitation by Marxist ideology. Similarly, insofar as the balance-of-power principle reflects a view of the dynamics of power that emphasizes political and moral factors over economic ones, it provides warrants for Niebuhr's rejection of Marxist theories of imperialism and his affirmation of greater justice and peace through the responsible exercise of hegemonic power. In view of these applications of his theological framework for social ethics, there can be no question of the consistency with which Niebuhr's political perspective reflects the central tenets of Christian realism.

What remains in doubt, however, is the adequacy of that perspective and, by implication, the validity of those tenets. From what we've seen so far, the suspicion arises that in the postwar years Christian realism lost its capacity to provide any independent definition of the political situations that it addressed. In short, by failing to provide a critical perspective for questioning the fundamental assumptions behind America's involvement in the cold war, it betrays a tendency toward ideological drift. But this suspicion itself raises some questions: Should Christian realism have been able to provide a critical analysis of the whole notion of an American "hegemony"? Or was its perspective properly restricted to accepting the "reality" of hegemony, while working to reform it in the interests of greater justice and peace? While it is clear that these are the sorts of questions at stake in trying to determine whether or not Christian realism is rightly regarded as an ideology of the Establishment, it is not clear how they are to be answered. The fact that Niebuhr's postwar perspective is consistent with the principles of Christian realism does not provide an answer, since the question is one not of consistency but of adequacy. Furthermore, Niebuhr's perspective on the cold war may not be the only possible one consistent with these principles. If it is not, then a rejection of his postwar perspective does not necessarily preclude an affirmation of the principles behind it. These questions may be explored more intelligently in light of further evidence of Christian realism's use as a critical social theory. Such is provided by the analysis of the prospects for democracy in Latin America, which Paul E. Sigmund did in collaboration with Niebuhr.

Latin America: The Prospects for Democracy

Prior to the publication of *The Democratic Experience: Past and Prospects*, Niebuhr had little to say about Latin America. Aside from a few passing remarks on Spanish colonialism in *The Structure of Nations and Empires* (Niebuhr, 1959:201–16) and a brief analysis of the Spanish-American War in *A Nation So Conceived* (Niebuhr and Heimert, 1963:128–34), this area remained on the periphery of his concern. When he did occasionally mention Latin America, typically he presented American involvement there as an example of "hypocrisy" in foreign policy. Thus in an address delivered in 1928 to the Evangelical Brotherhood, "Christianizing International Relations," Niebuhr underscores the self-righteousness of American proposals to outlaw war by pointing to the presence of American troops in Nicaragua (Niebuhr, 1977:206–7). The United States was willing to impose "Christian standards" on others which it would not abide by itself. Over the years, most of his observations are like this one; they are made in passing, and exhibit only a superficial awareness of the problems of the area. All the same, Niebuhr's lack of interest is understandable, given the focus of his work as a whole. Recall that his view of international politics was inspired first by his concern with social conflict in the United States and later by his support for the struggle against Nazism in Europe. Since Latin America—along with the other "non-industrial nations"—was only peripherally related to these developments, he apparently took for granted its relationship to the American "hegemony." Only after the relationship was challenged, as it was by the Cuban Revolution, did Latin America become a problem for Christian realism.

The new concern is evident from the attention given it in *The Democratic Experience: Past and Prospects,* a book jointly written by Niebuhr and Paul E. Sigmund. Although it first appeared in 1969, the book is actually the result of a course taught by the two at Harvard in 1962 (Stone, 1972:204). It thus reflects fears and hopes more characteristic of that earlier period. Moreover, the fact that the chapter on Latin America was written by Sigmund means that its relation to Niebuhr's position cannot be presumed; nevertheless, since Sigmund's views closely correspond to Niebuhr's general perspective, it may be taken as representative of Christian realism's approach to Latin America.

The book starts from a premise that Niebuhr had argued for in *The Children of Light and the Children of Darkness:* free democratic institutions are morally necessary for achieving social justice. Niebuhr's contribution to *The Democratic Experience* therefore is an analysis of the complex historical factors that shaped the development of democracy in Western Europe and North America. His study suggests that there are three "constant prerequisites of free governments." Democracies require

(1) the unity and solidarity of the community, sufficiently strong to allow the free play of competitive interests without endangering the unity of the community itself; (2) a belief in the freedom of the individual and appreciation of his worth; and (3) a tolerable harmony and equilibrium of social and political and economic forces necessary to establish an approximation of social justice. [Niebuhr and Sigmund, 1969:73]

Niebuhr concedes that these factors have emerged amid the contingencies of history, and therefore cannot be taken as absolute; nevertheless, they do provide an agenda, a set of goals to be promoted in any strategy for political and social development.

The factors themselves should be familiar by now. The first represents Niebuhr's assessment of the constructive role of ethnic and linguistic communities in providing an infrastructure for democratic institutions, what in his later work he discusses as the "organic" dimension to society (Niebuhr, 1955:163–82).[5] The second factor is religious and ideological. Although the appeal to "individual freedom" has been a "bourgeois" panacea, the indispensable half-truth hidden in this ideology may be retrieved by returning to the understanding of "selfhood" nurtured by "the Judaeo-Christian faith" (Niebuhr and Sigmund, 1969:77). This strategy, of course, reflects the critical intention of *The Nature and Destiny of Man*. The third factor represents Niebuhr's conception of the balance of power. The conflict of social interests can never be eliminated, but must be institutionalized so that issues may be resolved more or less "tolerably" as they emerge. Obviously, this factor requires the political organization of less powerful nations and groups within nations, so that they might both represent their own interests more effectively and act as a check upon the inevitable excesses of the more powerful. Niebuhr's contribution therefore is an attempt to develop a critical social theory from his reflections on human nature and history. The point to this theory is practical: by analyzing the factors required for the development of democracy, Niebuhr hopes to promote its institutionalization in the Third World.

The section of the book written by Paul Sigmund, "The Prospects for Democracy in the Developing Areas," applies Niebuhr's theory to the political situation beyond North America and Western Europe. Sigmund's analyses tend to proceed systematically on the basis of Niebuhr's three prerequisites. Thus the chapter "Latin America: Democracy Imposed on Feudalism" discusses the prospects for developing "genuinely prosperous and free societies in Latin America" (Niebuhr and Sigmund, 1969:152). Not surprisingly, his conclusions are ambivalent: on the one hand, Latin America is in crisis, a situation made more acute by "the Communist threat"; on the other hand, there are reasons for hoping that the crisis may be overcome:

> If the modernized sector can develop the political will and the economic surplus to bring the semifeudal and depressed areas into the national community through education, welfare, and reform, the impending crisis may be averted. If it does not, the rural areas and the downtrodden urban masses will rise up to destroy those who refuse them their economic rights. [Niebuhr and Sigmund, 1969:152]

Sigmund begins his analysis with the thesis that Latin America's problems stem mainly from the remnants of "an essentially feudal hierarchical economic and social structure," the legacy of Spanish and Portuguese imperialism. The effects of this structure are compounded by "the racial amalgam of Iberian conquerors and Indian natives" in which the *mestizos,* the descendants of both peoples, form "a politically unstable intermediate group, estranged from the traditional Indian community but lacking the economic and political power of those of European racial extraction" (Niebuhr and Sigmund, 1969: 128). The peculiarities of Iberian political and cultural history made it inevitable that when the movements for independence actually emerged in Latin America they were "only superficially

democratic": "Democracy in these circumstances could not slowly transform feudalism. It became merely a superficial facade concealing the real
power of the oligarchs" (Niebuhr and Sigmund, 1969:129). The result is
that although Latin America today exhibits sufficient ethnic and linguistic
cohesiveness, and is uniquely situated among developing areas in its relation to at least one form of the Judeo-Christian faith, still it is "defective in
the possession of a tolerable equilibrium of social and economic power." In
view of its "feudal" origins, the social structure in many parts of Latin
America is "dangerously akin to the situation in European nations at the
beginning of the nineteenth century, and the plausibility of the Marxist
indictment of bourgeois democracy is correspondingly strong" (Niebuhr
and Sigmund, 1969:130).

Latin America's history thus is the source of problems relative to the
three requirements for democracy formulated by Niebuhr. (1) The positive
contribution to be expected from the possession of a common language is
blocked by massive illiteracy in many areas. Basic education may not of
itself assure the survival of democratic institutions, but it remains an
essential prerequisite. (2) The religious and cultural advantages normally
associated with the Judeo-Christian tradition are restricted in Latin
America because of the peculiar history and structure of the Catholic
church there. The ethos of the Counter-Reformation and the fact that the
church hierarchy traditionally was associated with either the Spanish
monarchy or the local oligarchies have contributed to a situation that
emphasizes traditional authority to the detriment of individual responsibility (Niebuhr and Sigmund, 1969:136–37). Despite the promising reform
movements that gained momentum with Vatican Council II, the church's
stand on birth control means that "the most serious economic and social
problem in Latin America today—the population explosion" has not been
faced (Niebuhr and Sigmund, 1969:138). (3) Coupled with the failure to
institutionalize a "tolerable harmony and equilibrium" of power in the
pursuit of social justice, these problems mean that the moral basis for
sustaining democratic political institutions is weak in Latin America.

In addition to these internal factors, Sigmund tries to assess the impact of
external factors, notably the history of the United States' intervention in
the area. Conceding that the record of American economic and military
involvement "is not an encouraging one" (Niebuhr and Sigmund, 1969:
146), he cites the exploitative and corrupting practices of "foreign business" in league with local oligarchies and the way in which "the over-
whelming military, economic, and political power of the United States"
has undermined the independence of the Organization of American States.
In Sigmund's view, even American resistance to "Castro and Communism" has had the ironic effect of strengthening the very social groups and
practices most in need of reform. Nevertheless, he rejects the thesis
that American influence is the sole cause of injustice in Latin America.
Thus he also insists that the effects of American involvement vary accord-

ing to the relative size and strength of the Latin American nations. As a result, he argues, "Whether the U.S. desires democratic government or stable authoritarian regimes will have little influence on large nations whose political processes are primarily determined by domestic factors rather than foreign influences" (Niebuhr and Sigmund, 1969:148). Moreover, the negative features of American intervention may be balanced by occasional examples of "enlightened conduct" in the face of Latin American programs nationalizing various American-owned industries. On the whole, then, Sigmund's assessment of American influence in Latin America is moderately reformist and thus entirely consistent with the thinking behind the Alliance for Progress.

Given this view of the internal and external factors, the prospects for democracy rest upon the creation of "an increasingly powerful middle class," which will trigger reform movements motivated by a concern for social justice. Accordingly, Sigmund is cautiously optimistic about the "democratic-left" parties—most conspicuously the Christian Democratic party of Chile—who "share the belief that government-sponsored reform can bring about changes in the present economic system that will promote democratic development and permit incorporation of previously excluded sectors of the population into the political process" (Niebuhr and Sigmund, 1969:142). In particular, he sees an affinity linking the policies of the Christian Democrats with the perspective of Christian realism. The party's sponsorship of the Popular Promotion program in Chile, for example, represents a strategy that, in theory, is consistent with Niebuhr's balance-of-power principle: "This plan gives government support to the formation of neighborhood, community, and peasant organizations, which can act to involve the deprived classes in government and to express their grievances" (Niebuhr and Sigmund, 1969:145). By advocating such strategies, the Christian Democrats may be able to forge the progressive sectors of the emerging middle class and the organizations of the "deprived classes" into an effective political coalition for reform. Largely on the strength of such a possibility, Sigmund concludes that "the prospects for free government seem more favorable in Latin America than in most other parts of the less developed world."

Sigmund's discussion of "the prospects for democracy in the developing areas" not only illustrates Christian realism's use as a critical social theory, but also raises some questions about it. Consistent with the priorities detected in Niebuhr's own reflections on international relations, Sigmund's analysis reflects Christian realism's anthropological bias. In other words, the theory emphasizes the moral basis for democratic political institutions and resists efforts to interpret these as simply a reflection of socioeconomic interests. While this emphasis is historical insofar as the moral basis is analyzed in terms of the vicissitudes of certain cultural values, it is also universal insofar as it assumes a normative anthropology according to which these cultural values, free political institutions, and socioeconomic development are closely linked.

The normative character of this analysis, in short, presupposes an ideal conception of human nature and destiny which, in turn, provides the basis for a political agenda, not only the politics of domestic reform but also the politics of foreign intervention—both of which represent the politics of "hegemony" responsibly exercised. Nevertheless, Christian realism's anthropological bias has two different tendencies, when Sigmund's analysis is compared with Niebuhr's cold war reflections. In the latter, the view of human nature serves as the basis for a moral appeal to policymakers for greater humility and restraint; but in the former, this same view tends to become the premise for a new activism seeking to extend the benefits of democracy to "the developing areas." *The Democratic Experience,* in other words, so simplifies the principles of Christian realism that they become virtually indistinguishable from the American moral idealism that Niebuhr criticized throughout his career. In this work it is hard to detect the influence of Niebuhr's paradoxical vision; and as a consequence, the tension between Christian realism and typical American common sense is relaxed. Apparently, the perspective of irony has given way to one of not-too-cautious optimism.

From the point of view of those who denounce Christian realism as an "ideology of the Establishment" this difference may seem overly subtle and finally irrelevant. But to those who continue to see merit in Christian realism, it may be considered as evidence of ideological drift, in other words, as an indication that Niebuhr's paradoxical vision was misunderstood and his principles misapplied. The final section of this chapter, at any rate, will assume this hypothesis and will seek to account for this drift in terms of the weaknesses of Christian realism.

The Weaknesses of Christian Realism

In recent years, even studies basically sympathetic to Niebuhr have expressed uneasiness about Christian realism's perspective on the postwar world. In light of the war in Vietnam and the demise of the Great Society, and as a part of the historical reassessment of the cold war and the imperial presidency, Christian realism has come to seem more a part of the problem than a part of the solution. It has been criticized not only for lacking any genuinely prophetic insight into these events, but also for sponsoring the policies that led to them. Critics who take this position, of course, may appeal to the discussions just presented as sufficient evidence for repudiating Niebuhr's work. But there are others who, while reading Niebuhr in light of these events, still seek to commend him. Recently, two full-length studies have appeared which evaluate Niebuhr's work in this way. Since their strategies differ significantly, I shall review them both to provide some context for my own observations.

Although it reads at times like an intellectual biography, Ronald H. Stone's *Reinhold Niebuhr: Prophet to Politicians* is actually an essay in the history of Christian social ethics. The book's perspective transcends the historical, for its purpose is to evaluate "the prospects for Niebuhr's social ethics," not only in his day but also for the present and the foreseeable future. In the course of his analysis, Stone presents a chapter on Niebuhr's views of "The United States' Role in International Politics since World War II" (1972:168–217) in which he argues that even in the postwar period Niebuhr maintained a critical stance on American foreign policy. While acknowledging his role as the "father of political realists," Stone tries to show that Niebuhr's views were more nuanced and thus generally more perceptive than those of his disciples. In this way he hopes to commend Christian realism's continued relevance to politics.

Nevertheless, the difficulty in establishing Niebuhr's superior perceptiveness is apparent as soon as his thinking on Vietnam is discussed. Stone shows how Niebuhr expressed reservations about the United States' role in Vietnam, beginning with a feeling of "vague uneasiness" in 1955, to doubts about the wisdom of supporting the "unjust and unpopular" Diem regime in 1962, to skepticism about President Lyndon Johnson's policy of escalation in 1966. Even with these reservations, Stone argues, the war in Vietnam was a difficult issue for Niebuhr. On the one hand, the United States had certain legitimate "imperial interests" in Southeast Asia; but on the other hand, since these interests were not worth the cost of defending them, the war was morally wrong because it "failed the test of proportionality." The depth of Niebuhr's perplexity, however, is perhaps unwittingly revealed in the metaphor he frequently used to describe the war: during the late 1960s he spoke of the "quagmire" of Vietnam (Stone, 1972:194). Even if Niebuhr's perception of the quagmire was more nuanced and perceptive than that of other realists, it is hard to see how this view would merit for him the title "prophet to politicians."

Thus despite his generally sympathetic attitude, Stone is not prepared to defend Niebuhr's perspective without criticism. He lists five "deficiencies" in Niebuhr's thought that must be corrected if Christian realism is to provide an adequate perspective on politics: (1) The relationship between morals and politics must be made more explicit, with less concentration on the "pinnacles of morality" and more on "prescriptive and goal oriented considerations." (2) The "equivocal usage" of many of Niebuhr's concepts, for example, "national interest, power, imperialism, liberalism, conservatism, idealism, and realism," must be cleared up. (3) Christian realism's failure to develop "case studies of how foreign policy is actually made and executed" must be remedied. In short, Niebuhr's proposals for the institutionalization of social conflict have not been reflected in his analyses of how "tolerable solutions" are actually worked out. (4) Attention must be given to ending the cold war rather than simply enduring it. Niebuhr's "irony" is helpful in coping with its frustrations, but where is "the courage to change the course of the conflict"? (5) Christian realism's skepticism regarding "the illusions of world government" must not be used as a pretext for throwing roadblocks in the way of building a genuinely international community. Since the bilateral conflict between the American and Soviet hegemonies has given way to a new and more pluralistic situation, creative effort is needed in this "flux" to bring the goals of justice and peace ever closer to realization.

In criticizing Niebuhr, Stone therefore is not proposing a revision of the principles of Christian realism. Instead, these are to be applied more effectively, first, by taking account of the changed situation of the 1970s, and second, by subjecting them to more rigorous philosophical and ethical reflection.

By contrast, Paul Merkley's *Reinhold Niebuhr: A Political Account* does not propose to assess the relevance of Christian realism for social ethics today. Nevertheless, his study—"a contribution to political history"—is evaluative in effect, if not in intention. Merkley is sympathetic to Niebuhr's perspective in the 1930s and 1940s, and thus focuses on "the formative years." To his credit is a very detailed and insightful account of that period, one which provides important information about Niebuhr's political activities while relating them to his theological reflections. All the same, Merkley's treatment of the postwar period is less helpful. Although he remains personally sympathetic to Niebuhr, he wishes to be critical of the "new realism" with which Niebuhr is associated. Thus regarding "the One Great Issue," he characterizes Niebuhr as "perilously close to becoming a Cold War ideologue" (Merkley, 1975:193). Yet extenuating circumstances, he argues, help account for this lapse.

In a chapter, "The Uses and Abuses of Reinhold Niebuhr," Merkley makes much of the series of illnesses that struck Niebuhr from 1952 until his death in 1971. The impression is created that his declining physical strength was the cause of a lack of "intellectual verve" in his later works. But in view of the fact that his following among American politicians and intellectuals reached its peak at that time, Merkley must argue that the physically debilitated Niebuhr was unable to resist being courted so indiscriminately (Merkley, 1975:206). The result of this situation was that Niebuhr became "cheaply appropriated": his defenders distorted the subtleties of his paradoxes to fit their own political commitments.[6]

Merkley to the contrary, Niebuhr's personal circumstances hardly explain either the merits or the weaknesses of his later works. The theories that he advocated then are just too consistent with his theological framework for social ethics to be dismissed so easily. Merkley's explanation is especially puzzling in view of his ringing endorsement of Niebuhr's bold attempt to make "the Christian Gospel" relevant to politics. Indeed, what Merkley likes about Niebuhr—as opposed to European theologians like Dietrich Bonhoeffer—is precisely his ability to formulate middle axioms, "the *theological* principles upon which American secular ethics stands." Apparently, he doesn't realize that his criticism of Niebuhr's later work implies a further criticism of the middle axioms upon which it rests. If Niebuhr's view of the cold war is questionable, then, for example, so is his understanding of the balance of power. In short, Merkley's appeal to Niebuhr's declining physical strength is unconvincing because the principles of Christian realism and the main outlines of their application were set before his illnesses struck.

If Merkley thus must be accused of evading the issues implicit in a critique of Christian realism's praxis, Stone must be criticized for not pursuing them far enough. Beyond the obvious demand made in his fifth point that Christian realism must continue to respond to historic changes in our common political experience if it is to remain "realistic," Stone's other recommendations require deeper reflection:

1. While his first point calling for greater explicitness in the definition of the relationship between morality and politics is certainly correct, it may be that clarity alone will not suffice as a corrective for the weaknesses of Christian realism. Even with more precise definition, it may still be necessary to recognize that the weaknesses of Christian realism as a social ethic are intrinsically related to its strengths as a religious vision, that its more or less intuitive approach to ethical issues cannot be corrected without also jeopardizing the spirituality symbolized by the paradoxical vision. Christian realism's weaknesses, in other words, may not be strictly formal; and consequently they may not be overcome by a greater degree of philosophical precision.

2. Similarly, his second point concerning the equivocal nature of Niebuhr's concepts is indicative of a real problem, but perhaps not exactly the one that he imagines. The difficulty is not that Niebuhr failed to define his political concepts, but that the concepts have meaning in reference to an anthropological construct whose primary theoretical value lies not in the area of critical social theory but in Christian moral psychology. Since social ethics involves more than the moral dispositions of politicians, such concepts—however suggestive—may never be adequate to define the conflict of social interests reflected in these dispositions. The equivocal nature of Niebuhr's concepts, in short, may require not just clarification, but a reexamination of their anthropological reference point and its theoretical capacity to explain societal conflicts.

3. Stone's third point also is correct, but too narrowly focused. The failure to do "case studies" of the sort he describes is not surprising, given Christian realism's tendency to use "national character" as a framework for political analysis. Since the concept "national character" is simply a secularized version of Niebuhr's theological anthropology, its inadequacies will not be overcome just by incorporating case studies into the analysis. By mapping the processes by which conflicts of interest are actually resolved, such studies inevitably will raise the issues just discussed regarding the adequacy of an anthropological—as opposed to a critical social—theory as the definitional framework for social ethics.

4. Finally, the "courage to change" demanded by Stone is only what one should expect from a theology designed to sustain a responsible radicalism

in politics. But in view of his career as a whole, Niebuhr's difficulty was never the courage to change but the perception of the need for change. The cold war, unlike the challenges of the 1930s for example, represented a situation that Christian realism had helped to define both politically and theologically. The question becomes whether or not Christian realism has the resources for criticizing perceptions that it has helped to shape. As in the previous points, this question initially concerns the adequacy of Niebuhr's anthropological focus for defining the issues of social ethics; at a deeper level, however, it asks whether Niebuhr's appeal to the "circular relation of the presupposition of faith and the facts of experience" allows for the kind of ideological criticism that makes for a change of perception.

When pressed further, each of Stone's points of criticism thus yields the same weaknesses previously detected in the theoretical structure of Niebuhr's theology and ethics. By pursuing Stone's criticisms, I have tried to show that these theoretical weaknesses have practical consequences, and vice versa. Assuming that this point is clearer now than it was before, let us proceed to a systematic critique of the praxis of Christian realism.

The fundamental theoretical problem originates with Niebuhr's theological anthropology and its relation to his theology of history. His "Christian interpretation of human nature" was and is a promising way to establish the reference of his paradoxical vision of a Hidden God, since without a correspondingly paradoxical understanding of human selfhood, this religious vision cannot be translated into theology. Nevertheless, a difficulty emerges as Niebuhr attempted to elaborate his anthropology into a theology of history. Through a process of metaphorical extension, the concepts defining human "selfhood" and "society" were made virtually interchangeable. But while the metaphors of "selfhood" are psychologically illuminating, they may be less adequate as a framework for social theory. In short, it is one thing to elaborate these anthropological insights into a dispositional ethic for guiding the consciences of politicians and social activists; but it is another, to use these same insights—as Niebuhr eventually did—to construct a model of "national character" from which to interpret the vicissitudes of international politics.

"National character"—whether it be American, Russian, Asian, or whatever—is a concept that illuminates some realities and obscures others. While it reflects national unity and helps create the sometimes necessary illusion of a collective psyche with its own "national interest," it also obscures the processes of social conflict that give this national interest its dynamism. Moreover, the danger of mystification—or ideological distortion—inherent in the concept of national character is intensified when this concept is stabilized according to the quasi-universal themes of a theological anthropology. Niebuhr's success in making those themes seem so relevant politically may have had the unwitting effect of obscuring the processes of social conflict that he meant to take seriously. As a result, Christian realism's critical perspective on international relations typically exhausts itself in a highly abstract discourse about policies of "expansionism," "adventurism," "isolationism," inspired by political motives of "cynicism," and "fanaticism," which themselves reflect the anxieties of "national character."[7]

Despite its abstract quality—or perhaps because of it—Christian realism's perspective does have its strength. Since its anthropology for a time did correspond to American public opinion—what Niebuhr referred to as "experience" or "common sense"—it was able to provide a framework in which the unprecedented complexities of American foreign policy could be made plausible to a national electorate, represented by that mythical American, "the man in the street." Given Niebuhr's commitment to the maintenance of "free democratic institutions" during a time of hegemonic conflict, it was crucially important to construct a public discourse that allowed some kind of popular participation in foreign policy decisions. While there are serious questions about the quality of that participation, there can be no doubt about Christian realism's enabling role as a form of public discourse.

Yet Christian realism's strength is also the key to its weakness. Its very success in reflecting—while also shaping—American common sense in the postwar period meant that it had become a part of the "reality" that it interpreted. When that reality entered a new stage of crisis, as it did with the war in Vietnam, Christian realism could only generate expressions of "vague uneasiness." Had Niebuhr faced the 1960s with the physical strength and intellectual vigor that possessed him in the 1930s, perhaps he would have had more to offer than the almost forlorn hope that a decent way out of the "quagmire" would be found. But in that case, he would have been the first to realize that among the "illusions" needing to be criticized so that "tolerable solutions" might be pursued were those fostered by Christian realism itself. How Niebuhr might have approached this problem without dismantling his whole theological framework must remain a matter of conjecture.

Besides the problem of ideological drift created by the use of Christian realism's anthropology as a mode of political analysis, there are a host of secondary difficulties related to it. In concluding this chapter, I shall mention two: one is the limited scope of Niebuhr's substantive view of human nature; the other is the problem created by the subtle shift in the kind of audience envisioned for Niebuhr's works. Both of these difficulties are pertinent to the question of Niebuhr's relevance to Christian social action today.

1. *Niebuhr's view of human nature:* Since human nature is manifest in a variety of cultures and is expressed in the structures of various languages and the themes of diverse intellectual traditions, no substantive perspective on it is universally valid. Theological anthropologies are no exception to this rule. While they seek to define the features of human nature considered most significant for understanding the One and Universal Divinity

active in our one and universal history, they perceive these features within particular religious traditions. Niebuhr, however, was well aware of this fact. He understood the limits of his "Christian interpretation" of human nature, and he was not about to deny the perspectival character of Christian faith. Thus it is apparent that Niebuhr's view of human nature has its perspectival limits. But what is the meaning of those limits for praxis?

A psychological profile on Niebuhr's anthropology would probably suggest that he was concerned with the aggressive personality and its problems. He assumes a high level of "vitality" and an almost spontaneous tendency to think and act in one's own interests. His "human nature," in short, is an active, dynamic "self," driven by anxiety, but also capable of a high level of personal integration—perhaps a model of the successful urban American of his day. For the most part, Niebuhr's counsels seek to channel constructively the force of this type of personality, by challenging him or her to adopt a measure of self-restraint and an attitude of self-criticism. "Humility" and "sacrificial love" thus are commended as the resources of Christian faith for social action.

No doubt, Niebuhr's diagnosis has the ring of truth for most of his North American readers. But his "self" is not the only personality type, and for today's social activists perhaps not the most immediately relevant. Recent psychological studies suggest that persons suffering the effects of oppression tend to react submissively to their situation.[8] Typically, their aggression is directed not against oppressors but against themselves. It is as if they must become "selves" in Niebuhr's sense before they can begin to change their situation. Thus the oppressed may have to overcome moral paralysis more often than the self-righteousness emphasized by Niebuhr. If this is true, then it is not surprising that many social activists find his "realism" stifling, an opportunity for indifference rather than responsibility. This response would certainly be understandable among those who read Niebuhr in the context of Latin American liberation theology.

Nevertheless, the perspectival limits of Niebuhr's view of human nature do not necessarily render Christian realism irrelevant. Niebuhr's characteristic emphases may be complemented by developing certain of his other insights. It should be possible, for example, to develop a more discerning interpretation of moral paralysis in politics by rethinking his dialectical understanding of pride and sensuality.[9] At any rate, the fragmentation of the "self" characteristic of oppressed peoples merits deeper reflection, if Christian realism is to address the situation of social activists today. Niebuhr, however, may still be uniquely qualified as a prophet to North American politicians. As long as the aggressive personality type continues to predominate among us, his dispositional ethic remains indispensable.

2. *Niebuhr's audience:* However abstract their reflections, religious thinkers do not work in a vacuum. Their writings inevitably are addressed to an implied audience or community of discourse for whom they may have some plausibility. Niebuhr himself understood this and presupposed it, for

example, in his approach to the problem of ideology. Nevertheless, over the years the character of the audience that he addressed shifted in important ways. As was noted previously, his works reflect changes from a denominational focus at Bethel, to a close identification while at Union Seminary first with religious socialists and later with the so-called vital center of American politics. In view of the critique of Christian realism's praxis, what is the significance of these shifts?

What happened to Niebuhr's thought, in other words, when it succeeded in attracting a broad but rather ill-defined national audience? While the obvious result was that this "circuit rider" now had the nation as a whole for his congregation, it is not just coincidence that his emphasis on national character emerged at this time. In short, Niebuhr's success in addressing a national audience actually may have undercut his ability to apply the balance-of-power principle effectively. For according to that principle, if the government is the organizing center in an equilibrium of power, then churches and other groups committed to humanitarian values must sponsor political organizing efforts so that—in Kenneth Thompson's words—"the public [can] give national leaders the grounds for transcending national interest" (Thompson, 1975:108). In theory, this is the strategy of Christian realism: it calls for the institutionalization of religious and humanitarian values in politics, because it recognizes that left to themselves "policymakers seldom, if ever, [can] rise above the national interest." But in practice, Niebuhr's later writings tend to speak directly to the policymakers in terms of a "generalized national character" without specifically encouraging such efforts at political organization. By failing to emphasize the institutionalization of perspectives at variance with those of policymakers, Niebuhr thus inadvertently may have compounded the weaknesses of Christian realism.

Niebuhr's inadvertence, however, cannot be attributed simply to the shifting character of his audience. While it is true that many of the activists who formed his audience in the 1930s became the policymakers of the late 1940s and the 1950s, and that together with Niebuhr they made a political odyssey from militant socialism to "piecemeal reformism," there are theological reasons that help to account for it as well. Consistent with the previous analysis, this weakness must be understood in relation to Niebuhr's anthropology. His understanding of the conflict of grace and pride, in other words, made him deeply suspicious of the utopian illusions and the self-righteousness all too common among religious leaders and secular moralists. Furthermore, he insisted that these spiritual problems manifest themselves even more acutely in the activity of human organizations, including the Christian churches. Thus his anthropological perspective unwittingly may have created an atmosphere that undermined an essential organizational strategy for maintaining a balance of power. At any rate, given the tensions introduced by his "religious reservation" regarding all forms of religious and political organization, the broadening of his audience meant that all too often these tensions were relaxed to such an extent that the balance-of-power principle was not applied effectively.

Any attempt to make Christian realism relevant once more to the concerns of American social activists will have to overcome these and similar difficulties. At the moment, however, the point is that they have been interpreted as resulting from certain theoretical weaknesses in Christian realism's theology and ethics, and not as indicating any fundamental inadequacy in Niebuhr's paradoxical vision of humanity before a Hidden God. Nevertheless, in view of these difficulties many social activists and religious thinkers have begun to look for alternative models for practical theology based on other religious visions. Much of the enthusiasm for Latin American liberation theology in the United States, for example, is understandable as a search for radical Christian alternatives. Whether these activists and thinkers are justified not only in repudiating Christian realism as an ideology of the Establishment but also in abandoning Niebuhr's paradoxical vision, is a question that finally cannot be answered until liberation theology's own merits have been discussed. In the chapters that follow, its claims as a model for practical theology will be subject to an analysis paralleling the one just made of Christian realism.

NOTES

1. Niebuhr's analysis of the United States' relationship with the Spanish Empire in the nineteenth century consistently reflects the theme of irony. Thus America's self-definition as a "messianic nation" is never challenged as such, but the nation's mixed "motives" and "temptations" are criticized in the following manner: "It did reveal some very telling manifestations of the temptation to screen the political lust and ambitions of a healthy young nation behind the ideal purposes with which our sense of mission had endowed us. That is the significance of the idea of manifest destiny under the cover of which we occupied our portion of our hemisphere" (Niebuhr and Heimert, 1963:128). Whatever the historical validity of this analysis, it clearly illustrates Niebuhr's tendency to interpret America's international relations in terms of the vicissitudes of national character.

2. In Niebuhr's opinion, racism is not necessarily linked to imperialism. He cites the difference between British and Latin imperialism, arguing that Latin imperialism was not racist. In view of its relevance for understanding Niebuhr's attitude toward imperialism in general and Latin America in particular, here is the passage in full: "A comparison favoring British over Latin imperialism would be neither fair nor complete without presenting a characteristic of Anglo-Saxon imperialism which presents us with a moral perplexity and illumines the curious relation between individual and collective standards and between the moral and the political order. Anglo-Saxons exhibit more race pride than the Latins, whether French, Spanish, or Italian; and all the achievements of British rule cannot obscure the fact that British dominion insisted on a separation of the dominant and the subject peoples, while Latin rule allowed intermarriage more consistently and made little of the distinction between white and colored peoples. The Latins were not more just to the subject peoples but they were more tolerant of intermarriage. Thus Spanish imperialism both enslaved the indigenous Indian population and mingled with them. The consequence was a half-Indian, half-Spanish culture, politically reproducing the ancient feudalism of Europe with the difference that the class or caste system was ethnically colored and determined. Our Puritans, on the other hand, while engaging in sporadic missions to the Indians, assumed that they were building a 'new England' on American territory. Not all the Indians were liquidated, but it is significant that remnants of

the Indian tribes now exist as wards of the Federal Government on their reservations. Some of the difference may be found in the higher degree of culture among the Indians of Mexico and Peru than among our North American Indians. But this does not explain the whole difference in strategy. Some of the difference may be due to different emphases in Catholic and Protestant cultures; and other differences may be explained in terms of the weight given to ethnic feeling in Latin and Anglo-Saxon cultures. It is sobering to observe that race prejudice is so intimately related to Anglo-Saxon achievements in empire that, indeed, it may even be basic to its success'' (Niebuhr, 1959:213–14).

3. At this point Niebuhr's philosophy of religion with its polemical categories "mystical" and "mythical" religions, as well as his reading of Western intellectual history, directly influences his political assessment of Asian values. Since biblical religion, in his opinion, is the distinctive source of the Western emphasis on the individual, it follows that cultures lacking that source will also lack that influence. Whatever the merits of Niebuhr's view, this line of reasoning illustrates some of the theoretical difficulties in using Christian realism as a framework for the analysis of non-Western cultures.

4. Niebuhr's conclusion regarding America's legitimate hegemonic responsibilities on the periphery of Asia, of course, is one of the reasons why in later years he regarded opposition to the Vietnam War as a difficult moral issue.

5. Niebuhr himself regarded his later emphasis upon the "organic" dimension of society as a corrective to his earlier stress upon the "mechanical." In short, his later work is more concerned with cultural than with socioeconomic factors. Yet even though his formulation of the balance-of-power principle in *The Nature and Destiny of Man* is tacitly critical of economic theories of political power, it does recognize the importance of both factors, at least in principle.

6. As examples of those who reread Niebuhr to fit their own commitments, Merkley cites both Walter LeFeber and Ronald Stone. LeFeber, he claims, brings Christian realism into "lock-step conformity with official Cold War policy," while Stone tries to "prove a case for Niebuhr's exceptional independence of judgment." Both are chastised for having "a certain gift for selectivity in quotation from Niebuhr's published word" (Merkley, 1975:207). Given the voluminousness of Niebuhr's published word, it would be difficult to prove Merkley wrong on this point!

7. Niebuhr's assessment of the prospects for Asian development and Sigmund's analysis of democracy in Latin America are only apparent exceptions to this general tendency. While they do introduce considerations of socioeconomic structure, their purposes in doing so are either to allay the anxieties of policymakers who may feel that American "national interest" is threatened or to promote policies—like the Alliance for Progress—that represent the nobler aspirations of American "national character."

8. For example, see Franz Fanon's groundbreaking study, *The Wretched of the Earth* (1968). This book is the chief source for the psychological profile of the oppressed that Paulo Freire outlines in *The Pedagogy of the Oppressed*. Freire's work will be criticized in Chapter 7, below, insofar as it forms the methodological foundation for liberation theology.

9. Given the fact that Niebuhr understands the sin of sensuality not as self-love but as a dissolution of the centered self, it should be possible to expand this notion to include the pathologies of oppression, for example, the "fear of freedom," which Paulo Freire identifies. Interpreting the psychology of oppression in this way, however, would place Freire's insights into the context of a theological anthropology representing a fundamentally different view of human nature from the one presupposed in the theory of conscientization. For a discussion of Freire's view, see Chapter 7, below.

6

Liberation Theology in Context

The Latin American Church has a message for all men on this continent who "hunger and thirst after justice." The very God who creates men in his image and likeness, creates the "earth and all that is in it for the use of all men and all nations, in such a way that created goods can reach all in a more just manner," and gives them power to transform and perfect the world in solidarity. It is the same God who, in the fullness of time, sends his Son in the flesh, so that He might come to liberate all men from the slavery to which sin has subjected them: hunger, misery, oppression and ignorance, in a word, that injustice and hatred which have their origin in human selfishness.

Thus, for our authentic liberation, all of us need a profound conversion so that "the kingdom of justice, love and peace," might come to us. The origin of all disdain for mankind, of all injustice, should be sought in the internal imbalance of human liberty, which will always need to be rectified in history. The uniqueness of the Christian message does not so much consist in the affirmation of the necessity for structural change, as it does in the insistence on the conversion of man which will in turn bring about this change. We will not have a new continent without new and reformed structures, but, above all, there will be no new continent without new men, who know how to be truly free and responsible according to the light of the Gospel.

—The Medellín Conference Document on Justice, 1968

Latin American liberation theology, among Roman Catholics at least, claims the second general conference of the Latin American Episcopal Council (CELAM) assembled at Medellín, Colombia, in 1968, as its authoritative point of departure. The conference met to develop continental strategies for implementing the program of renewal outlined at Vatican Council II. There is nothing extraordinary about the conference itself; various regional bishops' meetings were being held throughout the Catholic world in order to implement the new style of episcopal leadership authorized by Vatican Council II. All the same, the documents approved by the bishops at Medellín had an extraordinary impact. The reason is that,

131

although they assume the stance already laid out by the Council's *Pastoral Constitution on the Church in the Modern World (Gaudium et spes)*, and Pope Paul VI's encyclical letter of 1967, *On the Development of Peoples (Populorum progressio)*, they transform it in the direction of more radical and more explicit criticism of the injustices of Latin American society and politics. Medellín's impact was due not simply to the forcefulness of its criticisms; the conference also outlined a program of pastoral action that, among other things, encourages "the people to create and develop their own grass-roots organizations for the redress and consolidation of their rights and the search for true justice" (Gremillion, 1976:462). The impression created by Medellín was of a church suddenly awake to its moral responsibilities, now preparing to mobilize its considerable resources for the pursuit of social justice and peace. That this awakening should have happened in a part of the church commonly identified with cultural stagnation and reactionary politics prompted one sympathetic observer, John C. Bennett, to describe the event as "a miracle of the spirit" (Bennett, 1975:132).

It would be a gross mistake, however, to see liberation theology only in the context of the bishops' conference at Medellín, or to see Medellín itself only in the context of the shift toward collective episcopal leadership, or "collegiality," encouraged by Vatican Council II. Such a reading, still oriented to the internal development of ecclesiastical structures and strategies, would miss the distinctiveness of liberation theology as well as its explosive potential vis-à-vis both "the church" and "the modern world." The context of liberation theology is anything but narrowly ecclesiastical; it must be understood in relation to the history of Christianity in Latin America and its impact on society and politics in that area. Indeed, perhaps the most significant claim to be made for liberation theology is that it summons the reader to recognize the importance of its broader context. This new way of doing theology is a deliberate attempt to respond to the challenge of historical consciousness. But unlike Christian realism, which perceives that challenge differently, liberation theology seeks to rethink the meaning of Christian faith in light of "the Latin American reality," a term used to summarize the dramatic impact of recent history upon the Catholic church in that area. As we shall see, the historical consciousness in question here is defined by a new sense of Latin America's destiny, where for the first time the region is creating its own role on the stage of world history as a decisive contribution to humanity's struggle for liberation. This great expectation overshadows even the hopes raised by Vatican Council II; or rather, it transforms those hopes and channels the Latin American response to them.

In what follows I shall present only a rough sketch of this context, since my purpose is limited to a comparative analysis of two models of practical theology. In keeping with the format used to present Reinhold Niebuhr's Christian realism, I shall focus on four interrelated contexts: historical, sociological, ideological, and theological. The chapter will conclude with a comparison of the contextual differences between liberation theology and Christian realism, and their significance for practical theology.

Christianity and the Latin American Reality

In approaching liberation theology's historical context, the critic is not restricted to the biography of any one theologian, nor even to the dimensions of a collective portrait. The personal histories in this case are not as important as the social history of Latin American Christianity. The reason is that liberation theologians do not see themselves as thinkers exploring a personal religious vision. They claim to represent the collective experience of communities dedicated to "the process of liberation in the oppressed and exploited land of Latin America" (Gutiérrez, 1973: ix). Their theological horizons are developed in "solidarity" with these communities, and their intention is "not to betray" their commitment to them. Consequently, the question of historical context must focus upon these communities: where they come from, and what their significance is in the history of Latin American Christianity.

Christianity in Latin America, of course, is a part of the legacy of Spanish colonialism. When Christopher Columbus waded ashore at San Salvador in 1492, he planted the cross as well as the flag of Spain. When Hernando Cortes addressed Montezuma, the Aztec emperor of Mexico, and when Francisco Pizarro captured the Inca, Atahualpa, they demanded submission to the Christian God as well as to the king of Spain. This much probably is remembered from history lessons in grammar school. Less familiar is the pattern of development once the *conquistadores* had established themselves. The Christianization of Central and South America was administered as part of Spanish colonial policy, an arrangement that had its roots in the distinctive history of Catholicism in Spain. For over four hundred years the Catholic faith had been identified with the struggle to liberate the Iberian peninsula from the Moors. By the time of the final defeat of the Moors and the discovery of the New World in 1492, a permanent link had been forged uniting Spanish imperial aspirations and the cause of Catholicism. It comes as no surprise, then, that this pattern should be impressed upon Latin America at its foundation.

In the New World, Catholicism thus came to represent an ideology of liberation and conquest. The Indians were to be liberated from slavery to Satan, but in order to do so their overlords, the Aztecs, the Mayans, and the Incas, first had to be conquered. In a series of wildly improbable triumphs, the Spaniards liquidated the so-called pre-Columbian empires. Indeed, the *conquistadores* had good reason to believe that they had witnessed the triumph of the cross over the powers of darkness. Even so, the ensuing reorganization of the Indian tribes was designed to further the economic as well as the spiritual interests of the Spanish monarchy. Typical of this arrangement was the *encomienda* system, consisting of large land grants from the king to form plantations on which the Indians might be converted and civilized. In effect they were also reduced to serfdom.

The structure of the church in Latin America, in turn, was transformed by royal patronage in various ways. In addition to his traditional privileges, such as the right to nominate bishops, the king of Spain exercised a quasi-pontifical authority in the New World. Not only did he supervise ecclesiastical policy through church councils and synods, he also controlled the finances: "A papal bull in 1501 granted the Spanish crown the use of tithes in America as partial compensation for the heavy expenses incurred in the Christianizing mission of conquest" (Smith, 1970: 78). The result was a mixing of the revenues of church and state, which served to incorporate the clergy into the imperial administration. The convergence of economic and spiritual interests was complete.

There were, of course, exceptions to this pattern of Christian empire. Courageous individuals, such as the Dominican Bartolomé de las Casas, and innovative religious orders, for example, the Jesuits of colonial Paraguay (Pendle, 1963:58–61), tried to provide alternatives to the prevailing system. De las Casas denounced the *encomiendas,* arguing that the Indians were free, and that conquest was not a proper method of conversion.[1] The Jesuits, on the other hand, tried to provide an institutional alternative to the system. Organized as Christian villages in which the Guarani Indians were taught manual arts along with the new religion, the Jesuit *reducciones* were a model of humane but paternalistic treatment. By the end of the colonial period, however, both the protests of Fra Bartolomé and the communities formed by the Jesuits had come to precious little. De las Casas's argument was dismissed in favor of the *Requerimiento,* a text that defended the use of force to spread the faith (Gutiérrez and Shaull, 1977:63). Over the years, the very success of the Jesuit experiment in Paraguay generated greed and envy among neighboring *encomenderos,* or commissioners, who plotted against the *reducciones* in various ways. Finally in 1767 the *reducciones* were taken over by the crown, when the Jesuits were suppressed. Within a few years the *reducciones* were in ruins (Pendle, 1963:61).

At the beginning of the nineteenth century the struggle for independence in Latin America brought significant changes. Just as the various independence movements were occasioned by local grievances, so for the most part they were led by *criollos.* This group, an urban elite made up of Latin Americans of Spanish descent, found itself situated in a rigid social caste system dominated by the *peninsulares,* colonial administrators born in Spain. Below both groups were the *mestizos,* the people of mixed blood, and on the bottom were the Indians "who either laboured as serfs for the *criollos* and *mestizos* or lived in isolation among the highest mountains" (Pendle, 1963:85–86). The *criollos* wanted independence because the authoritarian and inefficient governments controlled by *peninsulares* prevented Latin American economic development. Once free from the antiquated mercantile policies of the Spanish Empire, they hoped to do business with the British. But over and above these economic considerations the ideals of the Enlightenment inspired many of the *criollos*. In short, they were enthusiastic about the religious and moral freedom as well as the political and economic changes they saw emerging in Britain, France, and the United States.

While the story of Latin America's struggle for independence is dramatic and complicated, what is of interest here are not the details, but the ambiguity of its results. In the first place, it did not immediately change the structure of society, since modern classes—notably, a genuine bourgeoisie—had yet to develop. Even so, the new political and economic climate opened the way for change by providing commercial opportunities, which in turn attracted the waves of European immigration characteristic of the nineteenth century. Second, the political situation became much more chaotic. The newly independent continent failed to achieve a political unity to complement its common cultural heritage. Moreover, the well-intended but unworkable constitutions inspired by the ideals of the Enlightenment soon gave way to the realities of *caudillismo*, a style of authoritarian personal leadership increasingly hostile to such ideals (Pendle, 1963: 125–37). Accompanying these social and political changes was the steady and pervasive economic penetration of the area, first by Britain and, after the turn of the century, by the United States (Pendle, 1963:161–86). Thus instead of fulfilling their expectations, Latin Americans found that the independence struggle had resulted in substituting one form of domination for another: Spanish colonialism had given way to British and American neocolonialism.

As this situation unfolded with a logic of its own, slowly but surely the cultural symptoms of modernization became evident. Among these, the role of the Catholic church changed from that of an imperial chaplaincy to that of a still formidable advocate of traditional values and conservative social policies within the new republics. Once the imperial connection was broken, the church had to contend with militant anticlericalism and a radical secularism bent on eliminating its influence from public life. At the same time it was challenged for the first time by the spiritual attractions of a Protestant mission associated with the progressive image projected by Britain and the United States (Arias, 1978:19–28). Placed on the defensive in Latin America, as elsewhere prior to World War I, the church reacted by denouncing "modernism" and by entering into alliance with various conservative political forces. Nevertheless, relations between church and state varied from one country to another, and from one regime to another in the same country. Thus, for example, the church was persecuted during the Mexican revolutions of the early twentieth century, but in Colombia its privileged status was secured in 1888 by a concordat with Rome (Smith, 1970:80–84, 118–21). These represent the extremes; in most places, the fortunes of the church oscillated with the alternation of conservative and liberal regimes. With the worldwide economic depression of 1929, however, the pattern shifted once more. The secular ideologies inherited from the nineteenth century came under intensive criticism, and a new kind of theologically conservative but socially progressive Catholicism began to emerge. Inspired by the social teachings of the modern papacy since Pope Leo XIII, and given institutional form in the Catholic Action movement (Smith, 1970:133), this twentieth-century Catholic renaissance represented an alternative to the stalemate reached by conservatives and liberals. It was to achieve mature political expression in the Christian Democratic parties organized after World War II. Thanks largely to this movement, the church could no longer be identified with cultural stagnation and the political status quo.

Two other developments since World War II need to be mentioned, both of them symptomatic of modernization and both of them demographic. The first is the trend toward urbanization; the second, a dramatic decline in infant mortality rates.[2] Taken together these have made for a "population explosion," resulting in a concentration of slums and social problems around the major urban centers of each country. More than any other single factor, the new demographic trends typify "the Latin American reality" invoked by the bishops at Medellín, a reality that exhibits both continuity and discontinuity with the patterns of Spanish colonialism and Latin American independence.

Medellin: A Rendezvous with Destiny?

It is clear that the 1960s marked a turning point in Latin American history. Three figures, Premier Fidel Castro, President John F. Kennedy, and Pope John XXIII, symbolize the hopes that many Latin Americans cherished for the new era. Castro's Cuban Revolution and Kennedy's Alliance for Progress represented fundamental political options for the future of the hemisphere. Both of these events raised expectations that old patterns could be broken in favor of social justice and peace. Among its most enthusiastic supporters, the Alliance for Progress meant prosperity and a new level of political maturity, approaching actual partnership with the United States. The strategy of development enshrined in the Alliance was to expand and stabilize a broad middle class as the basis for socially progressive democracies. The Cuban Revolution, on the other hand, promised real social equality based on the elimination of governmental corruption and the distorted economies of neocolonialism. Its strategy involved the abolition of class differences and the socialization of all productive wealth in the name of the people as a whole. As the implications of these two fundamental options were being explored, a third figure, Pope John XXIII, called for an ecumenical council to update the Catholic church's relation to the modern world. Pope John's personal image, one of openness, warmth, and a passion for social justice and peace, symbolized the hopes that were raised by the call for a council. For many the renewal of Catholicism under the inspiration of such an attractive leader promised to unleash an incalculable force for good in the world. There were days when all sorts of things seemed possible, such was the general euphoria of the early 1960s. In particular the events dramatized by these three figures suggested that perhaps for the first time Latin America stood on the threshold of a historic destiny.

This expectation remains unfulfilled. Within the space of a few years the images projected by both the Cuban Revolution and the Alliance for Progress had been tarnished. The Cuban missile crisis suggested that American neocolonialism might be eliminated only at the price of accepting Soviet imperialism. On the other hand, the partnership promised by the Alliance for Progress did not extend the benefits of middle-class life very far; instead, it appeared to bring increasing American interference in the political economies of various countries. For many Latin Americans it was discredited by the Brazilian military coup of 1964, the United States' military intervention in the Dominican Republic in 1965, and the political failure of Eduardo Frei's Chilean "Revolution in Liberty." Pope John's call to council was heeded, but the changes that it authorized did not add up to the renewal that many had hoped for. His successor, Pope Paul VI, supervised the work of the Council in an orderly fashion, making sure that its reforms were in continuity with the mainstream of modern papal social teaching.

Despite the mixed legacy of these initial hopes, the second general conference of Latin American bishops met at Medellín in 1968 in an atmosphere still influenced by them. Heartened by Pope Paul's opening address to the conference, the bishops projected a dramatic vision of the fundamental problems confronting Latin America and the Catholic church's role in solving them. The bishops denounced oppression and expressed hope for the future in the idiom of liberation.

The Medellín documents denounce oppression in terms of both "internal colonialism" and "external neocolonialism." The former refers to the exploitative conditions generated by the economic and political practices of local elites (Gremillion, 1976:455–56); but the latter links those same conditions with the impact of foreign economic domination:

> We wish to emphasize that the principal guilt for economic depend-
> ence of our countries rests with powers inspired by uncontrolled
> desire for gain, which leads to economic dictatorship and the "inter-
> national imperialism of money" condemned by Pope Pius IX in
> *Quadragesimo anno* and by Pope Paul VI in *Populorum progressio*.
> [Gremillion, 1976:457]

The analyses that accompany these denunciations, however, are neither thorough nor specific. Thus, for example, the "powers inspired by uncon-trolled desire for gain" are not identified; nor is any discrimination made between the economic and social interests that are captive to "the international imperialism of money" and those that are not. Despite this lack of precision, the documents do endorse a perspective from which more rigorous analysis might proceed.

Equally suggestive is the adoption of the idiom of liberation to express the church's hope for the future. The doctrinal section of the document on justice frames the denunciations just mentioned within a new theological language:

> Only by the light of Christ is the mystery of man made clear. In the economy of salvation the divine work is an action of integral human development and liberation, which has love for its sole motive. . . . We have faith that our love for Christ and our brethren will not only be the great force liberating us from injustice and oppression, but also the inspiration for social justice, understood as a whole of life and as an impulse toward the integral growth of our countries. [Gremillion, 1976:447]

The bishops, however, do not develop the theme of liberation systematically. In fact, their references to it are ambiguous. For example, the phrase linking "integral human development and liberation" may be read as a superficial attempt to reconcile the ideologies of both the Alliance for Progress ("development") and the Cuban Revolution ("liberation"). Moreover, the words "integral human" themselves suggest the social philosophy of Jacques Maritain, and therefore may be read as lending support to Eduardo Frei's Christian Democrats. In any case, the documents are not as unequivocal in their use of this idiom as liberation theology later will seek to be. Nevertheless, in summoning the church to heed the cry of the poor, the bishops do identify liberation with the mission of Christ:

> Christ, our Saviour, not only loved the poor, but rather "being rich He became poor", He lived in poverty. His mission centered on advising the poor of their liberation and He founded His Church as the sign of that poverty among men. [Gremillion, 1976:473]

In imitation of Christ, the bishops preach "our duty of solidarity with the poor." The specific forms this solidarity may take are left open, but at least they involve a renewal of the practice of voluntary poverty, especially among the clergy.

The sincere desire to share the burdens of the poor in some form of solidarity is perhaps the most impressive feature of the bishops' statements. It seems to inspire their effort to understand the Latin American reality from the perspective of the oppressed. One significant example of this is provided by their discussion of violence:

As the Christian believes in the productiveness of peace in order to achieve justice, he also believes that justice is a prerequisite for peace. He recognizes that in many instances Latin America finds itself faced with a situation of injustice that can be called institutionalized violence, when, because of a structural deficiency of industry and agriculture, of national and international economy, of cultural and political life, "whole towns lack necessities, live in such dependence as hinders all initiatives and responsibility as well as every possibility for cultural promotion and participation in social and political life," thus violating fundamental rights. The situation demands all-embracing, courageous, urgent and profoundly renovating transformations. We should not be surprised, therefore, that the "temptation to violence" is surfacing in Latin America. One should not abuse the patience of a people that for years has borne a situation that would not be acceptable to anyone with any degree of awareness of human rights. [Gremillion, 1976:460]

This statement echoes Pope Paul VI's sympathetic remarks about "the temptation to violence" published in the encyclical *Populorum progressio* (Gremillion, 1976:396). Still more significantly, it adopts the idea of "institutionalized violence," that is, a description of the ordinary workings of the police powers of the state in protecting an economic system that perpetuates gross inequalities. Usually this idea provides a point of departure for analyzing the options available to the oppressed and their would-be liberators. For some theorists the situation of "institutionalized violence" justifies the use of "counter-violence" against the system. The bishops, however, neither endorse the "counter-violence" of resistance and revolution nor do they explicitly condemn it. They label it, instead, a "temptation." Their own hope is that some other solution may be found:

If we consider then, the totality of the circumstances of our countries, and if we take into account the Christian preference for peace, the enormous difficulty of a civil war, the logic of violence, the atrocities it engenders, the risk of provoking foreign intervention, illegitimate as it may be, the difficulty of building a regime of justice and freedom while participating in a process of violence, we earnestly desire that the dynamism of the awakened and organized community be put to the service of justice and peace. [Gremillion, 1976:461]

The bishops therefore hope to awaken and organize "the dynamism" of the community as an alternative to violence. The vagueness of this alternative is partially overcome in a strategy involving "conscientization" (consciousness-raising) and the formation of "basic communities." Apparently, the bishops see the church playing an educational role in a process from which they hope new options will emerge. They pledge themselves to a program of religious and social conscientization meant "to awaken in individuals and communities, principally through the mass media, a living awareness of justice, infusing in them a dynamic sense of responsibility and solidarity." This effort is directed first of all toward the church's own institutions, seminaries and universities, but also toward "our governments and upper classes." So far, then, the bishops are simply extending the exercise of their traditional role as moral teachers, with possibly some effort to lobby the governments on behalf of the poor. But this is not their only pledge. They also stand committed to a new kind of community organization. They promise "to encourage and favor the efforts of the people to create and develop their own grass-roots organizations for the redress and consolidation of their rights and the search for true justice" (Gremillion, 1976:462). This commitment is the point of departure for the "basic communities" (comunidades de base) in which liberation theology will emerge.

Such was the bishops' response to Latin America's new sense of historic destiny. Encouraged by the Vatican Council's fresh approach to "the modern world," and inspired by Pope Paul VI's increasingly pointed appeals for social justice and peace, the bishops denounced the evils of oppression and embraced the continent's desire for liberation. Their sense of the historical moment, however, was conveyed in a perhaps deliberately ambiguous idiom that made the church appear more leftist than it actually was. In any case, when stripped of their provocative language, the Medellín documents continue the basic strategy of modern papal social teaching in criticizing both liberal capitalism and totalitarian communism as threats to "the dignity of the human person" (Gremillion, 1976: 449). In the context of the Latin American reality, they clearly imply a critical attitude toward both the Alliance for Progress and Castro's Cuban Revolution. The constructive alternative, however, remains obscure. Although the bishops hoped to awaken the dynamism of community by encouraging conscientization, it is not surprising that—given the ambiguity of the alternative— they were unable to control that dynamism once awakened.

Despite this ambiguity—or rather because of it—Latin American theologians like Gustavo Gutiérrez were quick to take Medellín as an endorsement of the various social movements with which they were involved: "Medellín, despite its imperfections and lacunae, legitimates newly-created phenomena in the Latin American Church; efforts at renewal now therefore enjoy unexpected support. Above all, Medellín provides an impulse for new commitments" (Gutiérrez, 1973:135). But just three years after the conference, the interpretation of the Medellín documents was already in dispute. Gutiérrez notes that "in the post-Medellín period (like in the postconciliar one) some groups would like the surprising consequences of positions they took to be forgotten or mitigated" (Gutiérrez, 1973:135). Gutiérrez thus is not prepared to admit any ambiguity in the documents, but sees in them a clear mandate for liberation theology. The source of this clarity is "the praxis of the Christian community." Accordingly, let us shift our attention to the sociological context for liberation theology, the so-called basic communities where this praxis takes place.

The "Basic Communities" and Their Theologians

Over the past century the Catholic church has encouraged the development of various forms of community organization as part of its strategy for coping with the modern world. Since the church has been consistently critical of both individualism and collectivism—the latter usually identified with Marxist socialism, and the former with liberal capitalism—it has also tried to sustain communities resistant to these values. Constructively, the church's proposals therefore have fallen into the category of a " 'middle way' or third alternative way *(tercerismo)* over against capitalism on the one hand and socialism on the other" (Fierro, 1977:68). In theory, *tercerismo* has been evident in a variety of ideological strategies: in the social teaching of the modern papacy, in the ideal of "new Christendom" advanced by Jacques Maritain, and in the progressive European theologies encouraged by Vatican Council II. But in practice, *tercerismo* has meant that the church has acted as the promoter and protector of various intermediary institutions, structures of genuine community that stand beyond the control of the state yet transcend the limits of primary institutions like the family.

In providing a rationale for these forms of association, the church formulated the principle of "subsidiarity," which forbids assigning to a "greater society of higher rank" responsibilities that can be "performed by lesser bodies on a lower plane."[3] In other words, if the family or a local community can cope with a situation, then it is wrong for the state to intervene. This is not the place to discuss all the implications of this principle. It is sufficient here to note its consistently personalistic and antitotalitarian intention, and the kinds of community that exhibit it. Thus, for example, the church has promoted consumers' and producers' cooperatives, some forms of labor organization, church-related youth groups, and the Catholic Action movement, which was meant to educate laypersons to their political responsibilities "as Christians" and to coordinate their efforts to defend the church's "religious interests" in a secularized society.[4] Common to all of these is a strategy designed to reinforce the family's role as the primary element in human relationships and yet to promote Catholic participation in the affairs of society as a whole. In fostering these institutions, the church seeks to exercise a kind of chaplaincy role involving various degrees of relatedness to its ordinary structures, the local parish and the diocese. With the basic communities, however, a new pattern may be emerging.

The basic communities represent a convergence of different trends in Catholic ecclesial development since Vatican Council II. At Medellín they were identified according to their form: "a community, local or environmental, which corresponds to the reality of a homogeneous group whose size allows for a personal fraternal contact among its members'' (Dulles, 1977:13). This definition, of course, fits most of the Catholic associations ever promoted under the principle of subsidiarity. But the basic communities are characterized by a distinctive blend of religious and social concerns. Unlike Catholic Action, the basic communities are not well integrated into the hierarchical structure of the church, nor are their political activities restricted to the defense of the church's ''religious interests'' in society. On the contrary, their activities range from prayerful Bible study to providing ''infrastructural'' support for guerrilla warfare (Assmann, 1976:137). More typical, perhaps, is the experience of the MEB (Basic Education Movement) sponsored by the Catholic bishops of Brazil and the Brazilian government prior to the military coup of 1964. The MEB directed a highly politicized literacy training program for Brazilian peasants using Paulo Freire's technique of conscientization. Eventually, as the Catholic laypersons who led the movement became divided over matters of strategy, they fell into two camps: ''the reformists who sought the integration of the depressed groups in society so that a major upheaval could be averted, and the militants whose object was nothing less than a revolutionary transformation of society'' (Smith, 1970: 167). The military coup, in more ways than one, put an end to this division, but the MEB's experience was transmitted to the rest of Latin America as a model for the basic communities and the kinds of projects to which they might aspire. They also bequeathed to liberation theology the root-metaphor of conscientization and a similar ambivalence over matters of strategy.

The church's primary intention in endorsing the basic communities was not narrowly political. Although the Medellín documents clearly affirm their role in the church's witness to social justice and peace, this role is understood as part of a broader commitment to new forms of evangelization. This is the context in which the basic communities were discussed at the 1974 Synod of Bishops in Rome, and this is how they are understood by North American theologians. Avery Dulles, for example, describes them as ''an alternative or complement to parish life'': ''In the United States such 'base communities' frequently grow up in connection with student associations, Marriage Encounter groups, and prayer groups, especially charismatic. Often the members not only worship and pray together but also live and work together'' (Dulles, 1977:14). Given the fact that Dulles makes no mention of their political role, the critic may wonder how the religious and social concerns of these communities are related. One sympathetic observer, Phillip E. Berryman, describes the situation:

> We have presented these two strains of reflection, the revolutionary and the pastoral, as though they were quite separated. In practice there is often a convergence. Often a pastoral team working at evangelization with peasants or barrio dwellers is radicalized by

events and reflection, so that what begins as biblical circles evolves toward some kind of confrontation with the power structure. Similarly, any kind of conscientization which touches major points of the culture must eventually get to a conscientization of religiosity. [Berryman, 1976:41]

It is apparent that in the context of the Latin American reality, any religious movement may quickly find itself involved in the struggle for justice.

Nevertheless, this process of radicalization is not simply spontaneous. The basic communities are defined ideologically rather than sociologically.[5] What makes these groups homogeneous is not some uniformity of social class background or occupational status, but a common social commitment, presumably as defined by the pastoral guidelines of the church. The "fraternity" called for by the bishops thus is not an end in itself; it is directed explicitly toward the struggle. Within these groups the theology of liberation is thought to emerge from the processes of reflection and action. The theologians of liberation, priests like Gustavo Gutiérrez and Juan Luis Segundo, see themselves simply as spokesmen for these communities. In theory, their works present a well-edited and systematized transcript of the groups' reflections. In practice, however, the theologian's role is more directive; he is more of a social theorist than a spiritual advisor. The question then becomes: Who are these theologians who speak for the basic communities?

Their personal histories are not as significant as the common response they have made to the situation confronting this generation of Catholic priests in Latin America. Some perspective on this situation may be achieved by recalling the life and death of the priest-revolutionary Camilo Torres. Torres may be taken as representative not because his actions are typical, but because his life and thought dramatize the context in which these theologians operate, and the options open to them. As is well known, Torres joined the National Liberation Army of Colombia (ELN) toward the end of 1965, and within a month or so he was killed in a skirmish involving governmental forces and guerrillas. For many in Latin America he is regarded as a revolutionary saint, a martyr in the struggle, a Christian brother to Che Guevara. These facts do not make him representative. His relevance here is based on the characteristic features of his situation. His family was part of the ruling elite of Colombia. He was a priest educated in Europe. A social scientist dedicated to political action as well as to research, he was radicalized in the course of his pastoral ministry.

From the beginning his was an exceptional career as a priest. Having acquired a law degree before entering the seminary, upon ordination he was sent to study social and political science in Louvain, Belgium. The fact that he was asked to serve as vice-rector of the Latin American College there is indicative of the high esteem he enjoyed with his superiors (Houtart and Rousseau, 1971:188). After his return to Colombia in 1959 he was named chaplain of the National University of Bogotá, where in addition to his pastoral responsibilities he taught sociology and continued his research. Always something of an activist, Torres was radicalized at the university. Thus, after becoming involved in a student strike, he was forced by the archbishop to resign his university post. Later, however, he was appointed dean of the Institute of Social Administration, where he helped to train personnel for government service (Houtart and Rousseau, 1971:189). In that capacity he continued his studies on the problem of social change. His research reinforced his political commitment, and in March 1965 he published a "Platform for a Movement for the Unity of the People" (Houtart and Rousseau, 1971:190). In essence, the platform denounced the politics of "developmentalism" advocated by the "liberal" government and called for a majority party on the Left. He saw his own role as that of an educator, one who would help build a popular revolution by raising class-consciousness in relation to the struggles of daily life.

Torres's platform "elicited an unprecedented response throughout the country." The archbishop, however, was not impressed. Although the platform was consistent with positions taken a few years later at Medellín, the fact that Torres had developed a systematic criticism of the church's role in Colombian society in particular was resented (Houtart and Rousseau, 1971:199). The archbishop retaliated by denouncing Torres for departing from the social teachings of the church. But more to the point, he made the incident a matter of principle: "A priest may not intervene in politics" (Houtart and Rousseau, 1971:200). Ever sensitive to the tension between his priestly duties and his political commitments, Torres finally requested laicization on June 24, 1965. In his letter of resignation he observed that "the present structures of the Church make it impossible for me to continue to exercise my priesthood." He also announced his intention of joining the guerrillas: "I believe that the revolutionary combat is a Christian and priestly combat. . . . It is the only way, in the concrete circumstances of our country, for us to love our neighbor as we should" (Houtart and Rousseau, 1971:200).

Despite the ultimate outcome of his personal struggle, Torres remains an appropriate symbol of the situation faced by liberation theologians. Most of them share much in common with him. They all seem to be within the same age-group as Torres. Most, if not all, come from bourgeois families, the descendants of *criollos* or the European immigrants of the nineteenth century. Most, if not all, have received theological and professional education in the Catholic centers of Europe. Many have expressed profound dissatisfaction both with progressive European theology and with their lack of preparation for the realities of the pastoral ministry in Latin America. Their relation to the social sciences often parallels Torres's, since invariably they combine theoretical interests with an intense moral commitment to liberation. Many of them are involved in specialized ministries, in university chaplaincies, college professorships, church-related research institutes, and in various social agencies sponsored by the church. Inevitably they have attached themselves to basic communities within these contexts, and there in immediate contact with the Latin American reality they have been radicalized. None of the major theologians has withdrawn to the mountains to join the guerrillas, but the pathos of their situation is similar to that of Torres. His strengths are their strengths; his weaknesses, their weaknesses.

Conflicting Ideologies

Beyond these similarities, liberation theologians share with Camilo Torres a common ideological presupposition. They are united in rejecting the ideology of "developmentalism" *(desarrollismo)* and in seeking an alternative under the banner of liberation. In taking a forthright stand on the ideological issue, liberation theologians have gone beyond the bishops' statements at Medellín. For although the bishops adopted the new idiom of liberation, they also continued to speak in terms of integral human development. They did this with no apparent awareness of any ideological conflict between the two. Liberation theologians, on the other hand, are acutely aware of it. Indeed, it is difficult to see how anyone could really act in solidarity with the basic communities unless they, too, shared the theologians' hostility to developmentalism. Thus contrasting polarities development/underdevelopment and dependence/liberation serve to define the ideological conflict. An essential presupposition of liberation theology, the paradigm of dependence/liberation entails a view of the world as divided between oppressors and oppressed, and an ethos based on "solidarity with the oppressed." As is true of most ideologies, this perspective can be summed up in a few convenient slogans. But what reasons may be given to justify this option?

The concept of "development," originally a term used in philosophies of history to suggest the complexities of human social evolution (Gutiérrez, 1973:23), in Latin America has taken on a more specific and highly controversial reference. "Development" refers to economic growth, not just any economic growth, but the kind of controlled upward spiral promised by advanced industrial capitalism. The Western industrial democracies, especially the United States since World War II, are presented as models of development and thus become a paradigm for analyzing problems of underdevelopment. "Underdevelopment" is a condition characterized by a chronic lack of economic growth, or at least not enough of it to reach a take-off point where the benefits of advanced industrial capitalism are supposed to begin. The paradigm is based on certain premises: that economic growth is the key to social progress, and that the factors promoting economic growth can be deduced from the experience of developed nations and reproduced among the underdeveloped. Consequently, the structures believed present in developed nations—free democratic institútions, secularized and pluralistic value systems, a middle-class majority educated to its political responsibilities, and an expanding industrial base—become the goals to be realized among the underdeveloped. These nations, however, are not to be left alone in their efforts to reach these goals. Thanks to the enlightened perception of self-interest among developed nations, whose prosperity depends on further economic growth, the underdeveloped nations receive the benefits of foreign aid and investment, strategically placed in order to promote development. This concept was popularized in Walt W. Rostow's *The Stages of Economic Growth: A Non-Communist Manifesto* (1960), and represents the underlying rationale of the Alliance for Progress.[6]

Liberation theologians, as well as many Latin American political economists, scornfully reject the paradigm of development as an ideological facade for American neocolonialism. Their reaction is due not simply to a lack of shared presuppositions. They also point to experience, to analyses of what actually went on during the so-called First Decade of Development (Gremillion, 1976:477–84). In practice, the panacea of economic growth either failed to materialize or had paradoxical consequences. Foreign aid and investment did not trigger the process of development, but increased the level of economic and political dependence. The decade actually witnessed a net economic loss for underdeveloped nations. Liberation theologians conclude, therefore, that "development" is not another name for peace, but for exploitation.

No less severe is their verdict on the social costs of developmentalism in Latin America. The middle-class majority, upon whom the hopes for economic justice and political responsibility were supposed to rest, did not materialize. Instead, an elite now habituated to modern consumer tastes managed to absorb most of the benefits without contributing much in turn to Latin American economic autonomy. The industrial base actually formed for the most part is controlled by the multinational corporations, and is directed toward the production of luxury goods and services for an elite, a strategy whose chief purpose is to maximize corporate profits. The expected corollary to development, the stabilization of free democratic institutions, did not occur. Instead, given the deteriorating economic situation, the fear of revolutionary socialism among the elite and their North American business partners, and the growing indifference to political responsibility fostered in part by the ethos of a consumer society, the trend shifted toward military dictatorships, which impose stability by suppressing civil liberties and ignoring basic human rights. In turn, the senior partner in this decade of development, the United States, went through an about-face in foreign policy. The moral idealism of the Alliance for Progress soon dissolved into a desperate cynicism capable of supporting any regime perceived to be favorable to American interests. These trends, in themselves damaging enough, appear to converge in the fates of those countries billed as "showcases for developmentalism," Brazil and Chile.

For liberation theologians this combination of factors is more than enough to discredit the paradigm of developmentalism. But the bitter scorn with which they reject it is a consequence of their ability to interpret it as an ideological facade for American neocolonialism. This they manage by shifting to the paradigm of dependence/liberation.

The two paradigms are interrelated in that the failure of developmentalism is read within the new framework as symptomatic of dependence. "Dependence" refers to a critical theory of neocolonialism interpreted from the point of view of those who have been colonized. It is based on the work of Fernando Henrique Cardoso and Enzo Faletto, *Dependencia y desarrollo en America Latina* (1967), which argues that the economies of the United States and Latin America are interrelated in a single oppressive system. Instead of the abstract polarity of development/underdevelopment, Cardoso and Faletto speak of the "center" and the "periphery": The center exercises domination, and the periphery is forced to submit to it. Within this theory the negative consequences of development no longer seem so paradoxical. They are seen as a result of certain imperatives built into the kind of economic growth generated by the capitalist system. In fact, the gross injustices at the periphery, namely the realities of exploitation in the so-called underdeveloped world, actually provide the profit margins that finance the prosperity of the middle-class majority at the center. Thus the factors contributing to economic growth even in the developed countries are secured through an exploitative system that makes it impossible to reproduce such prosperity among the underdeveloped. "Dependence" means not simply that the economies of the United States and Latin America are integrated; more to the point, it suggests they are related as a parasite is to its host.[7]

Given this interpretation of the situation, the imperative of liberation becomes virtually self-evident. The nations of Latin America must find ways to eliminate the parasite from their systems. Once that is done, they must work out strategies for social change according to their own definitions of human need. The paradigm of dependence/liberation, therefore, emphasizes social conflict in a way that developmentalism does not. Furthermore, in the absence of critical analysis of the class structure of society, economic growth must be rejected as a mystifying abstraction. By contrast, the critique of dependence is meant to demystify the situation by specifying the classes that actually are enriched or victimized by neocolonialism. The paradigm of liberation, however, is not simply a way to highlight the continued reality of the international class struggle. More to the point, it provides an alternative to capitalist economic growth by envisioning an indigenous Latin American socialism.

For liberation theologians, at least, the ideology of dependence/liberation represents more than just a paradigm for analysis. It also expresses a historic turning point for the peoples of Latin America, a worldview and an ethos in which various levels of meaning interact with one another. Gustavo Gutiérrez describes the three levels involved in the ideology of liberation:

> In the first place, *liberation* expresses the aspirations of oppressed peoples and social classes, emphasizing the conflictual aspect of the economic, social, and political process which puts them at odds with wealthy nations and oppressive classes. [Gutiérrez, 1973:36]

On this level the paradigm helps the oppressed to demystify their oppression by providing a critical understanding of their particular situation. This also represents the first step in the process of conscientization.

> At a deeper level, *liberation* can be applied to an understanding of history. Man is seen as assuming conscious responsibility for his own destiny. This understanding provides a dynamic context and broadens the horizons of the desired social changes. In this perspective the unfolding of all of man's dimensions is demanded—a man who makes himself throughout his life and throughout history. The gradual conquest of true freedom leads to the creation of a new man and a qualitatively different society. [Gutiérrez, 1973:36–37]

Here the paradigm provides a universal vision in which the aspirations of the oppressed are identified with the meaning of history as a whole. The substantive values expressed in this vision are those presupposed in the theory of conscientization, the recognition of which marks the second stage of the process. At an ultimate level,

> the word *liberation* allows for another approach leading to the Biblical sources which inspire the presence and action of man in history. In the Bible Christ is presented as the one who brings us liberation. Christ the Saviour liberates man from sin, which is the ultimate root of all disruption of friendship and of all injustice and oppression. Christ makes man truly free, that is to say, he enables man to live in communion with him; and this is the basis for all human brotherhood. [Gutiérrez, 1973:37]

Here the ideology of liberation is transposed into theology, thus providing the distinctive *raison d'être* for the basic communities. The ultimate stage of conscientization, for liberation theologians at least, is a communal experience of Christ the Liberator apprehended in the praxis of Christian faith. While it is clear that the idea of liberation and social movements embodying it may exist apart from the Christian community, the full meaning of liberation is recognized only in Christ. Without this reference to Christ, of course, there could be no liberation theology.

A Theology of Liberation

This claim concerning an ultimate level of meaning in liberation marks the transition from the ideological to the theological context. As in the case of Niebuhr's practical theology, there is a complex relationship between the two. Just as Christian realism is related but not strictly reducible to the ideology of reform adopted by the Americans for Democratic Action, so liberation theology—at least in its initial formulation—is not reducible to the ideology of dependence/liberation. In both cases the relationship must be characterized as some sort of elective affinity. Liberation theology, like Christian realism, seeks to present a distinctively religious legitimation of universal human aspirations insofar as they become meaningful in a particular religious vision of ultimate reality. What's more, the religious visions in question claim to be essentially biblical and Christocentric. Nevertheless, there is a closer and more explicit relationship between this theology and its ideological context. The paradigm of dependence/liberation and the historic vision of the Latin American reality implicit in it are constitutive for liberation theology in a way that the ideology of reform is not for Christian realism. The difference between the two and its consequences for them as models for practical theology is a major burden of the remainder of this analysis. For the moment, however, let us introduce the distinctive features of its theological context.

Liberation theology's basic intention may be described as an attempt to discern the meaning of "the signs of the times." The kind of historical consciousness required for such a project, no doubt, is something of an innovation in Roman Catholic theology. Although the supposition that Catholic theology is static and essentially unrelated to historical changes should have been laid to rest long before Pope John XXIII called the Vatican Council, the translation of historical consciousness into theological categories has proceeded slowly and hesitantly. The progressive theology of the Council sought to achieve a dynamic balance between permanence and change, between the permanent essential principles of Catholic faith and the historical vicissitudes within which they must be interpreted and lived. Thus the Council's *Pastoral Constitution on the Church in the Modern World (Gaudium et spes)* declared that "the Church has always had the duty of scrutinizing the signs of the times and of interpreting them in the light of the gospel" (Gremillion, 1976:246). For all its reassuring ambiguity, this statement generally has been understood as the authorization for a genuinely new kind of practical theology. The Latin Americans, going a step further than the Council, interpreted this abstract directive in the context of the basic communities professing solidarity with the oppressed. Liberation theology therefore asserts that the appropriate criteria for discerning these signs are to be derived from reflection and action based on such solidarity. This is what these theologians mean when they describe their theological method as "critical reflection on praxis."

Doing theology in the context of solidarity with the oppressed places great importance on the modes of analysis used to interpret the situation of oppression. Accordingly, the critical theories that support the paradigm of dependence/liberation are transposed into principles of theological interpretation. They circumscribe a "hermeneutic circle" (Gutiérrez: 1973: 13), which in turn is validated by the community's experience of and reflection upon the struggle against oppression. There is nothing surprising about this, when viewed in relation to the usual circular processes of modern ideological thinking. Questions are raised, however, whether or not there is any justification for this as a distinctively theological method.

Here a brief comparison with Christian realism may be instructive. Its theological categories are formulated in relation to a religious vision of the Hidden God whose meaning for humanity is paradoxically revealed in the general content and structure of human experience as confirmed through a pious reading of the Bible. Its insights are spelled out in a "Christian interpretation" of "the nature and destiny of man," which functions to provide a religious perspective on the ultimate limits of human thinking and acting. By contrast, liberation theology begins with a religious vision not of a Hidden God, but of One who emphatically stands revealed in the struggles of oppressed peoples. The figure of Christ is interpreted consistently from this perspective. The struggles of oppressed peoples—or at least, the liberation theologians' imaginative reconstruction of them—therefore function theologically in approximately the same way as the general content and stucture of human experience do for Niebuhr. To use the jargon, each has a different *locus theologicus* (Gutiérrez, 1973:12). History, not anthropology, serves as the primary reference point for liberation theology. The implications of this referential shift will be explored later on. For the moment, it is sufficient to recognize that the Bible is invoked as the ultimate warrant for this shift: through a highly selective reading of certain texts, liberation theologians understand their commitment as essentially an imitation of Yahweh's historic concern for the poor, the *anawim*. If, as they believe, Yahweh himself emphatically identifies his cause with that of the oppressed, then fidelity to Yahweh—as definitively revealed in Jesus Christ—requires no less of Christians. Practical theology based on anything less than this commitment inevitably becomes a betrayal not only of the oppressed but of God and his Christ.

Such a program for theology, not surprisingly, has critical as well as constructive dimensions. Just as Niebuhr's Christian realism first emerged in polemical relation to the Social Gospel, so liberation theology relates to Maritain's Integral Humanism. Niebuhr's objections to the Social Gospel were at first practical—it failed to grasp the "astute intelligence . . . needed to guide moral purpose in a complex situation"—but later became theoretical. So liberation theology begins its polemic against Integral Humanism by criticizing its practical consequences. Integral Humanism, it is alleged, restricts the scope of Catholic social action in ways that obscure and distort the church's involvement in politics. In other words, by making a distinction between what may be done "as a Christian" and "as a Christian as such," Maritain sought to involve the individual believer, but not the institutional church, in the vicissitudes of social action (Maritain, 1973: 294). As a consequence, the clergy's role was limited to educating the laity to defend the church's essentially "religious interests" (activities of "a Christian as such") and to exercise political responsibility (activities undertaken "as a Christian"). Maritain recognized that there was an area where these activities overlap, the sphere of "Catholic Action," which seeks to protect the church's institutions—for example, the Catholic school system—through the political process. This intermediary area was to be strictly supervised "*hic et nunc* by the Holy See and by the Episcopate" (Maritain, 1973:301), so that the church's "religious interests" might not be compromised by partisan political entanglements. Liberation theologians reject these restrictions because they are incompatible with the praxis of the basic communities. Their experience suggests that in fact the church has never confined itself to essentially religious interests in politics, and that the distinctions tend to obscure the church's historic collaboration with an oppressive *status quo*. Furthermore, the less formal and more intimate participation of priests in basic communities makes the distinction of clerical and lay roles in Christian social action seem untenable. To insist upon this distinction is to make it impossible for the clergy to achieve genuine solidarity with the oppressed.

These practical objections have led to theoretical criticisms of Integral Humanism as a theology. Liberation theologians claim that the practical problem results from Integral Humanism's obsolete distinction between the supernatural and the natural orders of existence. The basic question therefore becomes one of understanding God's action in history and humanity's proper response to it. Integral Humanism continues to interpret this relationship in continuity with the classical Thomistic distinction of nature and grace. While Thomism affirms that "grace builds on nature," grace represents an ontological change in human nature that prepares us for a heavenly fulfillment with God beyond history in the "beatific vision." Liberation theologians criticize this interpretation as "dualistic," proclaiming instead that "history is one," a formula meant to convey their distinctive view of religious transcendence and its relation to the struggle for liberation. History, not heaven, is the arena where ultimate fulfillment will occur, and its occurrence will mean humanity's total liberation. Consequently, they call for a new theology of history that will faithfully interpret the concrete dynamism of God's involvement in human thinking and acting. Since the figure of Christ the Liberator both symbolizes and effects this fulfillment, his historic reality thus dramatizes the inadequacy of what for them is only a so-called Integral Humanism.

Contexts in Contrast

In concluding this analysis of the context of liberation theology, let us compare it with the results of the one made on Christian realism. At each of the four levels there are similarities as well as differences. The similarities are significant enough to allow discussion of them as alternative models for practical theology. The differences are important enough to make the critic suspicious of any easy reconciliation between the two.

Historically, both theologies emerged as responses to major social changes accompanying the process of modernization. Since the dynamics of this process are different in the United States and in Latin America, it is not surprising that these theologies differ in their perception of the tasks confronting them. Niebuhr's agenda first emerged in relation to the transition from rural life to the complexities of modern urban America. In the United States religion was secularized with the founding of the republic, and Protestantism had already responded by developing a distinctively American denominational pattern. But the challenge confronted first by the Social Gospel and later by Christian realism was to find an equally effective response, institutional as well as spiritual, to urban life in an industrial society. By contrast, liberation theology takes shape in response to Latin America's historic struggle for genuine independence, economic as well as political. It also comes at a time when the Catholic church is attempting to respond positively to the process of modernization, after more than a century of unbending resistance to it. Denominationalism, as experienced in the United States, does not exist in Latin America; nor did that continent ever enjoy anything like the United States' original experience of agrarian democracy, with its powerful role in creating an American ethos. Liberation theology, instead, understands its context in terms of a great leap forward from colonialism to some sort of revolutionary socialism. Consequently, this theology is rooted in a historical consciousness of social conflict to an extent that is foreign to Niebuhr's thinking even in his early days as a socialist radical.

Sociologically, both theologies emerge from the context of the pastoral ministry. But the ministries in question differ not only according to the diverging patterns of modernization in society, but also according to diverging institutional patterns in the churches. Niebuhr's theology is a reflection on his experience as a pastor, ecumenical leader, and religious journalist. There is little concern for the kind of centralized policy-making bureaucracies that have become so important to modern Catholic pastoral activity. Niebuhr's parish, when compared to the Latin American basic communities, is heterogeneous ideologically as well as socially. Membership in the congregation is not based on a shared commitment to the struggle against oppression, but on the traditional religious aspirations of individual believers. Niebuhr's task therefore is to cultivate a Christian social imagination among these believers, rather than to interpret the theological meaning of a solidarity already experienced in collective political action. His later "vocation" as a "circuit-rider in the colleges" was merely an extension of his nonspecialized parish ministry. By contrast, liberation theologians generally operate from a base within the pastoral bureaucracies of the institutional church, and usually have professional training in the social sciences. These occupational differences are reflected theologically in various ways. One obvious difference is that liberation theologians take an institutional approach to politics, and are more interested in changing structures, while Niebuhr's approach is more concerned to challenge the hearts and minds of individuals. Compared to the Latin Americans, he showed little interest in organizing Christians or in changing the structures of the church. Liberation theologians, on the other hand, recognize the historic political and social involvement of the church, and therefore hope to organize its power in behalf of the oppressed. They expect more from the church, and their expectation is political.

Both theologies exhibit an elective affinity for certain ideological perspectives with which they interact. They differ, however, in that Christian realism emerged from Niebuhr's practical experience and theoretical criticism of a militant socialism that paralleled the theology of the Social Gospel, while liberation theology arose from dissatisfaction with both conservative and progressive forms of Catholic social thought. Since the reformist tendencies of both Christian realism and Integral Humanism were one in taking an optimistic approach to the Alliance for Progress, the ideological conflict between the Latin Americans and Niebuhr apparently is most acute. The major issue separating them boils down to this: Is American neocolonialism really the primary cause of the misery among the oppressed peoples of Latin America, or is it not? If it is, then the paradigm of dependence/liberation is probably the most suitable framework for analyzing the problems of the area. If it is not, then some other paradigm —not necessarily the one designated by "developmentalism"— will have to be adopted. Since the distinctive agenda of liberation theology is constitutively related to this paradigm, its rejection would entail at least a blurring of the differences that now separate this theology from Christian realism, not to mention its differences with progressive Catholic social thought. But as it stands, liberation theology is committed to this paradigm, and that commitment helps to define its theological agenda.

Finally, both Christian realism and liberation theology are meant to interpret "the signs of the times" theologically, in the sense that both seek to discern God's action in history and humanity's response to it. They differ, however, on what criteria they accept as indicative of God's action, that is, they look to different aspects of human existence for disclosures of the divine. Although Niebuhr's theological interpretations only reach maturity much later on in his career, it is clear that from the beginning his understanding of religion emphasized certain features of human nature in general. While Christian realism's agenda initially proposed to relate a "vital religious idealism" to a more "astute intelligence," it was the religious idealism that provided the basis for interpreting God's action in history. Thus from this point of departure Niebuhr moved toward the problematic of theological anthropology. By contrast, liberation theologians interpret God's action by identifying it with the historic aspirations of a particular group of human agents, the oppressed. This agenda represents a shift toward the problematic of a new kind of theology of history.

In the chapters that follow, the significance of these contextual differences will emerge as a conflict over the meaning of religious transcendence and its critical role in human historical action.

NOTES

1. Gustavo Gutiérrez is so impressed with Bartolomé de las Casas's work that he proposes him as a model for liberation theology, especially insofar as he criticized the "theology of oppression" represented by the *Requerimiento*, which tried to justify the conquest and forced conversion of the Indians (Gutiérrez and Shaull, 1977: 60–69). Ironically, in his zeal to save the Indians, de las Casas was one of the first to advocate the use of Black African slaves in the New World (Mannix, 1962: 2–3), a fact whose significance Gutiérrez minimizes in the footnote where it is mentioned, saying that Fra Bartolomé was "a man of his time." From the perspective of Christian realism, this irony is a perfect illustration of the fact that all too often in history one group's liberation entails another group's enslavement, a fact which might make one pause before he or she identifies liberation with the kingdom of God.

2. For a vivid description of the human impact of these trends, see Berger, 1976, especially the "interlude" pieces "Tableau in Garbage—Child with Vultures" and "A Tale of Two Slums." For an interpretation of the demographic statistics and an analysis of the "explosion's" impact on Latin America's capacity to provide subsistence for its own people, see Smith, 1976. It is interesting to note that neither the Medellín documents nor the liberation theologians seem to have grasped the significance of the "population explosion" and its economic impact. While the bishops recognize the problem, they also reaffirm the teachings of *Humanae vitae* on birth control (Gremillion, 1976:467–69). Their reticence on this issue is in marked contrast to their bold attempts to tackle questions of political economy. Nevertheless, an argument could be made showing that these demographic trends are more significant for developing an accurate picture of Latin America's problems than the paradigm of dependence/liberation. In this area, as in so many others, the situation is more complex than the ideologists would have it.

3. The principle of subsidiarity, one of the mainstays of modern papal social teaching, was first formulated by Pope Pius XI in the encyclical letter *Quadragesimo anno*: "This supremely important principle of social philosophy, one which cannot be set aside or altered, remains firm and unshaken: Just as it is wrong to withdraw from the individual and commit to the community at large what private enterprise and endeavor can accomplish, so it is likewise unjust and a gravely harmful disturbance of right order to turn over to a greater society of higher rank functions and services which can be performed by lesser bodies on a lower plane. For a social undertaking of any sort, by its very nature, ought to aid the members of the body social, but never to destroy and absorb them" (Gremillion, 1976: 322). It would be hard to find a more concise statement of the philosophical perspective underlying the strategy of *tercerismo*.

4. Jacques Maritain distinguishes three "planes" of Catholic social action: (1) action "as a Christian as such," which formally engages the institutional church, (2) action "as a Christian engaging only myself," and (3) action which in theory is related to the first "plane," but in practice takes place on the second. This "intermediary" plane of "the spiritual considered in connection with the temporal" defines the sphere of Catholic Action. Maritain elaborates:

"The whole work of 'Catholic action' takes place on the first and third planes. If, by the teaching which it dispenses and the spiritual formation which it procures, it *prepares* laymen to act *as Christians*, to participate in the struggles of the temporal and to participate there *as Christians*, to assume the social and political work to which they deem themselves called and to assume it *as Christians*, it guards itself with the greatest care from laying the shadow of a finger on this second plane. And it is not only because the Church does not want at any price to find itself enfeoffed to temporal things. It is because, also, with regard to the work proper to the second plane, with regard to a work which must descend to the ultimate contingent realizations demanded by the service of the temporal common good, the competence of an activity whose order is wholly spiritual quickly finds its limits" (Maritain, 1973: 298–99). As we shall see further on in this chapter, these distinctions are rejected by liberation theologians as inadequate to their praxis.

5. While the ideological factor is primary, the sociological profile on the basic communities must not be discounted. It is clear that these communities represent a militant minority of Latin American Catholics, recruited primarily from the urban middle classes (Berryman, 1976: 40). Within this group, they are most likely to be found at the universities where they represent a politically radicalized remnant of Catholic Action and Catholic youth movements (Antoine, 1973). Given their minority status, it is not surprising that much of the discussion of political strategy within liberation theology concerns the relationship between "masses" and "elites."

6. The paradigm of "developmentalism" shares both similarities and differences with the analysis of the prospects for democracy offered by Niebuhr and Sigmund, as summarized here in the previous chapter. Although both culminate in an endorsement of the Alliance for Progress, and acknowledge the same prerequisites for "development," they differ in that Niebuhr and Sigmund view democratic political structures as the key to economic progress, while the developmentalists tend to see economic progress as the key to stable political institutions. In other words, Christian realism's perspective tries to bring the moral basis of society into sharper focus. Furthermore, Sigmund's analysis concedes the negative consequences of United States' economic and political involvement among "underdeveloped" nations. These differences, however, do not warrant the claim that Christian realism provides a genuine alternative to "developmentalism." Instead, as defined by Niebuhr and Sigmund its perspective allows for "piecemeal" criticism of strategies emerging from that paradigm.

7. The explanation offered by the paradigm of dependence/liberation obviously has a different emphasis from that of Niebuhr and Sigmund, who place primary responsibility not on American neocolonialism, but on the cultural and historical consequences of Spanish imperialism. An alternative to both of these diagnoses recently has been proposed by Eduardo Frei, who seeks to do justice to both internal and external factors. By emphasizing the "very limited usefulness" of "the theory of dependence" (Frei, 1978: 143), Frei comes down much closer to Christian realism than to liberation theology.

7

Liberation Theology as a Method

Our purpose is not to elaborate an ideology to justify postures already taken, nor to undertake a feverish search for security in the face of the radical challenges which confront the faith, nor to fashion a theology from which political action is "deduced." It is rather to let ourselves be judged by the Word of the Lord, to think through our faith, to strengthen our love, and to give reason for our hope from within a commitment which seeks to become more radical, total, and efficacious. It is to reconsider the great themes of the Christian life within this radically changed perspective and with regard to the new questions posed by this commitment. This is the goal of the so-called theology of liberation.*

—Gustavo Gutiérrez, A Theology of Liberation, 1973

The question of method, once it is posed critically in theology, tends to be subversive of tradition. An unchallenged tradition has no need of methodological justification; but the attempt to criticize tradition does. Criticism in theology must engage in a form of methodological reflection because the task is to account for the tradition's theoretical incoherence and practical irrelevance in a way that will open up plausible alternatives. If greater coherence and relevance can be achieved thereby, the results of such criticism eventually will be regarded as constructive rather than subversive and in time will become part of the tradition. This eventuality represents the difference between prophets and heretics.

The critical intention of the question of method is sensed nowhere more acutely these days than among liberation theologians. In the context of Roman Catholic tradition, their concern is based on a disenchantment with what they regard as the academic theology of the seminaries and universities, especially as it has been shaped in Europe. One theologian, José Comblin, puts it this way: "Any Latin American who has studied in Europe has to undergo detoxification before he can begin to act" (Assmann, 1976: 56). His point is that the academic theology transplanted from Europe unwittingly serves as an ideological block that prevents Latin Americans from perceiving their actual situation and responding to it effectively. In order to overcome this block, theologians must learn how to criticize the ideological distortions built into their perspectives. Subversive criticism is necessary in order to liberate theology from such distortions. Otherwise, the constructive possibilities in liberation theology may be closed off before they have a chance to develop.

In a situation of ideological conflict, liberation theologians therefore are urged to take up the weapons of criticism. Ironically, these weapons also come from Europe. Liberation theologians either adopt the methods by which European progressives have already criticized Catholic tradition and give them a radical political content, or they adapt those of Latin American social theorists themselves inspired by European philosophy. "Detoxification," therefore, does not mean the wholesale rejection of European models but their critical transformation in light of the praxis of the basic communities.

In this chapter I shall trace the emergence of the method distinctive of liberation theology and analyze the direction in which it appears to be heading. It is clear that Paulo Freire's theory of conscientization provides the distinctive methodological principle. But since the logic of conscientization in itself appears to be more subversive than constructive, I shall argue that it promises not just to detoxify but to eliminate theological reflection entirely. If this point can be made persuasively, it will mean that liberation theology from the beginning is marked by an internal difficulty, a tension between its subversive method and its constructive theological intention, which makes it at once dynamic and yet vulnerable to dissolution. In any case, the chapter will conclude by comparing Christian realism and liberation theology on the question of method, so that the significance of this difficulty may be recognized.

"Critical Reflection on Praxis"

"Critical reflection on praxis," as we have seen, is generally the way in which liberation theology is described methodologically. But this slogan in itself is opaque. It may mean nothing more than a restatement of the truism that you must practice what you preach. Or it may sound suspiciously provocative, since there is some reason to think that, as someone once put it, "Praxis is just a German word for revolution." Gustavo Gutiérrez tried to clear up the confusion by offering a programmatic analysis of the tasks of theology. He reasoned that a definition of theology as "critical reflection on praxis" might provide a complement to the classical tasks, "theology as wisdom" and "theology as rational knowledge" (Gutiérrez, 1973:4). In Gutiérrez's thinking, all three forms stem from theology's "essential effort to understand the faith." They differ in that "theology as wisdom" centers on the quest for personal spiritual perfection, whereas "theology as rational knowledge" projects an ideal of divine science, "an intellectual discipline born of the meeting of faith and reason."

While Gutiérrez admits no intention of disparaging these traditional tasks, he does hope to transcend them in a renewed concern for praxis.

Nevertheless, he initially describes praxis itself in traditional terms as Christian action inspired by charity:

> This is the foundation of the *praxis* of the Christian, of his active presence in history. According to the Bible, faith is the total response of man to God, who saves through love. In this light, the understanding of the faith appears as the understanding not of the simple affirmation—almost memorization—of truths, but of a commitment, an overall attitude, a particular posture toward life. [Gutiérrez, 1973: 7]

Gutiérrez's understanding of praxis thus claims a basis in Catholic tradition and recent progressive theology. Indeed, he appeals to the *Spiritual Exercises* of St. Ignatius Loyola and the efforts of modern theologians like Yves Congar and M. D. Chenu to define an adequate spirituality for laity active in the church and the new directions advanced in Vatican II's *Gaudium et spes*. But more to the point, he cites Catholicism's "direct and fruitful confrontation with Marxism" (Gutiérrez, 1973:9).

On the face of it, there is nothing extraordinary about this general description of praxis. It merely reflects a commitment to Christian renewal. But when Gutiérrez goes on to give a detailed description of theology as "critical reflection on praxis," the interplay of subversive and constructive tendencies becomes apparent:

> Theology must be man's critical reflection on himself, on his own basic principles. Only with this approach will theology be a serious discourse, aware of itself, in full possession of its conceptual elements. But we are not referring exclusively to this epistemological aspect when we talk about theology as critical reflection. We also refer to a clear and critical attitude regarding economic and socio-cultural issues in the life and reflection of the Christian community. To disregard these is to deceive both oneself and others. But above all, we intend this term to express the theory of a definite practice. Theological reflection would then necessarily be a criticism of society and the Church insofar as they are called and addressed by the Word of God; it would be a critical theory, worked out in the light of the Word accepted in faith and inspired by a practical purpose—and therefore indissolubly linked to historical praxis. [Gutiérrez, 1973: 11]

In calling for "a criticism of society and the Church" based on "the Word of God," Gutiérrez means to use the foundations of tradition to criticize tradition itself. A new understanding of the foundations is promised in order to give theology "a necessary and permanent role in the liberation from every form of religious alienation" (Gutiérrez, 1973:12).

Notice, however, the strategy proposed for Gutiérrez's attempt to detoxify theology: theological method will no longer be based exclusively on "epistemological" questions, but on an "economic and socio-cultural" mode of analysis capable of illuminating "every form of religious alienation." No doubt, Gutiérrez's critical awareness of religious alienation is partly a result of his "direct and fruitful confrontation with Marxism." In that vein, he admits that religious alienation "is often fostered by the ecclesiastical institution itself when it impedes an authentic approach to the Word of the Lord." But, unlike Marxists, he assumes that there *is* "an authentic approach to the Word" which transcends the problematic of religious alienation. The "Word of the Lord," as Gutiérrez sees it, is to serve as the inspiration for a criticism of tradition using Marxist modes of social analysis; and yet the "Word of the Lord" itself is to be vindicated against the suspicion that it, too, is a form of alienation. But such an agenda, at once both subversive and constructive in intention, raises certain questions: Where is a Catholic theologian to find an "authentic approach to the Word of the Lord" that is critical of the church? What modes of analysis may serve to develop criticism of the church and society based on the "Word"? In short what are the criteria by which the program of "critical reflection on praxis" is justified theologically?

The answers to these questions are more easily repeated than understood. The ultimate theological criterion, of course, remains the "Word of the Lord." But what may that mean? Traditionally, Catholic theologians had a ready response: the Word of the Lord is known in Scripture as interpreted in the infallible magisterium of the church and defined by the popes and the ecumenical councils. This answer is unavailable, however, to liberation theologians. Like some Catholic progressives, they recognize that the church's reading of Scripture is subject to the vicissitudes of history. The Word of the Lord is not a cognitive absolute infallibly apprehended and faithfully taught by the church. Like every other word in history, it must be interpreted. Its meaning is always relative to context. Gutiérrez therefore condemns "a theology which has as its points of reference only 'truths' which have been established once and for all—and not the Truth which is also the Way" as "static and, in the long run, sterile" (Gutiérrez, 1973:13). As an alternative, he invites theologians to find the Word of the Lord in the struggle for liberation in history:

> To reflect on the basis of the historical praxis of liberation is to reflect in the light of the future which is believed in and hoped for. It is to reflect with a view to action which transforms the present. But it does not mean doing this from an armchair; rather it means sinking roots where the pulse of history is beating at this moment and illuminating history with the Word of the Lord of history, who irreversibly committed himself to the present moment of mankind to carry it to its fulfillment. [Gutiérrez, 1973:15]

Critical reflection on praxis, therefore, means thinking and acting in harmony with "the Lord of history," who is recognized at the point "where the pulse of history is beating at this moment." The Way, then, is also the Truth. The question becomes: Which Way? Where is the pulse of history beating at this moment? The answer to this and all similar questions is wherever oppressed peoples struggle for liberation. The Truth is discovered in praxis.

As a result, liberation theologians sometimes summarize their methodological innovation as a shift from criteria of orthodoxy to "orthopraxis" (Gutiérrez, 1973:10). "Academic theology" is generated by a method based on a static conception of truth and committed to a standard of "right thinking" or "orthodoxy." Liberation theology is generated by a method committed to a dynamic conception of "right acting" or "orthopraxis," a concept which claims a biblical warrant in the theme of "doing the truth" found in the discourses of the Johannine Christ (Assmann, 1976:76).[1] As interpreted by the Latin Americans, however, orthopraxis not only gives moral legitimacy to participation in the struggle for liberation, but it also asserts the cognitive authority of such participation. In other words, those who participate in the struggle are in a better position to interpret the Word of the Lord than are the "armchair" theologians of the church.

So far, then, the alternative proposed is clearly subversive of academic theology. It combines an allegedly biblical concept of truth with a mode of analysis that is critical of the abstract concerns of epistemology. Thus both "reason" and "revelation" lend authority to the attempt to liberate theologians from methods based on "static and in the long run sterile" conceptions of Christian truth. But it remains to be seen how this alternative is clearly constructive. In what way does it answer the suspicion that the Word of the Lord so understood is only the residue of a religious alienation, whose spell may have been broken in practice but whose illusory nature has not yet been understood in theory. If "the pulse of history" has already been located in the struggles of oppressed peoples, what historical necessity warrants the theologians' intention of "illuminating it with the Word of the Lord"? The fact that theologians have formulated a biblical notion of "orthopraxis" congenial to the ideological requirements of such struggles is not a sufficient answer to the suspicions of Marxist theoreticians regarding "the Word." Unless these suspicions are satisfactorily laid to rest, the constructive dimension of this method remains in doubt, since Marxist perspectives have inspired its subversive dimension. A way of reconciling these dimensions, which thereby would overcome the objections raised by purists of either the Marxist or the Catholic persuasion, may be possible, provided that a perfect identity of meaning linking the struggle for liberation with the divine Christ can be established. In order to explore that possibility, Gutiérrez gives liberation theology further specification as "a political hermeneutics of the Gospel" (Gutiérrez, 1973:13).

"A Political Hermeneutics of the Gospel"

This term designates Johannes Metz's methodological proposal for a "new political theology," which liberation theologians have tried to adapt to the Latin American reality. But in order to understand what they do with Metz's political hermeneutics, we must have some idea of its original meaning. This discussion will also serve to illustrate liberation theology's critical relationship to the progressive thought of European theologians and its methodological implications.

For the past generation at least, both Protestant and progressive Catholic theologians have insisted that the question of hermeneutics is central to theological method. They have done so because they have recognized the theoretical problem posed by historical consciousness as it impinges on the traditional claims of Christian theology. In short, they have confronted not only the theoretical issue of the historical relativity of all moral values —especially those claiming some sort of absolute religious sanction—but also its practical corollary: the question of interpreting historical texts that preserve these values in some sort of authoritative tradition. The problem, in other words, raises questions concerning the traditional methods of interpretation characteristic of Western humanism in general; but in particular, it casts doubt upon the validity of any religious reading of the Bible. Since historical consciousness undermines any assurance that a believer's pious reading of the Scriptures has an objective relationship to the values originally set down in the text, some form of theological hermeneutics becomes necessary.

In light of this problem, the recent history of methodological reflection in theology may be understood as a series of hermeneutic proposals related to the latest theoretical innovations in the tradition of Western humanism. Metz's proposal, "a political hermeneutics of the Gospel," is no exception to this rule. It can best be located in relation to the perspectives adopted by modern Protestants and progressive Catholics, who have been impressed by Martin Heidegger's philosophical response to the question of hermeneutics. The Protestant theologian Rudolf Bultmann, for example, finds the religious meaning of the Bible in the "Word of God," which is authoritatively given in the primitive gospel preaching, or *kerygma,* as apprehended in Christian faith. But the meaning of the kerygma constitutes a hermeneutic problem because in order to be accepted in faith it first must be understood. Since the kerygma originally was proclaimed in a context that is foreign to our own, it must be translated into terms appropriate to us. Given the distinctive features of a modern "self-understanding," Bultmann reasoned, the kerygma must be "demythologized."[2] In other words, the religious meaning of the New Testament had to be extracted from its context in a mythical world inhabited by supernatural powers if it were to become intelligible, let alone credible, to persons sharing a modern perspective on life.

Bultmann therefore developed a new form of hermeneutics to fulfill this task. The point was not to give a learned paraphrase of the kerygma, but to translate it creatively from its original context into our own. Believing that Martin Heidegger's philosophy afforded the right set of categories for making this translation, Bultmann used a Heideggerian "existential ontology" to explicate the symbolic structure of the human condition and its ultimate meaning. Since in Bultmann's view the kerygma could have religious meaning only in terms of this structure, Heidegger's philosophy was adapted as the framework for an "existential theology" of the Word of God—a proposal that finds an echo in Karl Rahner's attempt to reinterpret the tradition of Catholic dogma using the same philosophy.[3] The resulting existential theologies interpret Christianity's religious meaning primarily in terms of personal spirituality, conceived of as a quest for "authentic existence." Christian faith becomes a practical guide to this quest, which in confronting existential decisions of the utmost generality promises to transcend the vicissitudes of history, society, and politics.

Metz's new political theology accepts this general understanding of the hermeneutic question in modern theology, but rejects its existential resolution (Metz, 1969:110). The emphasis on personal spirituality is criticized as distorted, since it abstracts from the historical conditions and social structures in which persons actually live. In Metz's view, the problem is not simply philosophical, namely, the failure of Heidegger's ontology to give anything but the most abstract reflection of historical existence. More to the point, it is also theological: the Christian faith—whether as epitomized in the kerygma or as elaborated in the Catholic magisterium—has an essentially public or "political" dimension, which cannot be neglected. The political hermeneutics of the gospel, therefore, is an attempt to correct this fault in modern existential theologies.

Metz's proposal for a new political theology is a subtle and complicated one. It emphasizes the political significance of the Bible's eschatological symbols, for example, the kingdom of God; but it does so without directly identifying these symbols with any particular political program, for example, socialism. Instead, it calls for an indirect or "critical" relationship to politics, based on Christianity's "eschatological proviso." The proviso stipulates that the "eschatological promises of the scriptural tradition— freedom, peace, justice, reconciliation—cannot . . . be identified with any social situation that has been achieved" (Metz, 1969:153). Far from being an abdication of political responsibility, the proviso represents a religious repudiation of any form of political absolutism. In short, the "new political theology" is meant to resist the claims of totalitarian ideologies. Metz hopes that the church will fulfill this intention by taking up its role as "the institution of a socially critical freedom" (Metz, 1969:134).

The relevance of Metz's proposal depends upon his analysis of advanced industrial society, which is influenced by the German neo-Marxist Frankfurt School of Social Research. Metz and the Frankfurt School share the view that advanced industrial societies, in both their socialist and capitalist forms, are threatened with a new kind of totalitarianism, one based on the pervasive extension of the imperatives of technological rationality into questions of ethics and politics (Metz, 1969:132; Habermas, 1970:62–80). They fear that the uncritical extension of these norms is causing a "privatization" of all religious and moral values, a trend which increasingly restricts the relevance of these values to the private lives of individuals. They remain meaningful only as "consumer preferences." Thus, for example, a commitment to social justice based on religious and moral beliefs becomes politically irrelevant because it cannot satisfy the supposed standards of "critical reason," while a "cost-benefit analysis" of "social problems" is relevant because it reflects the imperatives of technological rationality. Ultimately, "privatization" means that politics, formerly conceived as a great moral debate concerning the choices that confront us as a society, now becomes obsolete. Political institutions, however, may be retained as a forum where consumers ratify the decisions already made by those who manage the technocracy. The totalitarian threat implied by this trend is that all forms of political life and thought will be sacrificed in favor of an allegedly rational society. The hard-won pluralism characteristic of modernity will give way to a new monolithic conformity, all in the name of a "scientific" planning of the future.

Both Metz and the Frankfurt School realize that the vision of a technological society is based on false premises, that in fact technical imperatives are never sufficient to resolve moral and political issues, and that questions of "ends" are just as amenable to reasoned reflection as questions of "means" (Metz, 1969:151–52). Nevertheless, they go their separate ways when it comes to developing a "post-critical" alternative to technocracy. The Frankfurt School—especially as represented in the work of Jürgen Habermas—seeks to retrieve a humanistic ideal of rationality based on the moral philosophies of Aristotle, Kant, and Marx. Thus Habermas hopes to provide a theoretical foundation for the renewal of public discourse, which will restore the primacy of moral values over technological imperatives and promote a rational decision to move toward a genuinely democratic socialism. Yet even for him religious beliefs at best have only private significance, and at worst are socially reactionary. Metz, by contrast, affirms the political relevance of religious beliefs, and therefore looks to the church as a special institutional resource for developing "post-critical" alternatives. The church, now freed by history of its traditional role in providing a religious legitimation for authoritarian societies,[4] may take up its proper role as an "institution of social criticism." Renewed in its commitment to the critical perspective of the kingdom of God, the church now may become a rallying point for sustaining the values upon which the political process depends and for criticizing the inadequacies of whatever policies may emerge from that process.

The new political theology, obviously, is highly abstract, and immediately responsive to certain theoretical issues currently debated among West German theologians and social philosophers. Despite its abstract quality, it does speak to a real concern among sensitive social critics who fear the consequences of the growing irrelevance of religious and moral beliefs to politics. In clarifying the church's role as an "institution of social criticism," it does give some direction to the vague progressivism of Vatican II. Nevertheless, Metz's political theology has been criticized in Europe on various grounds: for being too sketchy in its view of the church, for being too abstract in its analysis of society, and for going too far in the direction of a "theology of revolution." Among the Latin Americans, however, it has been criticized for not going far enough.

Liberation theologians, in short, see Metz's position as still tied too closely to the concerns of European progressives (Gutiérrez, 1973:224–25). Among liberation theologians, the theory of privatization does not correspond to the reality of the church's powerful position in society. The theoretical issues raised by a technological rationality are not as impressive to them as are the practical problems of overcoming oppression. They do not equate democracy with the ideal of a socially critical freedom; instead, they criticize it as merely "formal." Consequently, they are skeptical of democracy's capacity to effect the revolutionary changes necessary for genuine liberation. These differences may be explained by their fidelity to the Latin American reality; but they also call for theological interpretation. Far from symbolizing a restrictive "eschatological proviso," the kingdom of God must also represent—as Gutiérrez insists—a "utopia," a "projection" of the society toward which liberation movements are working. The church's role in bearing witness to Christ and the kingdom, therefore, cannot simply be a negative one, limited to denouncing the pretensions of ideologies. It must also be positive in the sense that it is active in announcing the establishment of the kingdom of God on earth in the struggle for liberation. Thus liberation theologians share Metz's premise that the Christian faith has a critical political dimension, but they define its "hermeneutic circle" differently. A political hermeneutics of the gospel for them must be positive as well as negative, incorporating strategies of "annunciation" as well as "denunciation" that offer utopian perspectives as well as criticism of ideologies (Gutiérrez, 1973:232–39).

Conscientization as a Theological Method

These contrasts make clear the direction in which liberation theologians hope to adapt Metz's political hermeneutics to the Latin American reality. But what theoretical resources do they use to accomplish this transformation? Is there a theory available that satisfies the methodological requirements of this new way of doing theology?

Once again, the Medellín documents provide a point of departure. The bishops had spoken favorably, the reader will recall, of a program of religious and social conscientization. It is doubtful, however, that the bishops understood precisely what they were endorsing, for their statements appear to link conscientization to two significantly different strategies. On the one hand, there are declarations that are fairly close to the spirit of Paulo Freire's *Pedagogy of the Oppressed*: "Justice, and therefore peace, conquer by means of a dynamic action of awakening *(concientización)* and organization of the popular sectors, which are capable of pressing public officials who are often impotent in their social projects without popular support" (Gremillion, 1976:461). On the other hand, there are declarations that identify conscientization with mass media campaigns addressed not just to "the popular sectors" but also to "key men, . . . to those persons at a decision-making level whose actions effect changes in the basic structures of national and international life" (Gremillion, 1976:452–53). The bishops' understandable urge "to establish a balance" in approaching both "the popular sectors" and the "key men" apparently ignores Freire's vision of a world divided between oppressors and the oppressed.

Despite this confusion, liberation theologians seized upon these statements as "an impulse for new commitments." Going beyond the bishops' more cautious endorsement, liberation theologians proposed a "conscienticizing evangelization" (Gutiérrez, 1973:116). While this slogan best describes the distinctive method of liberation theology, the question is whether or not it represents a program that is consistent with the logic of conscientization as proposed by Freire. In other words, can this theory be used to map out a coherent model for evangelization—a question that is crucial for assessing the claims that liberation theologians make for their own version of a political hermeneutics of the gospel.

The theory of conscientization, as Freire presents it in *Pedagogy of the Oppressed*, is fundamentally three things: (1) a description of the practice of a literacy training program designed to trigger a social awakening among oppressed peasants and barrio dwellers; (2) a revolutionary theory of education derived from this practice; and (3) a global perspective on history as a whole—what I shall call the "dialectical vision"[5]—which grounds the substantive values that inspire both the practice and the theory. When Gutiérrez proposes a conscienticizing evangelization, he is interested primarily in the constructive implication of the first and second meanings of this pedagogy. When I suggest that conscientization threatens to eliminate theological reflection entirely, I am interested primarily in the third meaning, the dialectical vision and its subversive implications for theology as such. The methodological question for liberation theologians—assuming that an analysis of conscientization will show that the dialectical vision is incompatible with the religious visions of Christianity in general and Catholicism in particular—thus is whether a conscienticizing evangelization can appropriate the first and second meanings without accepting necessarily the third and the problems of coherence that go with it.

1. As an educational practice, conscientization is designed to liberate oppressed peoples by promoting what Freire calls "dialogical action." This goal is to be achieved by restructuring the dynamics of basic education in such a way that the practice itself will enable people to become more fully human. Freire dramatizes this process by contrasting his "libertarian education" with "banking education" (Freire, 1970:59). In banking education, the teacher is active; the students are passive. The teacher knows; the students are informed. The banking analogy is used to suggest the ways in which knowledge is deposited. Implying that under capitalism even learning is reified as a commodity, banking education defines an alienating exchange system in which those excluded from ownership of the means of knowledge-production, namely, students, are exploited and further dehumanized. By contrast, "libertarian" or "problem-posing education" seeks to humanize the process by transforming it into a common effort in learning how to learn. Teachers become "coordinators," and students participate. The participants' own perspective on life becomes the context in which problem-posing goes on. The result is an educational process in which teachers no longer dominate and students no longer are alienated from their own world.

The genius of Freire's pedagogy is that its admirable goals are built into the dialogical action that occurs between the coordinators and the communities they serve. The agenda for basic education or literacy training thus emerges from the actual needs expressed by the participants. As basic skills are being acquired, a set of "codifications" is developed to identify significant structures in their everyday world. In analyzing these codifications, the coordinators serve as "co-investigators" with the people (Freire, 1970:97), and thus help them to map out the "thematic universe" in terms of which they live. Eventually the participants come to recognize the "generative themes" that provide the keys to "decoding" this "universe." While such generative themes may be general, such as the distinction between "nature" and "culture," they also are quite specific. Freire elaborates:

> Generative themes can be located in concentric circles, moving from the general to the particular. The broadest epochal unit, which includes a diversified range of units and sub-units—continental, regional, national, and so forth—contains themes of a universal character. I consider the fundamental theme of our epoch to be that of *domination*—which implies its opposite, the theme of *liberation*, as the objective to be achieved. It is this tormenting theme which gives

our epoch the anthropological character mentioned earlier. In order to achieve humanization, which presupposes the elimination of dehumanizing oppression, it is absolutely necessary to surmount the limit-situations in which men are reduced to things. [Freire, 1970:93]

The emphasis given to the theme of domination/liberation, of course, means that conscientization is not only a technique for literacy training but a praxis based on a revolutionary theory of education.

2. As a revolutionary theory of education, then, conscientization stems from an awareness of the dialectical relationship of domination and freedom, in which critical consciousness of domination is the first step toward freedom. Liberating one's own words becomes the basis for liberating one's own deeds. But liberation is not a gift; it must be conquered:

> Problem-posing education, as a humanist and liberating praxis, posits as fundamental that men subjected to domination must fight for their emancipation. To that end, it enables teachers and students to become Subjects of the educational process by overcoming authoritarianism and an alienating intellectualism; it also enables men to overcome their false perception of reality. The world—no longer something to be described with deceptive words—becomes the object of that transforming action by men which results in their humanization. [Freire, 1970:74]

Freire theorizes that the oppressed have internalized the oppressors' perspective to such a degree that, initially at least, they have difficulty in seeing their true situation. The oppressed, in other words, must overcome their "fear of freedom." Freire elaborates:

> The conflict lies in the choice between being wholly themselves or being divided; between ejecting the oppressor within or not ejecting him; between human solidarity or alienation; between following prescriptions or having choices; between being spectators or actors; between acting or having the illusion of acting through the action of the oppressors; between speaking out or being silent, castrated in their power to create and recreate, in their power to transform the world. This is the tragic dilemma of the oppressed which their education must take into account. [Freire, 1970:33]

It is precisely the technique of codification/decodification that assists the oppressed in resolving this dilemma.

The strategy of problem-posing and the tactics of codification/decodification, however, depend upon a particular view of human freedom and its "untested feasibilities":

Men, however, because they are aware of themselves and thus of the world—because they are *conscious beings*—exist in a dialectical relationship between the determination of limits and their own freedom. As they separate themselves from the world, which they objectify, as they separate themselves from their own activity, as they locate the seat of their decisions in themselves and in their relations with the world and others, men overcome the situations which limit them: the "limit-situations." Once perceived by men as fetters, as obstacles to their liberation, these situations stand out in relief from the background, revealing their true nature as concrete historical dimensions of a given reality. Men respond to the challenge with actions which Vieira Pinto calls "limit-acts": those directed at negating and overcoming, rather than passively accepting the "given."

Thus, it is not the limit-situations in and of themselves which create a climate of hopelessness, but rather how they are perceived by men at a given historical moment: whether they appear as fetters or as insurmountable barriers. As critical perception is embodied in action, a climate of hope and confidence develops which leads men to attempt to overcome the limit-situations. This objective can be achieved only through action upon the concrete historical reality in which limit-situations historically are found. As reality is transformed and these situations are superseded, new ones will appear, which in turn will evoke new limit-acts. [Freire, 1970:89–90]

Freire's view of human freedom as the overcoming of limit-situations through limit-acts represents the nucleus of conscientization as an educational theory. It provides the framework for "making it possible for men to enter the historical process as responsible Subjects" (Freire, 1970:20).

The pedagogical significance of this view is dramatized in still another of Freire's contrasts, this one between "decodification" and a process described as "mythicization." When limit-situations are not identified and overcome, "there is a tendency for reality itself to be mythicized." "In such a situation, myth-creating irrationality itself becomes a fundamental theme. Its opposing theme, the critical and dynamic view of the world, strives to unveil reality, unmask its mythicization, and achieve a full realization of the human task: the permanent transformation of reality in favor of the liberation of men" (Freire, 1970:92). The decodification of mythicized reality, in short, is the educational praxis which conscientization addresses as a revolutionary theory.

3. The dialectical vision that grounds this theory pictures the whole of history as a struggle for liberation. Freire clearly envisions a historic struggle in which human freedom as an "untested feasibility" is to be realized by overcoming alienation both in consciousness and in action. As the "dehumanization" represented by the structures of domination is overcome, the "new man" (Freire, 1970:30, 42) will emerge, a goal whose

meaning can be defined only by the historic struggle itself. In other words, what the "new man" will be is less important than what it represents, the collective image of the oppressed who, having overcome the "fear of freedom," stand fully commited to "a process of permanent liberation" (Freire, 1970:40).

The dialectical vision sees the "new man" emerging from the struggle between oppressors and the oppressed in history, a struggle which is best understood as a conflict over limit-situations:

> In sum, limit-situations imply the existence of persons who are directly or indirectly served by these situations, and of those who are negated and curbed by them. Once the latter come to perceive these situations as the frontier between being and being more human, rather than the frontier between being and nothingness, they begin to direct their increasingly critical actions toward achieving the untested feasibility implicit in that perception. On the other hand, those who are served by the present limit-situation regard the untested feasibility as a threatening limit-situation which must not be allowed to materialize, and act to maintain the status quo. [Freire, 1970:92–93]

Just as "liberation" means overcoming limit-situations, so "oppression" means being overcome by them. Freire underscores this point by defining "oppression" in opposition to "self-affirmation": "Any situation in which 'A' objectively exploits 'B' or hinders his pursuit of self-affirmation as a responsible person is one of oppression" (Freire, 1970:40). Since the "pursuit of self-affirmation," for Freire, is nothing other than "man's ontological and historical vocation to become more fully human" (Freire, 1970:41), to insist upon the reality of limit-situations is willy-nilly to oppress and dehumanize.

Freire makes this point clear by linking this vision of the "new man" with certain characteristics typical of "man" in general. While he does not develop the point systematically, he does affirm ". . . men as beings who transcend themselves, who move forward and look ahead, for whom immobility represents a fatal threat, for whom looking at the past must only be a means of understanding more clearly what and who they are so that they can more wisely build the future. Hence it (a "problem-posing education" corresponding to the "historical nature of man") identifies with the movement which engages men as beings aware of their incompletion—an historical movement which has its point of departure, its Subjects, and its objective" (Freire, 1970:72). Men, he goes on to say, "simultaneously create history and become historical-social beings" (Freire, 1970:91). And they become historical "as transforming rather than adaptive beings" (Freire, 1970:114). Man's ontological and historical vocation, in short, is to overcome limit-situations by performing limit-acts.

By now it may have occurred to the reader that the concepts of liberation/oppression are defined in a circular manner, and that the notion of the "new man" is formal rather than substantive. This does not mean that the dialectical vision is meaningless; it suggests, rather, that, despite its talk of "man," conscientization is less an anthropology than a radical theory of praxis in history. The dialectical vision, in other words, sees history as a struggle for freedom without defining the content of that freedom, save as overcoming all possible limit-situations. The untested feasibility is a process, pure and simple. Its content is realized only by participating in it.

Freire is hardly unaware of the practical implications of the dialectical vision. Since a liberating education entails not only consciousness-raising but also organizing communities to struggle for control of their own destinies, he gears his political reflections mainly to the problem of institutionalizing the dialectical vision without giving way to the strategies of domination. In short, the positive values emerging from conscientization —namely, cooperation, unity, organization, and cultural synthesis—are to overcome the negative values of conquest, division, manipulation, and cultural invasion that define the politics of domination (Freire, 1970:119–20). Freire contends that most self-consciously radical movements have not inspired dialogical action because they have incorporated these negative values into their own internal organization. But once the "new man" is awakened through conscientization, the struggle for liberation must begin in the communities dedicated to it. Unless this is done, revolutionary action will degenerate into a self-defeating "sectarianism," becoming either "activism" or "bureaucracy" (Freire, 1970:121). Both disorders fundamentally conflict with the strategy of conscientization, since both represent a failure to "trust in the people." They are distinct in that activism occurs when a revolutionary elite tries to act independently of the people, whereas bureaucracies are formed whenever the patterns of authoritarian leadership are reintroduced into radical movements. Although the two disorders feed on each other, Freire believes that they can be avoided if there is no discrepancy between the praxis of revolution and the theory of conscientization.[6]

The correspondences linking Freire's pedagogy of the oppressed at each level with liberation theology are as obvious as they are thought-provoking. Not only does his proposal for institutionalizing the dialogical action of conscientization provide a rationale for the basic communities, but his revolutionary educational theory confirms the centrality of the themes of oppression/liberation and gives them conceptual definition. Still more fundamentally, the method of liberation theology derives its notion of a conscienticizing evangelization from his pedagogy as a whole. Gutiérrez makes the correspondences explicit:

> This awareness of being oppressed but nevertheless of being masters
> of their own destiny is nothing other than a consequence of a well-

understood evangelization: "As we see it, a perhaps faulty presentation of the Christian message may have given the impression that religion is indeed the opiate of the people. And we would be guilty of betraying the cause of Peru's development, if we did not stress the fact that the doctrinal riches of the Gospel contain a revolutionary thrust." Indeed, "the God whom we know in the Bible is a liberating God, a God who destroys myths and alienations, a God who intervenes in history in order to break down the structures of injustice and who raises up prophets in order to point out the way of justice and mercy. He is the God who liberates slaves (Exodus), who causes empires to fall and raises up the oppressed." The whole climate of the Gospel is a continual demand for the right of the poor to make themselves heard, to be considered preferentially by society, a demand to subordinate economic needs to those of the deprived. Was not Christ's first preaching to "proclaim the liberation of the oppressed"? The context of the message itself, the process of liberation in Latin America, and the demands for participation on the part of the people, all determine the priority of a conscienticizing evangelization. [Gutiérrez, 1973:116]

This view of the correlation between the process of conscientization and the strategy and tactics of evangelization implies three things: (1) Liberation theologians will function within "basic communities" in a manner similar to the role of coordinators in a basic education project. (2) Doing liberation theology will mean primarily helping communities to "problematize" their experience by codifying and decodifying it according to its "generative theme" of oppression/liberation. As in Freire's pedagogy, the liberation theologian will help the participants to move from naiveté through an initial externalization of the everyday world to an increasingly critical analysis of the structures that actually constitute that world. A conscienticizing evangelization therefore involves problematizing the ideologies that legitimate oppression, including those based on traditional Christianity. So far the strategy is not essentially different from that of Metz's political hermeneutics of the Gospel. (3) But in addition—as the document quoted by Gutiérrez makes clear—a conscienticizing evangelization implies that the liberating God of the Bible is identified with the struggle of the oppressed. While this third move transgresses the "eschatological proviso" recognized by Metz, it also raises a question whether it is possible to speak of a liberating God and still remain faithful to the dialectical vision presupposed in the method of conscientization. In reference to Gutiérrez's remarks, the question is whether codifying the symbols of "the God whom we know in the Bible" according to the generative theme of oppression/liberation is sufficient to overcome "the impression that religion is the opiate of the people." Or to put the same issue in another way, by what criteria—if any—is this vision of a liberating God exempted from conscientization's dynamic opposition to mythicization? To understand this question, how it arises and its implications, it is necessary to look more deeply into Freire's distinctive view of limit-situations.

A Question of Limits

If a conscienticizing evangelization is to be theoretically coherent, then biblical Christianity and Freire's dialectical vision must be virtually identical. His hope for a "new man" must be the Christian hope; his understanding of the generative theme of oppression/liberation, the Christian understanding; his theory of limit-situations, to sum it up, must be theologically adequate. For if his theory is inadequate at this crucial point, then all the concepts dependent on it are inadequate as well. But what is it about Freire's theory of limit-situations that raises questions regarding its theological adequacy?

The problem is that conscientization in principle recognizes no genuine limit-situations. All of them are problematic in principle, since all of them are "obstacles to liberation," and in fact serve the interests of oppressors. But this view has critical implications for religion in general and Christianity in particular. In essence it raises the same challenge as the critique of religion which Marx adapted from Ludwig Feuerbach. The reality of God is an illusion, for Feuerbach, precisely because God is the alienated projection of the infinite possibilities represented by the "species-being" of "man." To restore these possibilities to "man" is to overcome the limit-situation defined by the reality of God. When Marx declared that religion is "the *expression* of real distress and the *protest* against real distress . . . the opium of the people" (Marx and Engels, 1964:42), he was merely reiterating Feuerbach's point: Limit-situations of distress or oppression, no doubt, are real; but their religious expression—including religious forms of protest against them—are illusory. Religion is an "opium" because a religious interpretation of limit-situations at some point must mythicize them as "given" by God. The believer is not invited to transform them by limit-acts but to interpret them as an occasion to contemplate or worship the mystery of God. Yet the attitude of worshipful contemplation is precisely what the critique of religion cannot abide. As Marx generalized the point in his "Theses against Feuerbach": "The philosophers have only *interpreted* the world, in various ways; the point, however, is to *change* it" (Marx and Engels, 1964:72).

The previous analysis of *The Pedagogy of the Oppressed* suggests that conscientization for the most part recapitulates Marx's "Theses against Feuerbach." In short, Freire's theory extends Marx's critique of traditional religion and classical philosophy to the whole question of hermeneutics, in such a way that hermeneutics is transformed into praxis. Humanization no longer involves recognizing the limits of human knowing and acting, but adopting a strategy committed to overcoming them. As a method of interpretation, "decodification" precludes any attempt to define those limits in a substantive idea of human nature. Indeed, its very purpose is to liberate "the people" from such idealizing abstractions. Even the "new man" is only apparently substantive, since in the end the concept is purely formal—an attempt to symbolize the process of conscientization itself.[7]

But granted that conscientization is a restatement of Marx's critique of religion, what theological consequences follow from it? If in principle there are no genuine limit-situations, it is difficult to see how the theologian is to understand an important dimension of biblical Christianity. How, for example, is God's relationship to the world as its creator to be understood, if not in relation to the limit-situation of being in the world? Similarly, how is humanity's theological identity as the creature made to "the image and likeness of God" to be understood, if not in relation to the limit-situation of being human? The recognition of God's role in creation—for biblical Christianity, at least—would seem to be the logical presupposition for any further understanding of God's role in history. This presupposition is clearly recognized, for example, in the structure of Niebuhr's Christian realism, in the priority given to theological anthropology as the constitutive principle of its theology of history. But if Freire is right about limit-situations, Christian realism could not be anything more than an interesting specimen of mythicization, since it points out and interprets the religious meaning of limit-situations that cannot be transformed by limit-acts.

The problem, however, is not just the difficulty of reconciling Christian realism and conscientization. For if it were, liberation theologians could dismiss this objection as a case of special pleading. The claim, instead, is a general one: if there are no genuine limit-situations, theological reflection eventually becomes meaningless.[8] If there are no genuine limit-situations, any discourse presupposing the reality of God—the biblical God, at least—necessarily is an instance of mythicization, however liberating its intent. As Marx said, religion may even be "the *protest* against real distress," but the sincerity of the protest makes its expression in religious symbols no less alienating and its theological reference no less illusory.

The difficulty with a conscienticizing evangelization, then, rests on a theoretical point: at the level of basic vision, as well as hermeneutic theory and practice, there is a serious tension between conscientization and evangelization. At the moment, this point must remain a suspicion based on the assumption that conscientization is a pedagogical restatement of the Feuerbachian humanism of Marx's youth, and that such Feuerbachian humanism is incompatible with Christian evangelization. The suspicion will either be vindicated or be dismissed, as the theology actually constructed with this method is analyzed. If the suspicion is correct, the reader should expect to find that such incoherence in method results in an unstable pattern of theological concepts. Thus as the logic of conscientization progresses, theology itself will be liberated, its myths decoded, leaving little more than a rhetorical invitation to share in the dialectical vision and its praxis. Before moving on to test this suspicion, the reader should have an initial idea of how conscientization transforms theology. Its consequences may be understood by returning to the question of the eschatological proviso.

Liberation theologians reject the eschatological proviso because it seems "to throw a dash of cold water" on the kind of "enthusiasm" (Segundo, 1976: 145) generated by a conscienticizing evangelization. Such diagnoses of the practical consequences of the proviso are essentially correct,[9] but the decisive issue is whether Christian evangelization is bound to set limits to such "enthusiasm," and if so, how those limits might be expressed theologically. While most Christian practical theologies prior to liberation theology have taken the eschatological proviso as a warrant for recognizing the limits of human thinking and acting in history, they have done so by formulating a variety of limit-concepts—metaphysical, anthropological, and historical—to symbolize these limits. The point may be illustrated by recalling the progressive theologies criticized by liberation theologians.

Integral Humanism, for example, on the basis of a neo-Thomistic metaphysics of nature and grace, distinguishes formally between human nature's "natural" and "supernatural" purpose or end. The biblical symbols of Christian eschatology, the Kingdom of God, the Resurrection, and the Last Judgment, are interpreted as pointing toward the "supernatural end," which is expressed in metaphysical limit-concepts like the "beatific vision." The concept of a supernatural end, in other words, defines a limit to human action and in so doing recognizes the relative value of history as an "infravalent end" (Maritain, 1973:134, 176). Since the church is the sacrament of this supernatural end, it cannot be identified with any political order in history. But since politics is a part of the natural or infravalent end, Christian social action is possible provided that the autonomy of both ends is respected. Thus for Integral Humanism, the eschatological proviso operates to restrict the political involvement of the institutional church while encouraging the participation of laypersons acting "as Christians." The kingdom of God is identified with no political program, but remains a symbol of "man's supernatural end."

Metz's political theology, on the other hand, defines these limits, not metaphysically but historically. Nevertheless, its eschatology seeks to interpret the meaning of history while pointing to a reality that transcends it. The biblical symbols constitute a "subversive memory" of the abyss that separates human aspirations and achievements, and of the sufferings created by that abyss. The eschatological proviso offers a perspective of "critical negativity" in history in which these aspirations and achievements are criticized. "Critical negativity," in other words, is a historical limit-concept insofar as it defines the perspective of a religious community involved in history. The church thus embodies "critical negativity" by bearing witness to a "subversive memory," namely, the kingdom of God in light of the cross of Christ. The eschatological proviso, in short, allows political theology to be informed by the memory of "the Passion," as well as by the aspirations of the oppressed. Its understanding of "humanization" proceeds from a different vision.

When they are consistent with their method, liberation theologians reject the eschatological proviso as an ideological distortion. In their view progressive Catholic theology does not recognize the utopian dimension of Christian eschatology. Its interpretation of the proviso as a limit to human thinking and acting inevitably reproduces a dualism that dissipates the liberating power of religious "enthusiasm." Nor is the problem unique to Catholicism. As Segundo insists, when liberal Protestant theology ". . . remains consistent with itself and its fonts, the revolution it speaks about is transformed into faith and hope in something metahistorical and a disgusted turning away from real-life history" (Segundo, 1976:147). The liberal Protestant understanding of justification by faith, in other words, is translated into an anthropological limit-concept, which relativizes "any and every political system in the name of God" (Segundo, 1976:144). Once again, these theological disagreements are rooted in a methodological difference over limit-situations and their interpretability. The methodological issue may now be joined by comparing the models provided by Christian realism and liberation theology.

Christian Realism and Liberation Theology: Methodological Issues

Christian realism, as we saw earlier, is founded on what Niebuhr called "the mythical method" of interpretation. Liberation theology has a methodological basis in the process of conscientization. Both approaches explore the role of the religious imagination in politics; both draw a certain kind of hermeneutic circle; and both are meant to engage spiritual resources for sustaining Christian social action. There are significant differences, however, in the way they go about these things.

1. Although both approaches may be understood as pedagogical, they differ regarding the way the teacher's role is conceived. As always, metaphors betray. Niebuhr's self-description as a "circuit-rider in the colleges and universities" entails a pedagogy that differs from what is expected from an educational "coordinator" involved in the conscientization of a basic community. While it would be unfair to interpret Christian realism as an example of banking education, it is clear that Niebuhr's approach does diverge systematically from Freire's. The circuit-rider, be he preacher, lecturer, or journalist, has a different relationship to the community that he serves. His impact is occasional; and the community in question is heterogeneous, in fact, practically anonymous. If he is effective, the circuit-rider will reach the hearts and minds of individuals, who may or may not form a community with one another. By contrast, the coordinator's goal is precisely to create a basic community, a deeply rooted spiritual consensus (ideological as well as religious and moral) that will lead to dialogical action.

These pedagogical differences are reflected in the different theological models. The relative anonymity of the circuit-rider's audience corresponds well with a model focused on interpreting human nature in general. Just as theological anthropology necessarily emphasizes certain allegedly universal human characteristics that are religiously problematic, so a circuit-rider in principle has little more than these characteristics in common with his audience. By contrast, the coordinator's participation in the community guarantees an intimacy that corresponds well with a model designed to reinforce the community's sense of its own historic destiny, since—in theory, as least—he codifies only what is known through solidarity with the oppressed. Liberation theology thus is a theology of history done from the particular perspective of a community engaged in a struggle to control its destiny. There are strengths and weaknesses in both approaches.

2. The question of method itself holds a different position in both models. Niebuhr was never interested in making explicit the method of Christian realism. He began with a basic agenda, a concern to bring together a "vital religious idealism" with "astute social intelligence," and this concern led him eventually to develop his "mythical method." By contrast, liberation theology begins with a vivid sense not only of the importance of method, but also of its critical role in consciousness-raising. Indeed, liberation theologians first adapted a method, and then began to construct a theology from it.

How significant is this difference in the location of methodological reflection in theology? The informality of Niebuhr's approach and the vagueness of his appeals to "experience" to verify the "abiding truths" of Christian myth suggest greater openness, an acceptance of "the given" as unproblematic until proved otherwise. Conscientization, on the other hand, is suspicious of "the given," since experience is distorted by the structures of oppression and must be codified/decodified in order to be criticized. As a consequence of this difference regarding experience, the two models exhibit different assessments of the problem of ideology. While ideology is primarily an existential problem for Niebuhr, it is primarily a cognitive problem for liberation theologians. If—as Niebuhr assumes—experience is more or less reliable, then ideological conflicts may be understood as more or less transparent expressions of the will to power inherent in human nature. If—as liberation theologians assume—experience is radically problematic, then ideological conflicts may reflect objective differences rooted in the structures of society. In either case, the function of method will be different. If an open attitude is assumed, method in theology need be no more than an *ad hoc* reflection of the circle of faith and experience. If a self-consciously critical attitude is assumed, theological method will have to be subversive in order to be constructive. Neither approach is without its risks. If an open attitude may lead to complacency and self-deception, so may the self-consciously critical attitude.

3. The methods that give structure to these approaches also differ in their theoretical foundations. This difference lies in the fact that Christian

realism is a hermeneutic based on a philosophy of religion, while liberation theology is a hermeneutic based on praxis. Although Niebuhr's "mythical method" emerges from a process of reflection informed by his social activism, that reflection proceeds at a high level of philosophical generality in exploring the role of religion in social change. Christian realism is not simply a theological critique of the Social Gospel. It proceeds from a comparison of ideal types of religions, based first on differences in social class but later and more characteristically on differences in spiritual orientation. Thus Niebuhr speaks of "mystical" and "mythical" religion, and later of "ahistorical" and "historical" religion. Within these categories he compares the practical spiritualities of Christianity and other religions for their adequacy to the "heights and depths" of human existence. The "mythical method" is simply a way to express the abiding truth that he discovered in the mythical religion of Christianity. By contrast, liberation theologians have stayed fairly close to the concerns of praxis. The call for a conscienticizing evangelization occurs as a critical response to the practical inadequacies of progressive Catholic theologies, and their theoretical implications. Seldom, if ever, do liberation theologians concern themselves with the philosophy of religion. Their political hermeneutics, instead, is dependent on conscientization, a method that—for them, at least—perfectly represents the intended unity of theory and praxis.

These foundational differences are most evident in their respective approaches to the challenge of Marxism. Christian realism views Marxism primarily as a mythology, which may be criticized in relation to "the heights and depths" of human existence. Its inadequacies are both practical and theoretical: practical, in that it promotes both "cynicism" and "fanaticism"—each of which defines polar opposites to a "realism" inspired by "religious disinterestedness"; theoretical, in that it fundamentally misunderstands human nature, thereby reducing humanity's paradoxes to half-truths instead of interpreting its abiding truth about both "finiteness" and "freedom." Its critique of religion is unwittingly ironic in that it, too, functions as a not very secularized form of "mythical religion." Given these inadequacies, the Marxist mythology cannot provide the foundations for any genuinely theological hermeneutic. By contrast, liberation theologians apparently ignore the "mythical" dimension of Marxism, emphasizing instead its critical insight into the "generative theme" of oppression/liberation. By adopting the method of conscientization, however, liberation theologians have introduced into their political hermeneutics precisely those elements of Marxism that Christian realism rejects as inadequate mythology, namely, the Feuerbachian humanism of Marx's youth, and as a result, Marxism's dialectical vision figures prominently in the foundations of a conscienticizing evangelization. Nevertheless, liberation theology's response to the critique of religion implicit in this vision is not theoretical. Its answer is not elaborated in a philosophy of religion, but in a praxis intended to overcome the alienation caused by the church's historic collusion in oppression. A theoretical answer to Marxism, based on the idealizing abstractions of a philosophy of religion, is suspect because inevitably—they claim—such answers themselves are a form of alienation.

Both strategies entail serious difficulties. As Niebuhr himself recognized, the repudiation of Marxist mythology does mean a loss in revolutionary fanaticism. But he saw this loss as potentially a step in the direction of a responsible political radicalism. The practical risk of diminishing enthusiasm was accepted rather than the theoretical risk of increasing confusion over theological foundations. Liberation theologians apparently have made the opposite choice. By insisting on the utopian dimension of the gospel, they have committed themselves to a method designed to reinforce solidarity with the oppressed at the risk of ambiguity about the theoretical basis of that solidarity. Unless one assumes that theoretical difficulties may be answered by repeated appeals to "orthopraxis," the risk they have chosen appears theologically unsound.

4. The methodological issues separating Christian realism and liberation theology finally boil down to a question of limits: limits to interpretability, limits to demythicization, limits to critical consciousness itself. In Niebuhr's "mythical method" the intention is to interpret these limits theologically in order to foster a spirit of religious disinterestedness. Conscientization, on the other hand, tries to overcome these limits by "decoding" them in order to instill a revolutionary "enthusiasm" for the "untested feasibility" of liberation. A critical attitude toward limit-situations is therefore a necessary first step toward liberation. But it also is a necessary first step toward realism. Where, then, do the two models differ regarding limit-situations?

The "mythical method" seeks religious wisdom about the heights and depths of human nature through a psychological and moral interpretation of the Christian myths of Creation, the Fall, and Atonement. The result is a paradoxical view of the limits of all human thinking and doing, a view structured in terms of "finiteness" and "freedom," the anxious, the sinful, and the gracious aspects of human existence. No particular situation fully exhibits these features, but each of these theological limit-concepts symbolizes what is common to all situations and tries to evoke a religious response to it. Genuine limit-situations must be accepted in faith, a response that leads, it is hoped, to repentance and a measure of serenity even in social conflict. Conscientization, however, is sharply critical of limit-situations. It seeks to "demythicize" them in order to overcome "fatalism." A conscienticizing evangelization assumes this strategy and redirects it as a theological critique of the church and society inspired by the Word of the Lord.

The problem is, does demythicization include the aspects of human nature interpreted mythically by Christian realism? By the same token, does it include the Word of the Lord as recognized in the praxis of liberation theology? Certainly, conscientization means to overcome the sense of inevitability attached to the structures of oppression. It cries out that oppression lies not in the nature of things, but in the historical decisions of various oppressors, social classes, and nations. Having been created by "man," it can be overcome by "man." Here liberation theology and Christian realism in principle agree: Christianity does entail a commitment to social justice and peace. But what about the "dimension of depth" alleged by Christian realism, or the vision of a "liberating God" proclaimed by liberation theology? Do these represent a limit to demythicizing, a limit to the "untested feasibility" of liberation? Or is conscientization focused on infinity?

Here Freire's theory is clear, but his intentions are ambiguous. If rigorously adhered to, conscientization recognizes no limit to demythicization, and in principle there is no reason not to demythicize any theology, including liberation theology. Thus from the theoretical point of view, conscientization has no criteria for distinguishing Christian realism's paradoxical vision of a Hidden God from liberation theology's vision of a liberating God. Both are mythical in the sense that both define the limit-situation of Christian action in the world. If so, how can there be a conscienticizing evangelization that doesn't decode the vision of a liberating God? The only answer to this seems to be that Freire does not recognize the critique of religion implicit in his theory, since he is personally sympathetic to liberation theologians (Assmann, 1976:73–74). Such personal sympathies may account for Freire's intentions, but they do not resolve the theoretical issue. If conscientization has no criteria for distinguishing genuine limit-situations from illusory ones, no criteria for distinguishing limits that summon persons to worshipful contemplation rather than political action, then the religious basis of liberation theology—not to mention any other form of theology—is jeopardized. Conscientization in theory creates a powerful suspicion that the heights and depths interpreted by Niebuhr's "mythical method" may be an illusion. But in so doing, it implies a similar suspicion against the vision of "a liberating God . . . who intervenes in history."

By contrast, Christian realism's "mythical method" in principle does distinguish limit-situations that are genuine from those that are illusory. The ability to recognize abiding truth in myths is contingent on making a distinction between "primitive" and "permanent" myth. While the definitions of permanent myth, its abiding truth, and their reference to a dimension of depth are not developed systematically, they do provide a framework for pointing to limit-situations that are not simply "obstacles to liberation." Their genuineness is recognized by a holistic appeal to experience and confirmed by philosophical reflection on the nature of religion. Within the framework provided by this method, Christian realism seeks to understand the distinctively religious resources of Christian social action. The theoretical dimension provided by its recognition of genuine limit-situations allows Christian realists to express the opinion that in practice religious disinterestedness is preferable to revolutionary enthusiasm.

The result of this comparison of the methodological dimension of the two models is a suspicion that the mythical method of interpretation is more adequate theologically than a conscienticizing evangelization. This suspicion is based not on a repudiation of the practical intention of conscientization, but on a recognition of the theoretical difficulties of reconciling it with evangelization. In view of these difficulties, a conscienticizing evangelization must be regarded as unstable methodologically, an instability which will be reflected in the ambiguity of liberation theology as theology. Ironically, liberation theologians have been less rigorous in their theologies than in their methodological manifestos. This lack of rigor, as we shall see in the next chapter, allows them to do liberation theology in spite of the apparent logic of conscientization.

NOTES

1. The most challenging and consistent formulation of this interpretation of the Gospel of John is found in José Miranda's *Being and the Messiah: The Message of St. John* (1977). Despite its polemical tone the book is illuminating, since Miranda works out his position in pointed debate with most of the major Johannine scholars.

2. Bultmann's program of demythologization differs from both Metz's attempt to deprivatize Christianity and Freire's attempt to demythicize reality. While all three are forms of critical hermeneutics, demythologization seeks to detach the kerygma from the New Testament's mythical worldview so that it may be understood as addressing "man's ontological condition." Freire's demythicization would have to regard Bultmann's program as insufficiently critical, since it still insists on understanding the kerygma in terms of an allegedly ontological limit-situation. Metz's deprivatization does not quarrel with Bultmann's intention, but criticizes the privatizing tendency of his understanding of ontology (Metz, 1969:110). Somewhat different from all three is Niebuhr's "mythical method of interpretation," which affirms the abiding truth of permanent myth while resisting efforts to either demythologize or demythicize Christian theology. The "mythical method," in short, sees the hermeneutic problem not so much as one of understanding the kerygma but of cultivating a religious imagination for practicing it as a way of life.

3. Rahner and Bultmann differ in ways that reflect the typical differences between modern Catholic and Protestant theologies. For Bultmann, that which is to be interpreted is the Word of God; for Rahner it is the magisterium of the church, which comprehends both Scripture and Tradition. While it is true that Rahner's ecclesiocentrism overcomes the religious individualism implicit in Bultmann's position, they both may be criticized for failing to take "the world" seriously. Hence, Metz's new political theology stands in a critical relationship to both their theologies.

4. Metz accepts more or less without question the theory that Christianity traditionally functioned as a religious legitimation of society and its institutions. He believes that the church is now in a position to serve as an "institution of social criticism," not only because modern society renders the previous function obsolete but also because the church possesses spiritual resources that were by no means exhausted by that function. His new political theology therefore seizes the opportunity to recover those resources, made possible by the basic trends of modern social change. For a helpful discussion of this theory and its relevance to developments in recent theology, see Gregory Baum's *Religion and Alienation: A Theological Reading of Sociology* (1975).

5. The term "dialectical vision" is taken from Lucien Goldmann's discussion of it in *The Hidden God*. As in Goldmann's study, the term refers to a global perspective that ultimately is accepted on a "wager" that must be made good in praxis. While this wager of faith is crucial for both the paradoxical vision and the dialectical vision, in neither case does it rule out the kind of rational analysis attempted here. Thus the wager involved in conscientization is evident from the way Freire connects the three elements of his pedagogy. There is no logical

connection, in my opinion, between the first and the second and third levels of this theory. While the practice of literacy training described in the first level may be justified on the basis of other theories, what links it to Freire's revolutionary theory of education and the dialectical vision is the emphasis given to the generative theme of oppression/liberation. But it is precisely the importance of this theme that is asserted in what amounts to an intuitive leap of faith (cf. Freire, 1970: 93). Of course, like any other leap of faith, this one will be recognized as successful if its praxis is successful (cf. Goldmann, 1964:300–302).

6. Given the Marxist orientation of the dialectical vision, the reader should recognize that the pathologies of activism and bureaucracy are exhibited in the organizational strategies sponsored by Leninism and Stalinism respectively. Curiously, while Freire quotes Vladimir Lenin and Georg Lukacs *inter alios* in support of his theory, he does not call attention to this critical application of it. Nevertheless, the point is made by other neo-Marxist theorists concerned with the problems of party organization (cf. Habermas, 1974:20–37). In view of Freire's failure to address this issue, it is not surprising that some observers have expressed skepticism about conscientization's relationship to the noble ideals of dialogical action (cf. Berger, 1974: 121–44).

7. One of the issues raised by this analysis of conscientization is how Freire can continue to speak of "man" when his theory precludes the development of substantive philosophical anthropologies. The apparent inconsistency is resolved by recognizing that Freire's understanding of "man" is purely formal, a symbol referring to a historic process and clearly not to an ontological substrate. Furthermore, Freire's usage merely reflects that of the young Marx who had yet to transcend anthropology in a critique of political economy. In contrast to the confusion of Freire and Marx's notion of "man," there is the clarity of Louis Althusser's criticism of all substantive doctrines of "man"—including that of Marxist humanism—as "ideology." While there is much that is questionable in Althusser—for example, his distinction of "science" and "ideology"—his work brilliantly exposes the theoretical problematic of Marxist humanism, and thus is useful for understanding the radical implications of conscientization (cf. Althusser, 1970:221–47).

8. I base this conclusion on a reading of David Tracy's *Blessed Rage for Order*. Given the fact that Tracy understands "the religious dimension of common human experience and language" in terms of the recognition of limit-situations, and grounds the possible "meaning, meaningfulness, and truth" of religious experience and language upon this recognition, it is clear—to me, at least—that if there are no genuine limit-situations, theological reflection eventually becomes meaningless (cf. Tracy, 1975:91–118).

9. Reinhold Niebuhr, for example, concluded as much in the article "The Problem of Communist Religion" (Niebuhr, 1934b), which in Chapter 2 of this book was discussed as representing the decisive step toward Christian realism.

8

The Theology in Liberation Theology

*To place oneself in the perspective of the Kingdom means to partici-
pate in the struggle for the liberation of those oppressed by others.
This is what many Christians who have committed themselves to the
Latin American revolutionary process have begun to experience. If
this option seems to separate them from the Christian community, it
is because many Christians, intent on domesticating the Good News,
see them as wayward and perhaps even dangerous. If they are not
always able to express in appropriate terms the profound reasons for
their commitment, it is because the theology in which they were
formed—and which they share with other Christians—has not produced the categories necessary to express this option, which seeks to
respond creatively to the new demands of the Gospel and of the
oppressed and exploited peoples of this continent. But in their commitments, and even in their attempts to explain them, there is greater
fidelity to the Lord than in the "orthodox" doctrine (some prefer to
call it by this name) of reputable Christian circles. This doctrine is
supported by authority and much publicized because of access to
social communications media, but it is not even strong enough to
abandon the Gospel. It is the Gospel which is disowning it.*
—*Gustavo Gutiérrez*, A Theology of Liberation, *1973*

If conscientization is as radical as it appears to be, there is question
whether it can ever yield constructive results in theology. More precisely,
can the meaning of a conscienticizing evangelization be expressed in a
more or less coherent theological doctrine? If one does succeed in formulating a theology of liberation, does this not also stand in need of critical
demythicization? Is the theology of liberation really free of the "myth-
making irrationality" that conscientization seeks to overcome? What
grounds are there to believe that liberation theology has transcended the
alienation that it charges against all other expressions of Christianity?
These questions represent the suspicions raised in the previous chapter
against the method of conscienticizing evangelization. They will now be
tested by examining the theology of liberation as proposed by Gustavo

182

Gutiérrez. If they are correct, the reader can expect to find the content of Gutiérrez's theology curiously ambiguous, given the radical implications of its method. In the analysis that follows, I shall argue that in fact this is the case. The chapter will conclude with a comparison between liberation theology and Christian realism so that the consequences of this ambiguity may be recognized.

Visions in Tension

Gutiérrez's conscienticizing evangelization is meant to proclaim the reality of Christ the Liberator, not as a religious symbol, but as the Divine Person who incarnates the fullness of liberation in history. Liberation is "the gift which Christ offers us . . . by his death and resurrection" (Gutiérrez, 1973:176). The "three levels of meaning" that Gutiérrez discerns in liberation thus are "all part of a single, all-encompassing salvific process" in which they "mutually effect each other, but . . . are not the same." Their unity as "the action of Christ and the gift of the Spirit" is what "gives human history its profound unity" (Gutiérrez, 1973:177), while their distinction represents the dynamic involvement of the Divine Person and human persons in the actual praxis of liberation. This simultaneous affirmation of unity and distinction allows Gutiérrez to bring the themes of liberation and salvation into the closest possible correlation (but not identification). Echoing the Medellín documents, Gutiérrez confesses:

"It is the same God who, in the fullness of time, sends his Son in the flesh, so that He might come to liberate all men from *all* slavery to which sin has subjected them: hunger, misery, oppression, and ignorance, in a word, that injustice and hatred which have their origin in human selfishness." This is why the Christian life is a passover, a transition from sin to grace, from death to life, from injustice to justice, from the subhuman to the human. Christ introduces us by the gift of his Spirit into communion with God and with all men. [Gutiérrez, 1973:176]

This is what Gutiérrez means at an ultimate level by "radical liberation."

These theological affirmations are rooted in a particular Christian religious vision, namely, the orthodox Catholic vision of the Incarnation. Christ is God become "man," the appearance of the Absolute in time, who redeems "man" from sin, who restores meaning to history. Since Gutiérrez's theology does not depart substantially from this vision, his Christ the Liberator remains the God-man of orthodoxy, even as its meaning is rendered more dynamic by understanding the Incarnation in the context provided by salvation-history. In other words, Gutiérrez's vision rests not on the single assertion that "the Word became flesh and dwelt among us" (John 1:14), but on a series of assertions that "in many and various ways

God spoke of old to our fathers by the prophets; but in these last days he has spoken to us by a Son" (Heb. 1:1–2). These "many and various ways" represent a series of "epiphanies," or historic encounters, between the divine and human persons, beginning paradigmatically in the Exodus of Israel from Egypt and culminating in the Incarnation of Christ. Given this emphasis on salvation-history, it is appropriate to say that Gutiérrez's theology is rooted in an "epiphanic vision." For him a conscienticizing evangelization encourages the oppressed to experience this vision in their struggles for liberation.

The question, however, is whether this vision is compatible with conscientization. If conscientization is based on a dialectical vision—in other words, if its foundational values are identical to those of the Feuerbachian humanism of Marx's youth—then there's a strong suspicion of incompatibility. The tension between Gutiérrez's epiphanic vision and Freire's dialectical vision is based on the fact that an orthodox understanding of the Incarnation simply cannot be reconciled with a dialectical interpretation of history.[1] No dialectical *tour de force* can integrate the epiphany of the Absolute in time with the vision of history as an ongoing struggle of the oppressed to realize the untested feasibility of liberation. This is so because the Incarnation makes God the primary agent or "Subject" in human history, while the dialectical vision makes "it possible for men to enter the historical process as responsible Subjects." If "history is one" in the sense required by the dialectical vision, then the Incarnation must be regarded as myth. An ennobling and enabling myth perhaps: a symbol of the aspirations of the oppressed for permanent liberation in history; but nevertheless, a myth. The epiphanic vision, on the other hand, sees the Incarnation as real history. Gutiérrez's theological affirmations must be construed as claiming that God really has intervened in history on the side of the oppressed, and that he can be expected to do so again, now and in the future. Incarnational realism, in other words, is the only way of making sense of Gutiérrez's correlation—but not identification—of liberation and salvation. Yet that correlation involves Gutiérrez in a tension between the two visions, one of which underlies the method, the other the content, of his theology.

The tension between the two is reflected in the theological hermeneutics actually proposed as a conscienticizing evangelization. In defending his correlation of liberation and salvation Gutiérrez rejects, for example, the traditional view that the New Testament has a "spiritualizing influence," which allows the biblical promises to be read not with reference to a "temporal redemption of Israel," but in terms of "the spiritual redemption of all men." The hermeneutic distinction between "carnal" and "spiritual" meanings of biblical texts derived from this view therefore is repudiated in favor of one that distinguishes "partial" and "total" fulfillments in history:

> The proper way to pose the question does not seem to us to be in terms
> of "temporal promise or spiritual promise." Rather, as we have

mentioned above, it is a matter of partial fulfillments through liberating historical events, which are in turn new promises marking the road toward total fulfillment. Christ does not "spiritualize" the eschatological promises; he gives them meaning and fulfillment today (cf. Luke 4:21); but at the same time he opens new perspectives by catapulting history forward, forward toward total reconciliation. The hidden sense is not the "spiritual" one, which devalues and even eliminates temporal and earthly obstacles; rather it is the sense of a fullness which takes on and transforms historical reality. Moreover, it is only *in* the temporal, earthly, historical event that we can open up to the future of complete fulfillment. [Gutiérrez, 1973:167]

Lest his meaning be missed, Gutiérrez goes on to specify what is entailed by this "total reconciliation" attributed to Christ:

It presupposes the defense of the rights of the poor, punishment of the oppressors, a life free from the fear of being enslaved by others, the liberation of the oppressed. Peace, justice, love, and freedom are not private realities; they are not only internal attitudes. They are social realities, implying an historical liberation. A poorly understood spiritualization has often made us forget the human consequences of the eschatological promises and the power to transform unjust social structures which they imply. The elimination of misery and exploitation is a sign of the coming of the Kingdom. [Gutiérrez, 1973:167]

The superficial clarity of the contrast drawn is not enough to gloss over the tensions underlying this "sense of a fullness which takes on and transforms historical reality." What does it mean, for example, to catapult "history forward, forward toward total reconciliation"? Can the dialectical vision allow for any "catapulting" in Gutiérrez's sense? In what way is this "catapulting" related to the efforts of the oppressed to seize control of their own destiny? Is the historical Christ one of the "partial fulfillments," or is he the "total fulfillment"? How can he be both, for a genuinely historical thinker? Once again, Gutiérrez's hermeneutic of history in fact presupposes an epiphanic vision of God's action while also claiming to be dialectical in its analysis. Either Christ is the definitive epiphany of God who decisively catapults history forward toward salvation, as orthodox Incarnationalists believe, or he is a symbol of human hope for liberation in the dialectical process of historical becoming, as a philosophy inspired by Hegel, Feuerbach, and Marx might interpret him. It is hard to see how he could be both, given Gutiérrez's premises; and yet he must be both, if the correlation between "liberation" and "salvation" is to work.

Furthermore, by fixing his focus on the "liberating historical event," Gutiérrez crosses the line separating Catholic progressives from a genuinely dialectical radicalism. But what warrants this exclusive concern for "the temporal"? Gutiérrez never makes his reasons explicit. Nevertheless, by insisting upon this concern, he gives much greater scope to the suspicion of "excessive spiritualization" than do progressives like Congar, whom he quotes in rejecting the traditional understanding of "carnal" and "spiritual" meanings. Apparently, for Gutiérrez those guilty of "excessive spiritualization" include anyone who objects to this correlation of liberation and salvation on theological grounds.

The basic agenda of Gutiérrez's theology of liberation, then, is both clear and difficult. He seeks to proclaim the reality of Christ the Liberator as the ultimate fulfillment of the struggles of the oppressed, by constructing a theology based on a correlation of the themes of "liberation" and "salvation." The difficulty is that each of these themes emerges from a distinctive world-vision which may not be reconcilable with the other.[2] The tensions between the epiphanic vision underlying the theme of salvation and the dialectical vision underlying the theme of liberation, in other words, make Gutiérrez's theology radically ambiguous or unstable. This, at least, is the suspicion that the following analysis will seek to confirm or deny.

Salvation and Liberation: A Theology of History

Despite this suspicion, there can be no doubt about the power of liberation theology to inspire a kind of revolutionary enthusiasm based on the Word of the Lord of history. Let us suppose, then, that liberation theology has genuine insight into "where the pulse of history is beating at this moment." How is this insight translated into theology? How is it codified so that the basic communities might come to experience it as the truth of their own praxis? The epiphanic vision, whatever its problems of internal coherence, provides the point of departure: liberation theology correlates "salvation" and "liberation" in a new kind of salvation-history. I say "a new kind," because its purpose is not simply a contemplation of the mighty acts of God as portrayed in the Bible, but the recognition of these acts as a process in which the basic communities participate, a process whose "goal is the creation of a new man" (Gutiérrez, 1973:146).

Mention of "a new man" may lead us to expect that Gutiérrez, like Niebuhr, constructs his theology first as a theological anthropology, and then as a theology of history. In fact, Gutiérrez on occasion does identify his understanding of the "Word of the Lord" as one that reflects "the anthropological aspects of revelation" (Gutiérrez, 1973:189). But there is no theological anthropology in his theology, no "Christian interpretation of human nature." Liberation theology is theology of history, pure and simple. What then does Gutiérrez mean by "anthropological aspects"? He writes:

But the Word is not only a Word about God and *about* man: the Word is *made* man. If all that is human is illuminated by the Word, it is precisely because the Word reaches us through human history; Von Rad comments that "it is in history that God reveals the secret of his person." Human history, then, is the location of our encounter with him, in Christ. [Gutiérrez, 1973:189]

The anthropological aspect is not some generalized model of the human self and its paradoxes, but human history in its concrete immediacy. The "new man" is the goal of history, the purpose intended by "the presence of God in the midst of his people."

Gutiérrez's theology, therefore, claims history as its reference point. More specifically, it focuses on the role of God's "people" in history. This people is to be identified, and its experience interpreted theologically. Such interpretation will mean reading the Bible in a new way, not for the wisdom with which it illuminates the paradoxes of human selfhood, but for a sense of direction by which God's people might carry forward their struggle today. Given the fact that the Latin American reality already discloses who God's people are, the reference point for this theology necessarily is the oppressed gathered in basic communities.[3] Consequently, the new kind of salvation-history offered by liberation theology must allow these communities to identify their praxis with the series of "epiphanies" they find in the Bible. Biblical history, in other words, becomes paradigmatic for understanding their struggle. So rendered, salvation-history provides a code by which the limit-situations of oppression are identified and overcome. This is possible, of course, only if the generative themes of "liberation" and "salvation" can be correlated.

Assuming that they can, Gutiérrez focuses his theology of history on those biblical narratives that dramatize "the presence of God in the midst of his people." The most characteristic of these is the story of Israel's liberation from Egypt. Gutiérrez conscienticizes the narrative, emphasizing the fact that the Exodus was a "political action" involving not only oppressors and oppressed, but also a "liberator," Moses, guided by "a liberating God," Yahweh, who "liberates the Jewish people politically in order to make them a holy nation" (Gutiérrez, 1973:157). The people once liberated, however, continue to show all the symptoms of "oppressor-consciousness":

And in the midst of the desert, faced with the first difficulties, they told him that they preferred the security of slavery—whose cruelty they were beginning to forget—to the uncertainties of a liberation in process: "If only we had died at the Lord's hand in Egypt, where we sat round the fleshpots and had plenty of bread to eat!" [Exod. 16:3] A gradual pedagogy of successes and failures would be necessary for the Jewish people to become aware of the roots of their oppression, to struggle against it, and to perceive the profound sense of the liberation to which they were called. [Gutiérrez, 1973:156]

They are reminded, in other words, that Exodus is "a historical-salvific fact, . . . a political liberation through which Yahweh expresses his love for his people and the gift of total liberation is received." With their consciousnesses properly raised by the liberator, God's people return to "the long march toward the promised land in which Israel can establish a society free from misery and alienation" (Gutiérrez, 1973:157).

Gutiérrez makes explicit how these narratives can be used to construct a liberating theology of history:

> The Exodus experience is paradigmatic. It remains vital and contemporary due to similar historical experiences which the People of God undergo. As Neher writes, it is characterized "by the twofold sign of the overriding will of God and the free and conscious consent of men." And it structures our faith in the gift of the Father's love. In Christ and through the Spirit, men are becoming one in the very heart of history, as they confront and struggle against all that divides and opposes them. But the true agents of this quest for unity are those who today are oppressed (economically, politically, culturally) and struggle to become free. Salvation—totally and freely given by God, the communion of men with God and among themselves—is the inner force and the fullness of this movement of man's self-generation which was initiated by the work of creation. [Gutiérrez, 1973:159]

The point to such paradigms, in other words, is to allow the basic communities to legitimate their praxis as part of the ongoing historical presence of God in the midst of his people.

Once the code is understood, the Exodus paradigm becomes crucial for understanding all the other narratives of the Bible. It is pivotal, for example, in Gutiérrez's interpretation of the stories of Creation and the Fall. The meaning of creation is interpreted not primarily in relation to the narratives of Genesis, but in relation to the discourses of Deutero-Isaiah (Gutiérrez, 1973:154). Consequently, the reference point shifts from an "abiding truth" concerning the image of God in human nature to an account of God's "first salvific act" in history. It represents a cosmic expansion of the liberating perspective disclosed in the Exodus:

> "Creation," writes Von Rad, "is regarded as a work of Yahweh in history, a work within time. This means that there is a real and true opening up of historical prospect. No doubt, Creation as the first of Yahweh's works stands at the very remotest beginnings—only, it does not stand alone, other works are to follow." The creation of the world initiates history, the human struggle, and the salvific adventure of Yahweh. Faith in creation does away with its mythical and supernatural character. It is the work of a God who saves and acts in history; since man is the center of creation, it is integrated into the history which is being built by man's efforts. [Gutiérrez, 1973:154]

For the moment let us ignore Gutiérrez's obscurantism regarding the supernatural and simply note where his emphasis rests: "The creation of the world initiates history, the human struggle, and the salvific adventure of Yahweh." Nothing here is said about human nature; the Creation story simply reinforces the historic consciousness dramatized in the Exodus paradigm.

Gutiérrez is silent regarding the story of the Fall. The topic of original sin is not even mentioned. This does not mean that he denies the reality of sin, but he does redefine it in terms of the struggle against oppression:

> Sin is regarded as a social, historical fact, the absence of brotherhood and love in relationships among men, the breach of friendship with God and with other men, and, therefore, an interior, personal fracture. When it is considered in this way, the collective dimensions of sin are rediscovered. . . . Nor is this a matter of escape into a flesh-less spiritualism. Sin is evident in oppressive structures, in the exploitation of man by man, in the domination and slavery of peoples, races, and social classes. Sin appears, therefore, as the fundamental alienation, the root of a situation of injustice and exploitation. It cannot be encountered in itself, but only in concrete instances, in particular alienations. It is impossible to understand the concrete manifestations without understanding the underlying basis and vice versa. Sin demands a radical liberation, which in turn necessarily implies a political liberation. Only by participating in the historical process of liberation will it be possible to show the fundamental alienation present in every partial alienation. [Gutiérrez, 1973:175–76]

This notion of sin does not depend upon an anthropological analysis of human anxiety. It depends, instead, upon a dialectical vision of the social relationships that constitute human history. The "breach of friendship with God and with other men" is attributed not to an alleged fault in human nature, but to a "fundamental alienation" produced historically by oppressive social structures. Nevertheless, Gutiérrez hesitates to identify it exclusively with these structures, insisting that "every partial alienation" must be distinguished from the "fundamental alienation" that is its "ultimate cause." This distinction parallels the previous one made between "partial" and "total" fulfillments, used for correlating the themes of "liberation" and "salvation." Like the previous one, it can be known only by participating in the struggle. But while its theoretical justification remains obscure, Gutiérrez's intention is clear. By asserting this distinction, he hopes to ensure that the role of "a liberating God" is not eclipsed by the demand for "political liberation."

In another passage Gutiérrez makes this point explicit:

> In describing sin as the ultimate cause we do not in any way negate the structural reasons and the objective determinations leading to these

situations. It does, however, emphasize the fact that things do not happen by chance and that behind the structure there is a personal or collective will responsible—a willingness to reject God and neighbor. It suggests, likewise, that a social transformation, no matter how radical it may be, does not automatically achieve the suppression of all evils. [Gutiérrez, 1973:35]

While orthodox in its intent, this statement does not resolve the problem of understanding the nature of sin. Granted, the problem concerns "a personal and collective will"; but what basis does Gutiérrez provide for understanding the condition of this will? Is it the "fundamental alienation"? If so, what is its source? Why is it bound "to reject God and neighbor"? These questions are difficult if not impossible to answer without some sort of theological anthropology. But since Gutiérrez is content to rely instead on what can be shown "by participating in the historical process of liberation," the questions go unanswered.

Whatever their ambiguity, these passages mark the point of departure for Gutiérrez's Christology. They imply that salvation from sin ultimately depends on the power of Christ the Liberator, and not exclusively on the political action of the oppressed. Gutiérrez elaborates:

The work of Christ is a new creation. In this sense, Paul speaks of a "new creation" in Christ (Gal. 6:15, 2 Cor. 5:17). Moreover, it is through this "new creation," that is to say, through the salvation which Christ affords, that creation acquires its full meaning (cf. Rom. 8). But the work of Christ is presented simultaneously as a liberation from sin and from all its consequences: despoliation, injustice, hatred. This liberation fulfills in an unexpected way the promises of the prophets and creates a new chosen people, which this time includes all humanity. Creation and salvation therefore have, in the first place, a Christological sense: all things have been created in Christ, all things have been saved in him (cf. Col. 1:15–20). [Gutiérrez, 1973: 158]

Gutiérrez's Christology thus for the most part is an Incarnationalism stripped of its overtly supernatural dimensions and recast according to the theme of liberation.

By transforming the orthodox Christology in this way, Gutiérrez provides a theological basis for understanding the positive and negative dimensions of the dialectical vision of history. "Liberation from sin" designates the negative pole of oppression; "new creation" designates the positive pole, a process of "permanent liberation" in history. Thus the fulfillment of salvation-history in the work of Christ is assimilated to the dialectical vision, and vice versa. This correlation of the themes of "salvation" and "liberation" would remain abstract—and perhaps unconvincing even for liberation theologians—were it not for the historical warrants to be found for it in the Bible itself: the legacy of Israel's prophets, and the actual ministry of Jesus of Nazareth.

Let us consider first Gutiérrez's understanding of the prophets. Essentially they serve to provide continuity between the major epiphanies of God, between the Exodus and the Incarnation. The message of the prophets is this: "To know Yahweh, which in Biblical language is equivalent to saying to love Yahweh, *is* to establish just relationships among men, it *is* to recognize the rights of the poor. The God of Biblical revelation is known through interhuman justice. Where justice does not exist, God is not known; he is absent" (Gutiérrez, 1973:195). The prophets, in other words, reiterate the meaning of the Exodus paradigm. Indeed, they sharpen it: without liberation, God is unknown. Gutiérrez summarizes the prophetic legacy for salvation-history as follows:

> What we have here, therefore, is a twofold process. On the one hand, there is a universalization of the presence of God: from being localized and linked to a particular people, it gradually extends to all the peoples of the earth (Amos 9:7; Isaiah 41:1–7; 45:20–25; 51:4; and the entire Book of Jonah). On the other hand, there is an internalization, or rather, an integration of this presence: from dwelling in places of worship, this presence is transferred to the heart of human history; it is a presence which embraces the whole man. Christ is the point of convergence of both processes. In him, in his personal uniqueness, the particular is transcended and the universal becomes concrete. In him, in his Incarnation, what is personal and internal becomes visible. Henceforth, this will be true, in one way or another, of every man. [Gutiérrez, 1973:193]

Through a series of "determinate negations" of the Exodus paradigm, the prophets thus point in the direction of Christ. The processes of "universalization" and "internalization" progressively clarify the issue of history as liberation. As the historic fulfillment of the prophetic legacy, Christ's coming marks a "point of convergence" in which the meaning of liberation is realized once and for all.

The second and most decisive warrant is the historic ministry of Jesus of Nazareth. Here the details of Jesus' life and death are used to confirm the correlation between "liberation" and "salvation." Gutiérrez thus alleges three historical facts for understanding Jesus' relation to political liberation: "the complex relationship between Jesus and the Zealots, his attitude toward the leaders of the Jewish people, and his death at the hands of the political authorities" (Gutiérrez, 1973:226). With regard to the first, Gutiérrez recognizes that Jesus was not a Zealot, but "even more revolutionary than the Zealots," insofar as he was not limited to the sectarian horizons that bound those "political militants" of first-century Palestine. In other words, the liberation that Jesus espoused was universal, and based on a "spiritual freedom" beyond the ken of such "fierce defenders of literal obedience to the Law." Second, the fact that Jesus "confronted the *groups in power* of the Jewish people" meant ". . . a radical option for the poor; one's attitude towards them determines the validity of all religious behavior; it is above all for them that the Son of Man has come" (Gutiérrez, 1973:228). Thus, finally, he appeared "as a dangerous traitor," and was executed "*at the hands of the political authorities*, the oppressors of the Jewish people."

The political implications of Jesus' ministry are confirmed and clarified by his preaching the kingdom of God. Gutiérrez interprets its meaning as follows:

> The Gospel does not get its political dimension from one or another particular option, but from the very nucleus of its message. If this message is subversive, it is because it takes on Israel's hope: the Kingdom as "the end of domination of man over man; it is a Kingdom of contradiction to the established powers and on behalf of man." And the Gospel gives Israel's hope its deepest meaning; indeed it calls for a "new creation." The life and preaching of Jesus postulate the unceasing search for a new kind of man in a qualitatively different society. Although the Kingdom must not be confused with the establishment of a just society, this does not mean that it is indifferent to this society. Nor does it mean this just society constitutes a "necessary condition" for the arrival of the Kingdom nor that they are closely linked, nor that they converge. More profoundly, the announcement of the Kingdom reveals to society itself the aspiration for a just society and leads it to discover unsuspected dimensions and unexplored paths. The Kingdom is realized in a society of brotherhood and justice; and, in turn, this realization opens up the promise and hope of complete communion of all men with God. The political is grafted into the eternal. [Gutiérrez, 1973:231–32]

In short, the kingdom of God as preached by Jesus means "the unceasing search for a new kind of man in a qualitatively different society." Even if this were a historically reliable paraphrase of Jesus' preaching, why should it be so compelling today? Is it true—as Gutiérrez asserts—that only Jesus "reveals to society itself the aspiration for a just society and leads it to discover unsuspected dimensions and unexplored paths"? But if others have also done this, what is so authoritative about Jesus' preaching? In interpreting the meaning of Jesus for salvation-history, Gutiérrez assumes the conclusions of orthodox Christology without actually defending them. Jesus' ministry is ultimately meaningful for political liberation because he is Christ the Liberator. His authority is that of the Messiah, the Son of God, the "Word made flesh who dwelt among us." Only on these premises does it make sense to say that "the political is grafted into the eternal."

Whatever the status of his premises, Gutiérrez sees the kingdom as the epitome of this new kind of salvation-history. The epiphanic vision culminates in an eschatological hope whose purpose is to inspire an ever renewable enthusiasm for "permanent liberation." But while the kingdom is utopian in the sense that it represents "an annunciation of what is not yet, but will be," it is not exhausted in any specific utopia. As the passage just quoted suggests, Christian eschatology and utopian aspirations are intimately correlated but not identified. They are one in that they have a common reference point: "history is one." They are distinct in that Christian eschatology remains in tension with all such aspirations. This tension is maintained not by pointing to a paradoxical fulfillment beyond history, but by insisting on the permanently revolutionary character of liberation in history. Thus although each achievement inevitably will be surpassed, the message of the kingdom is an invitation always to "discover unsuspected dimensions and unexplored paths." The eschatological promise, in other words, symbolizes transcendence, but a transcendence immanent to history itself: "The complete encounter with the Lord will mark an end to history, but it will take place in history. Thus we must acknowledge historical events in all their concreteness and significance, but we are also led to permanent detachment" (Gutiérrez, 1973:168).[4]

The practical consequence of this new kind of salvation-history is a radical freedom for basic communities to participate in the struggle for liberation. Gutiérrez explains:

Christian hope opens us, in an attitude of spiritual childhood, to the gift of the future promised by God. It keeps us from any confusion of the Kingdom with any one historical stage, from any idolatry toward unavoidably ambiguous human achievement, from any absolutizing of revolution. In this way hope makes us radically free to commit ourselves to social praxis, motivated by a liberating utopia and with the means which the scientific analysis of reality provides for us. And our hope not only frees us for this commitment; it simultaneously demands and judges it. [Gutiérrez, 1973:238]

While this hope clearly represents the goal of a conscientizing evangelization, its basis remains ambiguous. Consistent with the correlation of "liberation" and "salvation," being "radically free," for Gutiérrez, entails not only "an attitude of spiritual childhood" but also a commitment to a "scientific analysis" inspired by "a liberating utopia." The tensions implicit in this attitude apparently are overcome in the confident trust that Christ the Liberator is really making changes in history.

Myth or History?

This synopsis of Gutiérrez's interpretation of salvation-history should allow the reader to confirm or deny the suspicion previously raised, whether liberation theology itself is a form of mythicization, in other words whether the epiphanic vision—even as adapted to the Latin American reality—remains an instance of "myth-making irrationality." Note well, this question presupposes not Christian realism's view of myth and truth, but the perspective implicit in the theory of conscientization. The latter, therefore, must provide the criteria for resolving this suspicion.

Accordingly, the question is whether Gutiérrez's salvation-history is a religious myth about history or a dialectical analysis of real history? While Gutiérrez assumes that it is real history, given the theory of conscientization, must it not be criticized as myth? While Freire never gives a precise definition of "mythicized reality," occasionally he describes it as a rationalization "created in defense of the class of the perceiver" (Freire, 1970:37). This makes myth more or less synonymous with ideology. At other times, he defines it formally in contrast to a "conscienticized reality," and thus it refers to an "antagonism" within the thematic universe according to which "men" fail to see through limit-situations and fail to project limit-acts. A mythicized reality, in other words, places obstacles in the way of "men's" emergence as "responsible Subjects." Can Gutiérrez's salvation-history be construed in this way?

The fact that this theology proclaims the ultimate reality of "a liberating God . . . who intervenes in history" initially raises the suspicion that it can. The difficulty is not primarily an epistemological one of verifying these interventions according to any mode of analysis compatible with conscientization. It is, instead, an existential difficulty with theoretical implications: In what way can salvation-history promote the emergence of "man" as a "Subject" when God and his Son, Christ the Liberator, are the principal or ultimate Subjects in the process of liberation? If liberation is "a gift of God," in what sense must it be won in a struggle? As we have seen, this is the major difficulty in correlating the themes of "salvation" and "liberation." Gutiérrez does, however, provide a rule for interpreting this correlation. In describing the Exodus experience as "paradigmatic," he characterized it as a process governed "by the twofold sign of the overriding will of God and the free and conscious consent of men." But this rule raises as many questions as it answers. As Alfredo Fierro, one of the radical critics of liberation theology, sees it, "Gutiérrez feels no need to ask what it might mean to talk about the 'assent' of man in God's project and the 'force' of God in man's self-generation. Gutiérrez allows himself to overlook the fact that for two centuries Protestant and Catholic theologians have racked their brains to solve a question that goes to the heart of the debate with modern atheism" (Fierro, 1977:236–37).[5] Since conscientization is based on the dialectical vision that continues to inspire much of modern atheism, Gutiérrez's failure to clarify this rule may be seen as an evasion. In any case, until an explanation of this rule is given in a manner consistent with conscientization, Gutiérrez's correlation remains at best ambiguous, and at worst an instance of "myth-making irrationality," his intentions to the contrary notwithstanding.

Conviction on the charge of mythicization requires more than evidence of ambiguity. There must also be an objective antagonism within the thematic universe. Does Gutiérrez's salvation-history really overcome limit-situations with limit-acts? Its capacity to do so is based on the allegedly paradigmatic status of the Exodus: "It remains vital and contemporary due to similar historical experiences which the People of God undergo." Gutiérrez's point here is not the general one made by "the twofold sign," but a specific one based on analogies between the Exodus experience and any other historic situation characterized by the theme of oppression/liberation. But what is the nature of these analogies? Have the basic communities witnessed anything like the *magnalia Dei*, the plagues of Egypt, for example, or the crossing of the Red Sea? Do their coordinators enjoy the charism of divine revelation as Moses allegedly did? Should they be encouraged to expect divine assistance in their struggle against oppression? It is hardly likely that Gutiérrez had these things in mind when he spoke of "similar historical experiences." Instead, the analogies are based almost exclusively on a conscientization of biblical narratives. But how do analogies of this sort overcome limit-situations? Certainly they raise the consciousness of those who mistakenly assume that biblical religion legitimates oppression. But this is to overcome limit-situations in a very narrow sense, for a revolutionary praxis today neither stands nor falls on keeping the historical record straight regarding the dynamics of biblical religion.

Be that as it may, it is difficult to see how these analogies make the "Exodus paradigm" necessary. Presumably, the modes of analysis normally used in conscientization would be sufficient to establish the ideological tendencies of biblical narrative. On the other hand, it is arguable that this paradigm is superfluous and perhaps even distracting. It is superfluous in that it offers the oppressed no additional theoretical or practical resource not already implicit in conscientization. It is distracting in that it focuses on biblical narratives precisely when a scientific mode of analysis needs most to be developed. If the theologians object that the Exodus paradigm serves the indispensable function of reinforcing a commitment to the struggle, the counter-argument is that the dialectical vision has proved more than adequate in this regard. It thus may be argued that this paradigm overcomes limit-situations only as a rhetorical expansion of conscientization itself. But if that is the case, then it can be little more than a residue of "myth-making irrationality" invoked only for reasons of expediency. In other words, salvation-history must be regarded as an ideology or as a myth, perhaps tolerated because of the peculiarities of the communities who cling to it, but certainly distrusted as precisely the sort of "subjectivism" (Freire, 1970:35) that both Marx and Freire reject as an impediment to full humanization.

But let us assume that, if pressed, liberation theologians can show that salvation-history is neither superfluous nor distracting. Aren't the biblical narratives themselves more mythical than historical, even after Gutiérrez has conscienticized them? Two aspects of his theology of history suggest that they are. The first is the semantic problem involved in Gutiérrez's claims regarding the "supernatural character" of salvation-history. The second is the epistemological problem of presupposing the historical reliability of biblical narratives. The problems are interrelated.

Regarding the first, throughout his theology of history Gutiérrez claims to have overcome "the mythical and supernatural character" so often attributed to biblical events. Supernaturalism at best is a mistake, and at worst a form of idolatry; in any case, he does not find it warranted by the Bible. This claim, however, is hard to reconcile with his affirmation of "a liberating God . . . who intervenes in history." His point apparently is that God's epiphanies are not supernatural, since they are not "otherworldly." They have meaning and reference in relation to the one history of this world. But does that make them any less supernatural? They are still "epiphanies," dramatic divine interventions in what is normally considered the natural order of things. What Gutiérrez has actually done is to translate salvation-history from one form of supernaturalism to another. A "this-worldly" supernaturalism has been politicized in a manner consistent with the theme of "liberation." Whatever their theological significance, both forms of supernaturalism in theory must count as a mythicization of reality.

The second problem is related to the first. Neither form of supernaturalism can be verified according to the modes of analysis usually employed in the critical study of history. Historical claims regarding divine interventions in human events are *prima-facie* evidence of myth, however liberating their effect. This assumption is as true for historical studies inspired by conscientization as it is for any other mode of critical analysis. The epistemological problem in this case, however, is compounded by the way in which Gutiérrez conscienticizes specific biblical episodes. Besides the suspicion of mythicization, Gutiérrez's rendering of the Exodus paradigm and the ministry of Jesus, for example, are open to serious question on historical grounds. Sometimes Gutiérrez assumes the historical reliability of the biblical narratives without question; often he seems to know more about these episodes than any reliable historian would care to assert; and consistently he reshapes their details to fit the preestablished requirements of the theme of liberation. These tactics suggest that whatever the historical authenticity of the biblical narratives may turn out to be, Gutiérrez's use of them is not disciplined by the usual canons of historical scholarship.[6] On the contrary, they suggest that Gutiérrez's theology of history is an exercise in reconstructing a biblical myth.

All three of these points—first, the existential problem of reconciling "a liberating God" with the project of "man's" becoming the Subject of history; second, the inability to establish the relevance of salvation-history to the praxis of liberation except on "subjectivist" theological grounds; and third, the epistemological difficulty of reconciling the biblical narratives in question with the modes of analysis characteristic of critical history—all three suggest that Gutiérrez's theology of history itself is not an interpretation of history consistent with the logic of conscientization, but a religious myth about history. While this conclusion should come as no surprise, the interesting question is what it implies about the internal stability of liberation theology. If the content of this theology rests on a religious myth about history, how might a rigorously consistent method of conscientization demythicize it?

Conscienticizing Liberation Theology

The religious myth about history that emerges from this "antagonism" between the generative themes of liberation and salvation represents only a partial conscientization of the epiphanic vision of Catholic Incarnationalism. The theology of history that Gutiérrez develops to give this myth paradigmatic status therefore stands in need of complete demythicization if the logic of conscientization is to be adhered to consistently. What would a complete demythicization of liberation theology involve?

If the basic strategy of conscientization is to identify limit-situations in order to decode them for praxis, the first step is to identify these in the concepts of this theology. The most basic limit-situation is that represented by the antagonism between a world-vision that acknowledges God as the primary Subject of history and one that casts "man" in that role. Any theism that confesses God as really acting in history necessarily defines limits to human thinking and doing. Since Freire's dialectical vision sees such limits only as obstacles to full humanization, necessarily the form of theism represented by Gutiérrez's epiphanic vision must be regarded as a problematic limit-situation. This much should be clear from the previous analyses.

In Gutiérrez's theology this basic limit-situation generates a series of secondary limit-situations that also require decoding. The most striking of these are the distinctions he makes between "partial" and "fundamental" alienation and "partial" and "total" fulfillment. These distinctions are generated by the attempt to correlate the themes of liberation and salvation. Gutiérrez avoids a complete identification between the two by making distinctions that introduce religious dimensions of "sin" and "salvation" into the process of permanent liberation. But in either case the distinctions serve to reinforce the limit-situation represented by the epiphanic vision. The distinction between partial and fundamental alienation presupposes that sin is an evil reality not reducible to "oppressive structures"—which is overcome ultimately only through divine intervention. The distinction between partial and total fulfillment presupposes that salvation is a reality constituting the "ultimate level" of liberation, which can be possessed only as the "gift" of Christ the Liberator. In either case, the distinctions represent limit-situations in that they define dimensions of the process that are not amenable to the limit-acts of ''man.'' Granted, these limit-situations are not the object of systematic investigation in Gutiérrez's theology; nevertheless, they are presupposed as real if these distinctions are to be regarded as more than merely verbal.

Once these limit-situations are identified, they must be decoded as obstacles to liberation. A consistent application of the logic of conscientization would have to criticize them as a final residue of "oppressor consciousness." Liberation theology responds to the Marxist critique of religion, in other words, by trying to dissociate Christianity from its historic ties to oppression. Its strategy is to make a great leap forward into the praxis of liberation. Nevertheless, if Freire and Marx are right about theory and praxis, this leap cannot be made successfully if liberation theology still presupposes limit-situations in its theoretical framework. The conscientization of Christianity remains incomplete, so long as these limit-situations are left uncriticized. The logic of conscientization requires this criticism of the theory despite the rhetorical impressiveness of Gutiérrez's politicization of salvation-history. To rely ultimately even on a liberating God for help in the struggle is to prevent the emergence of a "new man." The "opium of the people" has not yet worn off completely.

If the epiphanic vision is a residue of oppressor consciousness, what happens once Gutiérrez's theology is conscienticized consistently? Liberation theology will be seen as a transitional phase in the process of permanent liberation, a phase made practically necessary by certain historical peculiarities of the Latin American reality. Given the legacy of Catholicism in Latin America, liberation theology will be tolerated as a subjectivist rhetoric having obvious practical advantages at this stage of the struggle. Decoding this rhetoric would mean the demythicization of liberation theology. It would entail, first, completing the process in which the themes of liberation and salvation are made identical, and then formalizing the theme of salvation to the point where its meaning is reducible to the dialectical vision. Nor would this process require any dramatic revision of liberation theology. Since its concepts are partially conscienticized already, the process would simply require consistent follow-through on the method of this theology.

Conscienticizing liberation theology would be fairly simple, given the ambiguity of these concepts, or the instability of their reference. Take, for example, Gutiérrez's discussion of "three principle reasons" for a "vigorous repudiation of poverty." His reasons are given in the context of a partial conscientization of the church's teaching, which traditionally commends poverty. "Poverty," he says, "contradicts the very meaning of the *Mosaic religion*, . . . goes against *the mandate of Genesis*," and is incompatible with a vision of "man" as "*the sacrament of God*" (Gutiérrez, 1973:294–95). The reference to Mosaic religion elaborates on the meaning of the Exodus paradigm, itself the result of a partial conscientization. More to the point is what he does with "*the mandate of Genesis*." Here the reference is to the text which declares that "man" is made "to the image and likeness of God," a text which is also the source of Niebuhr's reflections on the *imago Dei* in human nature. Gutiérrez interprets it as follows:

Man is created in the image and likeness of God and is destined to dominate the earth. Man fulfills himself only by transforming nature and thus entering into relationships with other men. Only in this way does he come to a full consciousness of himself as the subject of creative freedom which is realized through work. The exploitation and injustice implicit in poverty make work into something servile and dehumanizing. Alienated work, instead of liberating man, enslaves him even more. [Gutiérrez, 1973:295]

The nucleus of this interpretation is almost a paraphrase of Freire's notion of the "new man": "Man fulfills himself only by transforming nature and thus entering into relationships with other men. Only in this way does he come to a full consciousness of himself as the subject of creative freedom which is realized through work." So intimate is the connection between the "new man" and "the image of God" that complete demythicization would proceed from this nucleus and simply make identifications where correlations once stood. The residual elements of religious myth, such as the allusion to "man" as *"the sacrament of God,"* would then be formalized to the point that their reference would become indistinguishable from the trust in the people generated by a revolutionary enthusiasm. Once the code is broken, liberation theology may be overcome and employed constructively as a "subjectivist" rhetoric still useful in this transitional phase of the struggle.

Judging from their published remarks, neither Freire nor Gutiérrez is aware of the possibility of conscienticizing liberation theology. But is there any way to restrict the logic of conscientization once it is set in motion? Certain strategies are apparent. On the one hand, the theory of conscientization might be reformulated so as to admit a distinction between genuine and illusory limit-situations. But such a reformulation would mean the recognition of limits to action and limits to critical consciousness, in other words, limits to human freedom and the possibilities of liberation. To recognize such limits as genuine would open up the possibility for a constructive philosophy of religion, but it would also mean abandoning the dialectical vision and the critique of religion founded upon it. Conscientization, in short, could not be so reformulated and still remain conscientization. On the other hand, liberation theology might criticize the method of conscientization and clarify its own content by making explicit the genuine limit-situations that it presupposes. Its correlation between the themes of liberation and salvation, its rule for interpreting them according to the consent of human beings and the will of God, and its distinctions between partial and fundamental alienations and fulfillments would be explained by reference to religious limit-situations and interpreted by theological limit-concepts of a metaphysical, historical, or anthropological nature. But such a clarification would mean giving up the distinctive agenda of liberation theology and retreating toward Catholic progressivism. In view of these consequences, it is unlikely that liberation theologians would abandon their methodological commitment to conscientization.

This experiment in conscienticizing liberation theology could be dismissed as an academic exercise were it not for the actual development of this theology since Gutiérrez's seminal work. In a precarious situation marked by polarization within the church and political repression in society, two trends have emerged among liberation theologians: one conservative, the other radical. The conservative trend is represented by Jon Sobrino's *Christology at the Crossroads*. By invoking the theme of liberation without the critical perspective of conscientization, Sobrino's theology becomes indistinguishable in its structure and content from that of some European progressives. The radical trend is represented by Juan Luis Segundo's *The Liberation of Theology*. More than any other writer, Segundo grasps the implications of conscientization. His proposal furthers the demythicization of liberation theology by abandoning the epiphanic vision of Catholic Incarnationalism. These trends will be examined in the next chapter. For the moment they serve as evidence of the conceptual instability of this theological model from its very beginning in Gutiérrez's seminal work. The significance of this instability will now be explored through a comparison with the theology of Christian realism.

Practical Theologies in Conflict

Christian realism and liberation theology represent two Christian world-visions. But while the visions diverge as two different ways of being Christian in the world, the conflict between these theologies cannot be reduced simply to the typical differences between Catholic and Protestant thought. The issue goes deeper to a problem common to both, the question of whether the meaning of Christianity's common confession of faith that God acts in history can be expressed coherently. Christian theologians are committed in principle to an affirmative answer to this question. They differ, however, regarding their basic understanding of both the question and its possible answers.

The conflict between Christian realism and liberation theology may be symbolized as the difference between a paradoxical vision and an epiphanic vision interpreted dialectically. Christian realism affirms that God's relation to history is paradoxical. God is a Hidden God who both fulfills and transcends the meaning of history. His action in history must be understood as manifest in the paradoxical situation of the human self. In other words, God acts in a hidden manner through human agents who have opened their hearts to him in repentance, humility, and faith. This activity is never known with certainty: God is never possessed, neither in mystical illumination, nor in rational demonstration, nor in the sacramental life of the church; but his "abiding truth" may be recognized in "moments of prayerful transcendence" shaped imaginatively by Christian myth. God thus remains a Hidden God even in the lives of those who sincerely seek to live the paradox. By contrast, Gutiérrez's theology of liberation affirms that God's relation to history is not hidden but is directly manifest in the struggles of the oppressed. God is revealed in the Exodus, a paradigm for all other epiphanies insofar as he espouses the cause of oppressed peoples and their historic struggle for liberation. God's action in history is to be understood dialectically, since it is known only through participation in this struggle. The meaning of history is hidden only to those who refuse to act in "solidarity with the oppressed."

The conflict between these two world-visions is expressed in diverging theological strategies. Christian realism represents the abiding truth in Christian myth by constructing a theological anthropology that defines the meaning of its theology of history. Liberation theology is a theology of history constructed by conscienticizing the biblical narratives of salvation-history. The difference between these two strategies lies in the role of theological anthropology. Christian realism uses this genre to establish the reference point for its theological concepts and to summarize their theoretical meaning. These have meaning in terms of an allegedly universal structure of human selfhood, defined as the paradox of finiteness and freedom, which represents a genuinely religious limit-situation for human individuals and groups. All of Niebuhr's Christian interpretations of human nature and history presuppose it. By contrast, the praxis of basic communities serves as the reference point for liberation theology. The Exodus paradigm and other conscienticized biblical narratives provide historical analogies between this praxis and salvation-history. The genre of theology of history is used, in short, to legitimate this praxis as part of "the overriding will of God." Thus basic communities learn to overcome oppressive limit-situations through limit-acts. That is liberation theology's aim, at least.

Why is theological anthropology so central to Christian realism and so suspect to liberation theology? The reasons stem from the theoretical requirements of the conflicting world-visions.

Liberation theology suppresses this genre because it is incompatible with conscientization. Granted, the epiphanic vision of Catholic Incarnationalism customarily employs theological anthropology to explain what it means for God to become "man." But the tension between this epiphanic vision and the dialectical vision underlying conscientization entails a different approach. "Critical reflection on praxis" has no place for abstract doctrines of human nature. Praxis is historical, and critical reflection must be appropriate to the structures of meaning inherent in the historical moment. Theological anthropology pretends to transcend the historical moment by offering generalizations about human nature claiming a universal validity. Such abstractions can only be regarded as instances of "myth-making irrationality," since they promote an illusory form of transcendence. This methodological suspicion is reinforced by a critical reading of the Bible. In the hermeneutic circle created by conscienticizing biblical narratives, theological anthropology must be rejected as an example of "excessive spiritualization." By formulating abstract doctrines about the religious limit-situation, unliberated theologians will neglect precisely those historical analogies that make the Exodus experience so paradigmatic. Biblical narratives will be read only for their wisdom concerning human nature, and not for the hope they proclaim in history.

Christian realism, on the other hand, uses this genre to spell out the meaning of its paradoxical vision as a norm for human thought and action. The vision of a Hidden God acknowledges a paradoxical form of transcendence as real. Consequently, limits are recognized and possibilities defined. A religious imagination sensitive to the self's paradoxical reality as both finite and free is cultivated as a resource for Christian social action. Far from being "abstract," theological anthropology outlines a substantive interpretation of Christianity. Within the circle of faith and experience drawn by Niebuhr's "mythical approach," the biblical narratives of Creation, the Fall, and Atonement define the human situation as at bottom "a conflict of grace and pride." Since this conflict is not exhausted by any historical analogies in the external order of events, it must be situated in human nature in a way that is immanent to all human events and yet transcendent to them all as well. This must be true for each individual and every human community. Thus the paradoxical vision requires a theological anthropology to define the religious limit-situation of selves and societies. Christian social action is possible only if this situation is recognized for what it is.

The formal difference represented by the use or the suppression of theological anthropology is the key to certain substantive differences in theological interpretation. The most significant of these are their diverging perspectives on Creation and the Fall. Christian realism does not read these myths in terms of the Exodus paradigm. Instead of being "a work of Yahweh in history, a work within time," they represent a poetic expression of the fundamental limit-situation presupposed by all of history. Niebuhr once used the term *Urgeschichte* (Niebuhr, 1937a:25) to distinguish Christian realism's approach to them. As "primordial" or "foundational" history, *Urgeschichte* represents a mythical orientation to the background conditions of all historical acting and thinking. By construing these myths in this way, Niebuhr finds their meaning in human nature's creation as the "image of God" and its corruption through "sin." Creation and the Fall thus do not initiate history in Gutiérrez's sense, but describe its fundamental problem in mythical terms themselves amenable to substantive elaboration in a theological anthropology. By contrast, Gutiérrez incorporates these myths into the narrative structure governed by the Exodus paradigm. They confirm the fact that history is a struggle for liberation. Theological anthropology, in short, allows Niebuhr to establish a clear—even if disputable—reference point for Christian realism's claims concerning the religious dimension of the good and the evil experienced in history. "Sin" and "grace" therefore become meaningful categories for interpreting human experience. Lacking any similar framework for interpreting limit-situations, Gutiérrez's reading of the Exodus paradigm fails to provide a coherent basis for distinguishing between "partial" and "fundamental" alienations and liberations. Unless a substantively theological distinction between these can be established, his theology of history will remain curiously ambiguous in focus.

Even more intriguing are the differences between the two theologies of history. These differences are evident in their respective interpretations of the meaning of Exodus, the prophets, and the ministry of Jesus. The Exodus experience is paradigmatic for liberation theology; it is not so for Christian realism. The paradigmatic status of Exodus is evident in that the prophets are treated primarily as an elaboration of its meaning and an extension of its promise, while the ministry of Jesus is seen as the key to its ultimate fulfillment in history. By contrast, if anything in history has paradigmatic status for Christian realism, it is the cross of Christ. Thus both the Exodus experience and the legacy of the prophets are subordinated to the supreme paradox of a Suffering Messiah. The meaning of Exodus therefore manifests the logic of prophetic Messianism, exhibiting the ambiguity of both the "egoistic-nationalistic" and "ethical-universalistic" ideal types, which in turn serves to heighten the tension represented by the "supra-ethical religious element" as dramatized by the prophets. Niebuhr's understanding of their message is roughly similar to Gutiérrez's formulation of it: "to know God is to do justice." But in light of the persistent failure to do either, the prophets, for Niebuhr, deliver this message as a terrible judgment upon Israel in particular and human history in general, one that raises the question "how history can be anything more than judgment, which is to say, whether the promise of history can be fulfilled at all." "Ethical-universalism," in short, gives way to a "supra-ethical religious" dimension, which clearly recognizes that power and goodness cannot be perfectly reconciled in history. The ministry of Jesus is viewed as an "unexpected reinterpretation" of prophetic Messianism where the focus shifts from historical fulfillment to the religious problem of ultimate reconciliation with God. The cross of Christ, in other words, symbolizes Atonement, an ultimately paradoxical assurance of God's mercy, of a fulfillment of history that lies beyond history itself.

These differences regarding the meaning of the episodes of salvation-history result in two different perspectives on history as a whole. For Christian realism, history is an interim in which the conflict of grace and pride confirms the paradoxical logic of the cross. For liberation theology, history is a struggle in which the promises of the Exodus paradigm are to be fulfilled ultimately through the work of Christ the Liberator. The key to these perspectives lies in the control of meaning afforded by Christian realism's theological anthropology. Niebuhr's theology of history merely serves to illustrate the limit-situation already defined by it. As a symbol of the interim, the cross thus has direct reference to the plight of the human self confronted by the Hidden God, and invites that self to live the human paradox in humility and faith. It expressly criticizes as illusory any hopes for liberation in history that aspire to overcome that paradox. Gutiérrez's theology of history, by contrast, is a narrative proclaiming the liberating God's role in overcoming limit-situations of oppression. By conscienticizing that narrative, Gutiérrez allows the basic communities to identify their aspirations with the fulfillment promised by Christ the Liberator. The differences between Niebuhr and Gutiérrez at this point are substantive and clear.

In evaluating the relative merits of these two theologies, such substantive differences are less important than the theoretical consistency of the constructions based on them. For while there is no absolute perspective from which either perspective might be condemned as heresy, there are criteria of internal coherence and relative adequacy by which these theologies may be judged. The arguments suggesting that Christian realism is a more coherent model than liberation theology need not be repeated here; nevertheless, at this point two questions regarding their relative adequacy may be introduced—one theoretical, the other practical. The theoretical issue is the way in which these theologies respond to the problem posed by critical history in their respective readings of the Bible. The practical one involves a conflict over the role of religious transcendence in human action.

Critical history challenges theology to be intellectually honest in its use of biblical narrative. If the events alleged in the Bible cannot be verified, then theologians cannot present them as if they were historical fact. Since theology is not a paraphrase of history, but a recreation of Christianity's practical meaning for today, the burden of intellectual honesty is minimally discharged by taking care not to contradict the more or less assured results of critical history. Even this minimum entails enormous theoretical difficulties, but at the same time it presupposes that historians do not dictate what theology should be. Theologians, in other words, are free to respond to the challenge in any number of ways that might be consistent with their tasks. This generalization is reflected in the different strategies of Christian realism and liberation theology. The burden of proof that they accept in their differing approaches to biblical narrative represent two different responses to critical history.

Christian realism's mythical approach presupposes a clear awareness of the problem created by critical history, while liberation theology's conscientization of salvation-history does not. Christian realism in principle accepts the findings of critical historical scholarship, which cast doubt on many of the historical claims of the Bible. Interpreting the story of Creation as a historical account, for example, is rejected as taking it "literally but not seriously." Furthermore, Niebuhr understands myth not in opposition to historical fact, but as a form of poetic expression that uniquely serves to convey a moral or religious orientation for action in history. The religious meanings of the biblical narratives, in short, are not strictly tied to considerations of critical history. They disclose "abiding truths" that must be interpreted theologically. Finally, his distinction between "primitive myth" and "permanent myth" is simply an attempt to mark the difference between historical reminiscence, legend, and fable, on the one hand, and the "abiding truth" that Christian communities have discerned in these narratives, on the other. Gutiérrez, by contrast, does not explain the reasons for understanding salvation-history as paradigmatic of real history. Although he does base his scheme on the work of various theologians and biblical interpreters, he nowhere interrogates them concerning the discrepancies between fact and meaning in biblical history. Thus he accepts as historical fact conscienticized redescriptions of biblical events, which have been stripped of their miraculous elements but not their essentially theological structure. The structure of *Heilsgeschichte* is modified only by the assertion that salvation consists in an ultimate liberation in history. Thus salvation-history is not myth for Gutiérrez, but a series of real events that provide a privileged perspective on the meaning of history as a whole.

As these differences suggest, critical history presents a different theoretical challenge for the two theologies. By adopting a "mythical approach" Niebuhr concedes in principle any historical claims for these narratives. But while he thus tries to distinguish the "truth" of history and myth, he must also interpret their convergence in the figure of Jesus Christ. Whether his "historical Christology" in fact conforms to the criteria that he accepts in principle remains an unresolved—though hardly unresolvable—difficulty. Conscienticizing biblical narratives, on the other hand, compounds the critical problem for liberation theology. Not only must the details of these narratives possess a high degree of historical accuracy for Guitérrez's "analogies" to be meaningful, but also the paradigmatic relationship between salvation-history and real history must work for liberation theology to hold a genuine promise for historical praxis. But Gutiérrez can make good on neither of these claims and still remain accountable to critical history—unless, of course, he concedes that his theology of history is really the retelling of a religious myth about history. The theoretical issue involved in judging the relative adequacy of these theologies is thus a choice between a strategy that for all its weaknesses still addresses the critical problem and one that mistakenly assumes that the problem is solved by conscientization.

The practical issue, to conclude this chapter, is the role of religious transcendence in human action. The two world-visions offer two different perspectives on the nature of religious transcendence, which derive from their basic understandings of God and the human situation. Niebuhr's paradoxical vision of the Hidden God reflects the words of the prophet, "Are you not like the Ethiopians to me, O people of Israel? says the Lord" (Amos 9:7). Gutiérrez's epiphanic vision mirrors the meaning of the Divine Name revealed to Moses at Sinai, "*Ehyeh asher ehyeh*, I will be who I will be" Exod. 3:14). If Israel is no more favored than Ethiopia, then God's relationship to the world transcends even the history of his people. Religious transcendence, in other words, may be characterized as "vertical"; it means seeking to live the paradoxical relationship of the temporal and the Eternal in an attitude of repentance, humility, and faith. But if a liberating God will be who he will be, then God's relation to the world is realized primarily in his power to act on behalf of his people. As Gutiérrez remarks in explaining the Divine Name: "A new kind of transcendence is emphasized: God reveals himself as a force in our future and not as an ahistorical being" (Gutiérrez, 1973:165). In that case religious transcendence is primarily "horizontal": it means participating in the struggle for liberation in history.

The practical consequences differ with each perspective. Niebuhr's "vertical" transcendence is more readily recognizable as precisely the sort of "religious disinterestedness" he advocated as indispensable for exorcising "political religion," the demonic aspect of social action symbolized by the twin perils of "fanaticism" and "cynicism." Gutiérrez's "horizontal" transcendence represents the "enthusiasm" that is generated by "solidarity with the oppressed." Although the two forms of transcendence may be consistent with the theologies that espouse them, they seem to be mutually exclusive. Gutiérrez's "enthusiasm" is indistinguishable from the "fanaticism" that Niebuhr renounced as "political religion." Niebuhr's "disinterestedness" is but one of the forms of "excessive spiritualization" that Gutiérrez rejects as an evasion of a Christian attitude of "solidarity with the oppressed." The remaining questions as to which of the two is more Christian in its inspiration or more beneficial in its social consequences cannot be answered without involving one's own irreducibly personal intuitions regarding the two world visions. No doubt here, too, the differences are substantive.[7]

However these differences are resolved, the conceptual instability of Gutiérrez's theology of history by now should be apparent. Some may judge this instability as sufficient reason to dismiss it as a model for practical theology. Others may admit the difficulties involved, but also may see some advantages. What is instability to someone locked into a "static" theology, may appear to others as refreshingly "dynamic." After all, Gutiérrez's theology of history has been acclaimed as something of a Magna Charta. Nevertheless, if the analysis so far has been right, in the next chapter we should expect to see this instability give way to a dilemma, as the logic of conscientization unfolds within the praxis of liberation theology.

NOTES

1. The most significant attempt to work out this reconciliation, namely, Hegel's philosophy of religion, illustrates the difficulty. In order for the reconciliation to be successful, the orthodox view of the Incarnation must be seriously compromised, becoming more a symbol of history's meaning as a whole than the supernatural event traditionally confessed by Christians.

2. The term "world-vision," taken from Lucien Goldmann's *The Hidden God* (1964: 3–21), is introduced here for analytic purposes. In comparing the religious visions at stake in either the conflict between Christian realism and liberation theology or the tensions between liberation theology's method and its content, I am using this term to suggest that these visions are not simply world-views, i.e., intellectual perspectives best understood psychologically or metaphysically, but ideological phenomena whose meaning includes the social structures with which they interact. While this use of the term "world-vision" is not as rigorous as Goldmann's in positing a correlation between the various visions and specific social classes, it remains open to that suggestion. Rather than assume that class conflict explains the difference between Christian realism and liberation theology, or the tension between a conscienticizing evangelization and conscientization, I have made the more restricted claim that these differences may be understood in a sociological context that recognizes the variety of religious communities and the diversity of their institutionalized ministries. Thus in keeping with this use of the term, the tension between the epiphanic and the dialectical vision characteristic of liberation theology may be understood in terms of the conflict between the role of a sacramental priesthood and that of a professional revolutionary vanguard. As was noted in Chapter 6, the tension between these two world-visions is dramatized in the life and death of Camilo Torres.

3. Discussion among liberation theologians concerning the identity of "the people of God" is pursued further in Chapter 9, below.

4. Gutiérrez's invocation of "permanent detachment" is only superficially similar to Niebuhr's "religious disinterestedness." While both represent a sense of transcendence based on Christian eschatology, they have a different theoretical understanding of eschatology and its practical consequences. On the one hand, Niebuhr's paradoxical vision means that his "disinterestedness" is based on a perspective that claims to transcend history as a whole; on the other hand, Gutiérrez's epiphanic vision promises "detachment" from each moment of the historic past by identifying transcendence with the future. Thus liberation theology's "permanent detachment" is only a dialectical moment in its revolutionary "enthusiasm." That Gutiérrez's language at times bears superficial resemblance to Niebuhr's is another indication of the ambiguity of his theology.

5. While Alfredo Fierro's analysis of liberation theology in *The Militant Gospel* notes the same kind of ambiguity that I'm arguing here, his purpose in doing so is to develop a radicalized "historical materialist theology." In my view, his proposal has the same kind of basic inadequacies that I allege against Juan Luis Segundo's "liberation of theology" in Chapter 9.

6. As in the analysis of Niebuhr's "theology of history," the relevant criteria are available in Van Harvey's *The Historian and the Believer*.

7. My own position on this issue, while implicit throughout the book, is made explicit in Chapter 10. What is said there is necessarily sketchy and will require further development if it is to provide the basis for a constructive alternative in practical theology.

9

The Praxis of Liberation Theology

It would be naive, nevertheless, to claim that the revolutionary exigencies in Latin America do not bring with them the danger of oversimplifying the Gospel message and making it a "revolutionary ideology"—which would definitely obscure reality. But we believe that the danger is not averted simply by noting its presence. It is not evaporated by a climate of alarm. It is necessary to look at it face to face and lucidly to analyze its causes as well as the factors which make it important for the Christians committed to the social struggle. Are we not in this position because we have tried to hide the real political implications of the Gospel? Those who—without stating so—neutralized these implications or oriented them for their own benefit are those who have the least authority for giving lessons in evangelical "purity." We cannot expect the true and opportune counsel today to come from those who are "verticalists" in theory and "horizontalists" in practice. The problem exists, but the solution can come only from the very roots of the problem. It is where the annunciation of the Gospel seems to border on submersion into the purely historical realm that there must be born the reflection, the spirituality, and the new preaching of a Christian message which is incarnated—not lost—in our here and now. To evangelize, Chenu has said, is to incarnate the Gospel in time. This time today is dark and difficult only for those who ultimately do not know how or hesitate to believe that the Lord is present in it.
—Gustavo Gutierrez, A Theology of Liberation, *1973*

As the call for a conscienticizing evangelization was heeded by many clergy and laity in Latin America, Gutiérrez's theology became an indispensable point of departure for sincere and courageous persons seeking to form basic communities dedicated to the struggle for liberation. Although the activities inspired by this commitment have been various, in no way do they amount to a unified political movement. The plurality of responses, however, does not mean that the praxis of liberation theology has somehow failed. On the contrary, its purpose from the beginning was to promote grassroots organizations geared to local and regional conditions. Yet within this diversity, the basic communities have faced a new Latin American reality which makes it extremely difficult for them to realize their hopes. Characterized by polarization within the church and repression within society, the post-Medellín period has been a time for martyrs—some in a spiritual sense, others quite literally. Under these adverse conditions the basic communities and their theologians have confronted the antagonisms built into Gutiérrez's proposal for a conscienticizing evangelization.

In what follows I shall try to analyze the results of this confrontation. In light of the praxis of the basic communities, I shall argue that liberation theologians have responded to the ambiguities in Gutiérrez's theology by accepting either horn in what amounts to a dilemma. The instability of his theology, in other words, has been superseded by strategies that threaten either to trivialize liberation or to politicize theology. The burden of this chapter is to show how this dilemma results from the logic of conscientization.

Ethics and Praxis

The reader will detect at this point a break in the parallelism of this analysis of Christian realism and liberation theology. There is no chapter on ethics; instead, the discussion moves from theology to praxis. This break reflects a significant feature of liberation theology: its neglect of theological ethics. The point is not that liberation theology is still at such an embryonic stage that it hasn't had time to construct its ethics. Rather, liberation theology in its most consistent forms deliberately rejects the possibility of theological ethics as incompatible with "critical reflection on praxis." Its criticisms of the strategies of *tercerismo* characteristic of papal social teaching and Maritain's Integral Humanism have already been noted. Now these criticisms must be interpreted in light of the general problem of theological ethics and praxis.

Initially, the charge that liberation theology repudiates the possibility of theological ethics may generate some confusion. Obviously, its commitment to the struggle for liberation is some sort of moral commitment. Indeed, liberation theology exhibits all the general features of practical theology. It seeks to interpret "the signs of the times" in ways that bring religious resources to bear on the problems of social action. Yet it does not construct a theological ethic. What is it, then, about liberation theology that excludes theological ethics from its agenda?

The point can be made by recalling the place of ethics in Niebuhr's theology. While Christian realism in general is meant to make moral and religious sense of "mysteries without which man remains a mystery to himself," its purpose is not exhausted in reinterpreting the existential meaning of the religious vision of a Hidden God. Niebuhr also tried to sketch out a coherent set of moral ideals and principles in light of his understanding of love and justice. His interpretation of love and justice, as we saw in Chapter 4, stems directly from his theological anthropology. The tension between these two virtues is a reflection of the paradox of "original righteousness" and "original sin." Given that paradox, Niebuhr tried to formulate "a theological framework for social ethics" that defines (1) a dispositional ethic of love and justice geared to the moral perplexities of political decision-making, and (2) a set of middle axioms for resolving ideological and social conflicts of interest, principles that in turn presuppose an ethical analysis of the structure and dynamics of the political process: the various forms of power, the psychology of human interests, and the adequacy of political institutions relative to them both. While it is true that Niebuhr did not develop this framework systematically, he did illustrate its use extensively in his writings on American history, society, and politics. In translating Christian realism's religious vision into a more or less coherent framework for making moral choices in politics, Niebuhr thus completed his practical theology with an outline for theological ethics.

There is nothing comparable in liberation theology. The vision of history as a struggle for liberation is given theological legitimation through the figure of Christ the Liberator, and a fundamental moral option, solidarity with the oppressed, is preached with great religious zeal. Typically, liberation theology then refers its converts to the basic communities and their praxis for illumination concerning the actual requirements of solidarity. There is little, if any, ethical reflection on praxis. Situations involving possible moral conflicts for these communities are not investigated with any explicit set of ethical principles. The basic communities apparently are free to develop whatever conscienticized intuitions they can come up with, guided—it would seem—by the direct assistance of the Holy Spirit. When liberation theologians discuss Christian ethical principles in the context of praxis, usually they do so in order to criticize them as ideology. What reasons can be given for this rejection of theological ethics?

In the first place, there are certain theoretical considerations. Consistent with the method of critical reflection on praxis, liberation theology rejects "abstract" forms of moral and religious reasoning. To give either a theological or an ethical interpretation of the normative structures of human nature presupposes transcendent perspectives that are incompatible with conscientization. The theological anthropologies characteristic of neo-orthodox Protestant and progressive Catholic theologies are simply a religious version of the fundamental illusion of modern bourgeois humanism.[1] Moreover, the Bible's hostility toward "excessive spiritualization" also applies to theological ethics. These negative considerations are reinforced by a positive one. Since a conscienticizing evangelization means redefining Christian theology in light of the basic community's experience, its agenda must be focused in terms of those ideological conflicts that help establish the community's distinctive identity. As a result, ethical reflection tends to be exhausted in the critique of ideologies. Once the logic of conscientization is grasped, there is nothing surprising about the repudiation of theological ethics. Any other outcome would be inconsistent with the method of liberation theology.

Second, there are a number of practical considerations specifically related to the situation of praxis in Latin America. Liberation theologians view theological ethics with suspicion because in general they identify it with the academic "moral theology" of the Catholic seminaries and universities. In keeping with their analysis of the logic of *tercerismo,* they criticize moral theology for tacitly presupposing the ideal of "Christendom" and therefore unwittingly supporting various forms of reactionary politics. Moreover, faced with the diversity of the basic communities, liberation theologians generally are trying to maximize the range of options available in praxis. An evaluation of these options presented in an abstract mode of ethical analysis thus is regarded as a threat to the critical prerogatives of the communities actually involved in praxis. In other words, liberation theology's understanding of the unity of theory and praxis is subverted unless such evaluations as are offered remain *ad hoc* and open-ended. All the same, their hostility toward abstract ethical analysis is not incompatible with a zeal for criticizing Christian groups not acting in solidarity with the oppressed. Since the practices of those groups are necessarily distorted by alienation and motivated by illusory ideologies, they must be criticized continually in order to minimize the confusions that inevitably mark the difficult path of conscienticizing evangelization.

It cannot be said, therefore, that liberation theology lacks visibility in the area of theological ethics because it is still in a preliminary phase of development. On the contrary, its context and method, and the theological horizon that it constructs from them, all entail a rejection of the procedures and assumptions of theological ethics. Consequently, the significant feature of liberation theology is that it proceeds directly from praxis to theology and back again. Such a process of "critical reflection" ensures that this theology will be more dynamic than Catholic moral theology traditionally has been. But this very dynamism only increases the problem of conceptual instability. Since liberation theology begins and ends with praxis, it is to praxis that we must return to see how the resulting ambiguity is being resolved.

The Struggle Marginalized

The praxis of liberation in the post-Medellín period has developed under increasingly difficult circumstances. Both church and society have experienced changes that make the situation of basic communities desperate, if not tragic. The political climate has shifted: the once euphoric expectation of a new era has cooled considerably. As the enthusiasm inspired initially by the success of the Cuban Revolution and the failure of the Alliance for Progress has waned, the personal risks of those acting in solidarity with the oppressed have increased dramatically. Basic human rights are being violated as a matter of course. In the new Latin American reality, the "state of siege" has become a way of life.

The basic communities in many places now find themselves confronted by the ideology of national security and the reality of repressive military regimes. Modeled on recent Brazilian experience, these regimes are dedicated to stimulating economic growth while imposing a moratorium on political and social change. This moratorium has meant the suspension of basic democratic political institutions and the relentless persecution of all political forces opposed to the government. Frequently it also results in a significant restriction in the church's freedom of movement. Continual surveillance and severe harassment have dogged the steps of Catholic progressives as well as radicals inspired by liberation theology. Conservative forces hostile to both have been strengthened within the church.

The strategy followed by the national-security regimes has been to isolate the social activists from the rest of the church, in order to make them even more vulnerable to repression.[2] Once isolated and discredited, socially activist religious and clergy may be viewed as infidels who have betrayed their spiritual vocations. No longer recognized as "sacred persons," they may be tortured and murdered—like any other individual considered a threat to national security. This appalling situation has placed the church on the defensive, and has heightened the ambiguity of its own response to liberation theology and the basic communities.

An organized campaign against liberation theology thus has emerged from this atmosphere of defensiveness within the church. Policies authorized by the Medellín documents are being substantially modified in light of the new Latin American reality, now governed by the fear of Communist infiltration. Far from representing the inevitable backlash that accompanies too rapid an advance in the pace of social change, this campaign evidently has been the work of pressure groups exploiting the church's polarization. The Belgian Jesuit Roger Vekemans, who heads the Center for the Study of Development and Integration in Latin America (CEDIAL), for example, has been identified as the source of a formidable and often unscrupulous effort to "quarantine the contagion" of liberation theology, both in Latin America and in Europe. According to some observers,[3] Vekemans has been very effective among conservative circles in Germany and in the Vatican, especially in linking liberation theology with the much feared possibility of Eurocommunism.

Against liberation theology Vekemans brings the following charges: (1) a thinly veiled attempt to baptize Marxist-Leninism, liberation theology is really a "theology of revolution"; (2) it has abandoned the heritage of a genuinely Catholic spirituality in favor of a socialist humanism; (3) it encourages a social activism among priests that is incompatible with their true vocation. Given its rhetorical excesses and conceptual confusion, as well as the cult of the revolutionary martyrs Che Guevara and Camilo

Torres, and the solemn pronouncements on Marxism as the uniquely appropriate mode of social analysis, many conservative Christians find these charges plausible. Nevertheless, liberation theology cannot be dismissed as a "theology of revolution" if careful attention is paid to its relation to the basic communities. There an open-ended commitment to the struggle for liberation geared to the immediate needs of local situations remains the norm for Christian praxis. But this diversity in matters of strategy cannot be reconciled with the sinister conspiracy that Vekemans imagines. A theology of revolution responds to a single global imperative and functions as a religious legitimation for it. But while liberation theology is open to revolution in ways that differ significantly from other Christian perspectives, its purpose is not simply to provide religious legitimation. More precisely, its praxis is defined as an effort to promote and sustain basic communities in an objectively revolutionary situation.

There can be little doubt, however, that the effort to "quarantine the contagion" within the church and society is marginalizing both the praxis and the theological reflection of these communities. In some areas, like Brazil, the basic communities now provide one of the few means for organizing the masses and allowing them a modicum of political visibility. In other places, they now are identified as a Christian elite, composed of university students and members of the professional classes dedicated to social justice and more intimate forms of Christian community. As a result, "critical reflection on praxis" has focused on the tension implicit in the difference between "masses" and "elites." On the one hand, there are some who, despite the marginalization, still see the basic communities as a nucleus from which the masses represented by both church and society may once more be evangelized; but on the other hand, precisely because of the marginalization, there are others who see themselves as a remnant called out from the church to struggle for liberation. The theological meaning of these diverging views is first apparent in ecclesiology.

Who Are the People of God?

In keeping with the epiphanic vision that he inherited from Catholic Incarnationalism, Gutiérrez proclaims "the Church: the sacrament of history." This slogan is based on the expectation that the church as an institution will follow the lead of the basic communities in a renewal inspired by a conscienticizing evangelization. The church as an institution is to side with the oppressed in the class struggle, even as it proclaims its witness to universal brotherhood (Gutiérrez, 1973:255–78). In this way it will participate in Christ's "new creation," thereby becoming "a new chosen people, which this time includes all humanity." Gutiérrez's utopian hope for the church does not envision the polarization of masses and elites. On the contrary, the tensions between the two are obscured by his ecclesiological reflections on "the sacrament of history."

Although his ecclesiology is dominated by this theme, Gutiérrez also speaks of the church as "the People of God," a term hallowed by its association with the Exodus paradigm. He uses this slogan typically in analyzing the role of the church in the process of liberation. It provides a way of introducing the question of institutional strategies by which the church participates in the struggle (Gutiérrez, 1973:102). Once again, the ambiguity of Gutiérrez's correlation of "salvation" and "liberation" is reflected in the use of these two terms. "The sacrament of salvation" has meaning within the context of the generative theme of salvation; "the People of God," in the context of liberation. But with the polarization that marked the post-Medellín period, the meaning of "the People of God" has become controversial.

"The People of God"—originally a biblical designation for Israel in its special relationship to Yahweh—was taken up by Vatican II to indicate the mission of the church throughout history. The church is called to be "the People of God," a community of believers drawn from all nations and historical epochs, united in their loyalty to the gospel. But in liberation theology the term has taken on a specific political reference. "The People of God" are identified with the biblical *Anawim*, "the poor of Yahweh," whose poverty consists sometimes in social deprivation, sometimes in a religious spirit of humility and trust in God, but most often in a combination of both. To clarify the meaning of the *Anawim*, the term then undergoes conscientization: its reference is established by an appeal to the semantics of the struggle for liberation. There the term "people" frequently connotes leftist political sympathies. "The people" are the lower classes—the oppressed—and a "popular government" is one concerned to redress their grievances. Understanding the church as "the People of God," therefore, becomes a warrant for identifying the church with the oppressed. A "popular church," as opposed to the hierarchical-institutional church, is one that is for "the people." It is based on solidarity with the oppressed. This shift of meaning from Vatican II's "abstract" use of the term, of course, is another example of liberation theology's political hermeneutics of the gospel. The theological vocabulary achieves a new relevance as its concrete meaning is made explicit.

Once "the People of God" is identified with the popular church, it becomes a way of expressing ecclesiological tensions between the church and the basic communities. The Chilean theologian Pablo Richard, for example, criticized the preliminary documents of CELAM's Puebla conference[4] for using the term "people" as if it referred to "an all-inclusive social and political entity, beyond class differences and contradictions. It is an abstraction, undifferentiated, homogeneous and non-conflictive. It is in fact a geo-political totality much like the idea of 'nation' in the doctrine of national security" (Richard, 1978: 44). Richard's point is that the failure to recognize the concrete meaning of "the People of God" is willy-nilly to support the ideology of national security. "The people" becomes an all-inclusive term that mythicizes the reality of class conflict, in a manner similar to "the nation." On the other hand, Richard admits that there is a risk in identifying "the People of God" with the perspective of the oppressed: "the popular church . . . being the church of and for the poor, would have the character of a sect, contrary to the universal character and mission of the church" (Richard,1978:42). But this risk is dismissed as "abstract and ideological," since it involves not an "ecclesiological contradiction," but the "ecclesiological consequences" of the political situation in which the church seeks to be "the lived church of Christ." Richard, in other words, appeals to "the judgment of Christ against all sin, oppression or alienation" and the hope that "the church which rises from the people calls together the whole of humanity" (Richard, 1978:42–43). In short, the universal aspirations of the basic communities outweigh their sectarian tendencies.

Nevertheless, the sectarian logic implied by this view of "the People of God" is not so easily overcome. The risk of sectarianism is based not on the "political contradiction" defining the current situation of praxis, but on the special ecclesiological function that Richard envisions for the oppressed classes. In the popular church, the poor are regarded not as "objects either of evangelization or of the church's preferential love," but as "subjects who evangelize and build up the church" (Richard, 1978:42).

What does it mean to say that the poor are "subjects who evangelize" in the context of a conscienticizing evangelization? It can only mean that the poor are "a chosen people" within the church as a whole. Since the poor are defined as the oppressed locked in a class struggle with their oppressors, to make of them a chosen people means ascribing to them a certain cognitive and moral privilege simply on the basis of their class status. This is the "concrete meaning" proposed for "the People of God." It is they who determine not only the church's agenda for social justice and peace, but also the very definition of the church and its membership.

In making explicit the concrete meaning of "the People of God," Richard is simply following through on the logic of conscientization. If solidarity with the oppressed is the ultimate criterion for practical theology, this can only mean a cognitive privilege for the perspective of the poor. But is this not precisely an example of sectarianism, when viewed from the perspective of Catholic ecclesiology? In the hierarchical-institutional church the bishops, in communion with the pope, are the "subjects who evangelize" in virtue of their sacramental ordination. No special privilege in this matter is granted to any social class. While Catholic ecclesiology does not rule out the church's participation in the struggles of oppressed peoples, it does mean that the poor, defined as a social class, are not in a position to determine either the church's agenda or its membership. If the poor are "subjects who evangelize" in the ecclesiological sense proposed by Richard, then the basic communities must be regarded as sectarian in character.

All the same, Pablo Richard has identified the central issue confronting the basic communities and their praxis. In light of liberation theology, how are these communities to be related to the structure of the Catholic church? Surely they were authorized by the bishops at Medellín, but since then have they developed in an independent direction? Do they now represent Christian sects increasingly alienated from the church? Most liberation theologians either deny that the alienation exists or ascribe it to the church's continuing involvement with the social *status quo*. It is diagnosed as a "political contradiction," soon to be overcome by further praxis. This in essence is the response not only of Richard but also of Gustavo Gutiérrez. Their hope is that the basic communities will succeed in winning the masses to the cause of Christ the Liberator, so that the Catholic church may become in truth "the People of God." Given this aspiration, they tend to minimize the consequences of marginalization for the basic communities and their theology.

One theologian, however, has adopted a more tough-minded approach, and appears willing to accept the consequences of marginalization. Juan Luis Segundo's *The Liberation of Theology* is an attempt to radicalize liberation theology in light of the new Latin American reality. By continuing the program of conscienticizing evangelization, he goes a long way toward resolving the central ambiguities of liberation theology.

Segundo's proposal is based on a critical sociological analysis of the basic communities and their function in the struggle for liberation. Conscientization and praxis require high levels of personal commitment and energy that are beyond the capacities of most people. The basic communities, therefore, must not aspire to convert "the masses," but "to create minorities" (Segundo, 1976:210). To fail to take account of the "inertia" that dominates the conduct of "the masses," when reflecting on the basic communities and their praxis, is to fall prey to romanticism, a mystical identification with "the people" similar to the ideology of Peronism in Argentina. In arguing for the elitist character of the basic communities, Segundo must also address the problem of sectarianism. But his response to it is less evasive than the good intentions of Richard and Gutiérrez. He begins by denouncing the "verbal terrorism" (Segundo, 1976: 185) that enforces the pejorative meaning traditionally attached to the term "sect." The New Testament provides no warrant for this hostile attitude, but the history of Catholicism as a "Church of the masses" does. By exposing the ideological distortions in Catholicism's claim as a "universal religion," he intends to conscienticize the problem so that the basic communities may be free to create "an elite of mature Christians."

Segundo's frank recognition of the sectarian character of the basic communities has certain crucial implications for praxis. There is a greater sense of sociological realism about what political strategies and tactics are open to them. The inertia of the masses must be "manipulated" by the basic communities to revolutionize the condition of society as a whole. Arguing from the theories of Vladimir Lenin and Ortega y Gasset, Segundo insists that the proper role of an elite is to master the "mechanisms" of inertia in order to control them. (Segundo, 1976: 219). Since the basic communities are analogous to Lenin's "revolutionary vanguard," they are to channel the "spontaneities" of the masses—especially the aspirations expressed in "popular religion"—into the struggle for liberation. Not surprisingly, in order to fulfill this role, the basic communities must maintain the discipline appropriate to a vanguard. The strategic parallel to Leninism becomes most striking as the question of safeguarding "revolutionary consciousness" thus becomes the critical imperative guiding Segundo's proposal for the liberation of theology.

The reader will recall that the burden of this chapter is to show that the development of liberation theology follows the logic of conscientization. Although Gutiérrez's partial conscientization of Catholic Incarnationalism does succeed in politicizing salvation-history, Segundo's consistent conscientization will mean its virtual eclipse. Even so, this review of the situation of praxis in the post-Medellín period suggests that the logic of conscientization does not unfold in a vacuum. On the contrary, liberation theology was radicalized as the basic communities were marginalized. Nowhere is the impact of this process more evident than in the attempt to express the ecclesiological identity of these communities. Once the ecclesiology of Vatican II was rejected as "abstract," and "the People of God" identified with the oppressed classes, the way was open for a frank recognition of the sectarian character of these communities. That realization, in my opinion, constitutes a moment of truth for liberation theologians. When the ecclesiological implications of solidarity with the oppressed are grasped, liberation theologians must either advance with Segundo into the radical problematic posed by "an elite of mature Christians" or they must retreat theologically into a thematic treatment of "liberation" that ignores these implications. In the sections that follow I shall sketch out these options and try to interpret them as the dilemma of liberation theology.

Theologizing Liberation

Jon Sobrino's *Christology at the Crossroads: A Latin American Approach* is an example of what happens when these ecclesiological tensions are ignored. His book is everything that one might expect in a treatise on "historical Christology" today. It is scholarly, systematic, and skillfully worked out as a dialogue with the most advanced Christological thinking of Protestant and Catholic Europe. Nevertheless, it serves as a model for one horn of the dilemma facing liberation theology because it is difficult to determine precisely how it represents a Latin American approach. No doubt, the theme of liberation informs Sobrino's work, and he says many of the same things that other liberation theologians say about the relevance of the historical Jesus to praxis. The difficulty is not so much what he says, but whether what he says is compatible with the method of conscientization.

Sobrino's Christology is a form of conscienticizing evangelization in only a superficial sense. Critical reflection on praxis does inspire his attempt to respond to the charge that "liberation theology has continued to lack any Christology" (Sobrino, 1978:xi). It also helps to focus his "threefold suspicion" against classic treatments of Christology, namely, their tendency to (1) reduce Christ to a sublime abstraction, (2) see him as the embodiment of universal reconciliation, and (3) absolutize him while "neglecting the dialectical side of the matter" (Sobrino, 1978:xv–xvii). And it influences his "almost spontaneous" movement toward a "historical Christology," based on "a clearly noticeable resemblance between the situation here in Latin America and that in which Jesus lived," on the one hand, and that in which "the first Christian communities" interpreted him, on the other (Sobrino, 1978:12–13). Nevertheless, the crucial point of conscientization, its strategy of demythicizing limit-situations to overcome them with limit-acts, is passed over in silence.

The fact that Sobrino makes no mention of conscientization in itself is merely suggestive. More important is his proposal "to comprehend Christ as the limit-reality that provides the total meaning of life and history and that will also help us to interpret our historical experience as a Christian experience" (Sobrino, 1978:347). Clearly, whatever Sobrino means by limit-reality, it is not something to be overcome by limit-acts. While never explicitly defined, the term is used to suggest a "noetic" or epistemological rule for theology. Limit-realities like "transcendence, liberation, love, truth, justice, the sinfulness of the world, and the meaning of history"—in short, the generative themes basic to any practical theology—cannot be intuited "in themselves," but are known from "historical experience." This principle reflects "the dialectical side" of Christology that Sobrino emphasizes in contrast to classic treatments. It means that Christology must be "historical" in the sense that its "objective starting point" is "the historical Jesus" who is encountered by "following his historical life: i.e., through real praxis of faith motivated by hope and love" (Sobrino, 1978: 352). Thus even though the term "limit-reality" is used to explain the agenda for a historical Christology, it does not correspond to Freire's notion of limit-situations. Indeed, if anything, it presupposes that there are genuine limit-situations/limit-realities that Jesus "Christianizes." But unless these limit-realities can be reconciled with Freire's critique of limit-situations, Sobrino's Christology at best is only partially conscienticized.

This point is corroborated by his discussion of "liberation." Sobrino recognizes that contemporary yearnings for liberation are rooted in a process that began with "the Enlightenment, which specifically saw it as human liberation vis-à-vis theology." But there are two phases of the Enlightenment: (1) "the liberation of reason from dogmatic faith (Kant)," and (2) "the liberation of the whole person from a religious outlook that supported or at least permitted social, economic and political alienation (Marx)." In contrast with European Christology, which for the most part addresses the first phase, Latin American Christology responds to the second: "It seeks to show how the truth of Christ is capable of transforming a sinful world into the Kingdom of God" (Sobrino, 1978:349). While this objective expresses the intention of any form of evangelization, the question is whether it is conscienticizing enough. Does it, in fact, really address the challenge of this so-called second phase of the Enlightenment? Even more to the point, can any serious answer to the second phase be given that is not based on a satisfactory response to the first?

An example of this difficulty is Sobrino's attempt to ascribe a "class outlook" to the historical Jesus. His intention in doing this is clear: he seeks to redefine Christian discipleship in a way that answers the objections typical of the second phase, which traditionally dismiss Christianity as an "opium" that obscures the reality of class conflict. But if it can be shown that Jesus acted from a "class outlook," then Christian discipleship means following "his Way" in the class struggle. As Sobrino recognizes, the logic of this answer is valid only if the historical Jesus really had "a class outlook." But as soon as he asserts this as historical fact, he qualifies it by saying that "a class outlook is meant to be somewhat ambiguous . . . in Jesus' case." The reasons he gives unwittingly suggest that this ambiguity is downright equivocation. Jesus' "class outlook" is explained as follows:

> . . . There are certain elements that help us to see what his understanding of justice from a "class outlook" means. First, the poor are the people who understand the meaning of the kingdom best, even though their knowledge and understanding comes by way of contrariety. Second, Jesus reinforces his experience of the necessity for justice through his contact with the poor. Third, Jesus' service to the totality is concretized directly in his service to the poor. Fourth, in his own personal life he experiences poverty. At the very least it is a relative poverty that somehow includes him in the ranks of the poor. Fifth, Jesus undergoes the experience of class-identity, and specifically the consequences of his fellowship with the group known as the poor. The power wielded by the other major group in society is directed against him. [Sobrino, 1978:124]

If this is what Sobrino means by "historical" Christology, it is questionable whether he can respond successfully to the challenge of either the first or the second phase of the Enlightenment. Even assuming that it is historically true that Jesus experienced poverty in his personal life, such experience is not indicative of a "class outlook." Anyone who takes conscientization seriously will have to admit that here Sobrino "mythicizes" both the historical Jesus and the nature of class consciousness.

Other "historical" claims show similar difficulties. For example, he derives the political implications of Jesus' crucifixion from the fact that "he was executed as a Zealot" (Sobrino, 1978:211–12). This dubiously historical inference is qualified by a special understanding of "political": "In short, Jesus' love is political because it is situated in the concrete" (Sobrino, 1978: 214). Thus the political implications of the historical Jesus rest on the assumption that everything "concrete" is "political." And, of course, this is only too true—indeed, trivially true. But Jesus' political implications will have to rest on something more substantive if this historical Christology is to be taken seriously as a guide to politics—either Jesus' or our own.

Even more questionable is his appeal to the Enlightenment's second phase to justify belief in the resurrection of Christ and acceptance of the Christological dogmas of Chalcedon, the standard of Catholic orthodoxy. While the practical challenge of the second phase must be met by Christian praxis, such praxis is also given as the sufficient reason verifying the truth of Christological claims. The resurrection, in short, is believable because praxis requires "a radical hope in the future" (Sobrino, 1978:256). Similarly, the dogmas of Chalcedon may be "verified" by history:

> The dogma of Chalcedon could hardly be eternally valid if, historically speaking, the Christ of Chalcedon did not generate Christians. To put it positively, the ultimate verification of the truth of Chalcedon's christological dogma lies in the course of later history. It is true if we continue to find Christians in later history and in very different cultures and societies, if we continue to find people whose life finds its meaning in pursuing and continuing the life of Jesus and thereby becoming children of God. [Sobrino, 1978:342]

The reasoning here is circular in the bad sense. Granted, a Christian praxis is a necessary condition for responding adequately to the Enlightenment's critique of religion in either phase. But a Christian praxis is meaningful only if Christian claims be true.[5] The fact that believing these claims "generates Christians" testifies to the sincerity of belief, not to its authenticity. The "verification" that Sobrino speaks of may be sufficient for faith, but how it satisfactorily answers the Enlightenment's suspicions against theology as such remains a mystery.

Instead of taking up this point, Sobrino generalizes this strategy by appealing to "orthopraxis" to validate "orthodoxy": "Orthodoxy can be rendered concrete and Christian only through a specific praxis" (Sobrino, 1978: 391), which is the "concrete" following of the historical Jesus. But what is so validated is Catholic orthodoxy "historicized": "God is a trinitarian process that entered into history in the incarnation, immersed itself in the depths of history on the cross, marked out the direction of history in the resurrection, and will attain its ultimate synthesis only when God becomes all in all" (Sobrino, 1978:392). For Sobrino the totality of orthodox Christological affirmations is possible once "the dialectical side of the matter" is recognized.

Christology at the Crossroads thus is a mind-boggling exercise in Christian apologetics, but is it liberation theology? Does it really respond to "the deep yearning for liberation" that "found expression as far back as the Enlightenment"? Can "the liberation of the whole person" be achieved without "the liberation of reason from dogmatic faith"? Sobrino would like to answer the first question with an emphatic Yes, and the second with a resounding No. But whether or not he is entitled to these answers depends on the success of his historical Christology. For this Christology to work, the Way of the historical Jesus must be as he describes it, and the praxis of liberation today must be a "concrete" following of that Way. There are reasons, however, to think that this strategy succeeds only by distorting what fragmentary evidence there is about the historical Jesus or by theologizing contemporary aspirations for liberation to the point where they, too, become abstractions. The distortion is evident in Sobrino's abortive attempt to ascribe a "class outlook" to Jesus. The theologizing is evident when the praxis of liberation becomes synonymous with a life patterned after the Christological formulae of Catholic orthodoxy.

This, indeed, is one way to respond to the marginalization of the basic communities and the conceptual instability of liberation theology. The situation of praxis is invoked as a principle of verification, but the actual tensions that define that praxis—most significantly, the problematic ecclesiological status of these communities—is ignored. The result, in my opinion, is a strange new kind of "academic theology" in which the theme of liberation is displayed prominently, while the method of conscientization that gives this theme its critical cutting edge against both the church and society is either ignored or distorted beyond recognition. Nevertheless, to give it its due, Sobrino's *Christology at the Crossroads* should be read as a contribution to contemporary European theology exploring the kind of project represented among Protestants by Jürgen Moltmann's *The Crucified God* and among Catholics by the Christological sections of Hans Küng's *On Being a Christian*. The three differ among themselves on various points, but they are one in their conception of a historical Christology and its tasks. The only thing distinctively Latin American in Sobrino's approach is that its author happens to teach in El Salvador.

Liberating Theology

The other horn of the dilemma may be represented by Juan Luis Segundo's *The Liberation of Theology*. With Segundo, Gutiérrez's partial conscientization of salvation-history gives way to a consistent conscientization of liberation theology itself. Liberation theology becomes even more open-ended in the direction of an indefinite future process of liberation, and more focused on radicalizing that process among an elite of "mature

Christians.'' The result is a theology without a substantive norm save the process of liberation itself. Salvation-history no longer provides a framework for a political hermeneutics of the gospel. Instead, Segundo proposes a "hermeneutic circle" that relativizes both the formal authority and the substantive content of Christian tradition.

Given this sketch of Segundo's proposal, it may come as a surprise that he finds a warrant for "liberating theology" in the teachings of Jesus. The point to these teachings must not be equated simply with their content, such as the commandment to love our enemies; on the contrary, according to Segundo they must be understood as initiating a "deutero-learning process" by which further insights are generated within the historic struggle for liberation.

In order to clarify the meaning of this shift from the content to the process of Jesus' teaching, Segundo makes a distinction between the faith and the ideology of Jesus. The substantive content of Jesus' teaching is understood as ideology, and is authoritative only for its immediate historical context. The deutero-learning process implicit in the teaching of Jesus is understood as faith, and remains authoritative even for an elite of "mature Christians." Jesus' promise to send the Holy Spirit is taken as an appropriate symbol for this process. Segundo elaborates:

> What will be the relationship between these new ideologies and *faith*, the latter being understood as a divine revelation that entails recognition of its revealer? The logical answer is that the former revealer, Christ, is replaced by the Holy Spirit. But the Spirit is not a visible, identifiable revealer, which would seem to indicate that one can really have faith only in past revelation. The only coherent hypothesis is to have recourse once again to the notion of a *deutero-learning* process, a process of learning to learn. This process is by its very definition the opposite of any sort of deposit, for it involves an unending process of acquiring new pieces of information that multiply the previous store of information. That being the case, the only visible guidepost is the presence or absence of the teacher outside the pupil. At a certain point, however, the external teacher disappears from the scene; yet the internal process of learning goes on continually, based on external experience.

> This seems to be the obvious import of Jesus' promise. The Spirit of truth is not an external teacher as Jesus himself was. Or we might say instead that no external teacher after Christ will add any information to the educational process. The process will go on internally, as the pupil confronts reality with new ideologies. Jesus is saying that one stage of the process is ended, but he is also promising that the process can continue through its own proper means. And those means are nothing else but a succession of ideologies vis-à-vis the concrete problems of history. In short, after Christ history itself is entrusted

with the task of carrying on the process. The Spirit of Christ, that is, the dynamic, intrinsic result of the relevatory education process, ensures a process that will lead to the full and complete truth. [Segundo, 1976:121]

This passage should make clear that conscientization is no longer just a method for correlating the themes of liberation and salvation, but is itself the actual message of salvation.

Nor surprisingly, this attempt to liberate theology entails a different Christology. Unlike some liberation theologians, Segundo does not try to defend a political interpretation of Jesus. He concedes that "Jesus himself seems to focus his message on liberation at the level of interpersonal relationships, forgetting almost completely, if not actually ruling out, liberation vis-à-vis political oppression. The same would seem to apply to Paul and almost all the other writings in the New Testament" (Segundo, 1976: 111). Indeed, in what appears to be a rejection of the Christologies developed by Gutiérrez and Sobrino, Segundo says, "We could maintain that liberation was the only theme of the New Testament, I suppose, but only if we were willing to go in for a great deal of abstraction." He is willing to forgo that sort of intellectual *tour de force* because, for him, Jesus' own political views constitute an ideology that is not binding on the faith of mature Christians one way or another. In short, "the pedagogical intent of the whole scriptural process" (Segundo, 1976:112) is the key to liberation theology, not the contents of scriptural teaching.

While Segundo uses this pedagogical intent to reject historical Christologies that have been only partially conscienticized, he also sees his perspective as an adequate historical interpretation of the Bible. If its significance is not to be missed, interpreters must "rediscover the decisive importance of the (historical) density of the Bible":

Over a period of twenty centuries different faith-inspired encounters took place between human beings and the objective font of absolute truth. All these encounters were historical; hence each one of them was relative, bound up with a specific and changing context. What came to be known or recognized in each of these encounters was an ideology, but that is not what was learned. Through the process people *learned how to learn* with the help of ideologies.

Since conscientization thus must be recognized as the true meaning of the Bible, Christology may be reformulated to reflect this discovery. Segundo continues:

This deutero-learning has its own proper content, and when I say that Jesus had two natures, one human and one divine, I am saying something about the *content* of this learning process. But these contentual items cannot be translated into one or another specific ideology because they belong to a secondary stage or level of meaning. They are essentially methodological symbols. On the one hand they have no direct ideological translation; on the other hand they have no other function but to be translated into ideologies. [Segundo, 1976: 108–9]

But what is the meaning of this intriguing suggestion? Segundo's reference to the Christological formula of Chalcedon is decisive: "When I say that Jesus had two natures, one human and one divine, I am saying something about the *content* of this learning process. . . .They are essentially methodological symbols." This can only mean that the Christological "content" of the Bible is not the revelation of the Incarnation of God in Christ, but the discovery of the deutero-learning process itself. The Chalcedonian formula thus no longer serves as the logical presupposition for an Incarnational theology of Christ the Liberator—as it still does for Gutiérrez and Sobrino. Instead, these "methodological symbols" represent the strategy and tactics of conscientization. Jesus' claim as the authoritative embodiment of Christian faith rests not on the alleged fact that he is the Son of God made "man," but on the quality of his insights into the deutero-learning process.

The consequences of Segundo's "rediscovery" of "the (historical) density of the Bible" may be understood by giving an example:

If God's revelation never comes to us in pure form, if it is always fleshed out in historical ideologies, then we cannot appeal to the historical Jesus in order to throw out the solutions of the Old Testament. If circumstantial conditions and exigencies are decisive, then Jesus' remarks about turning the other cheek in no way correct the command of Deuteronomy to physically exterminate certain foreign peoples.

Our theory, in other words, assumes that there is an empty space between the conception of God that we receive from our faith and the problems that come to us from an every-changing history. So we must build a bridge between our conception of God and the real-life problems of history. This bridge, this provisional but necessary system of means and ends is what we are calling *ideology* here. Obviously each and every ideology presented in Scripture is a human element even though in the intensely unified psychological processes of human beings it may seem to be a direct and straightforward translation of the proper conception of God who has been revealed.

Consider the Israelites who arrived in the promised land. For them the extermination of their enemies was concretely the most clear-cut way of conceiving who God was and what he was commanding in the face of specific historical circumstances. Thus the extermination of enemies was the ideology that faith adopted, with or without critical thought, at that moment in history. And to be logical here, we must say the same thing with regard to the gospel message. When Jesus talked about freely proffered love and nonresistance to evil, he was facing the same problem of filling the void between his conception of God (or perhaps that of the first Christian community) and the problems existing in his age. In short, we are dealing here with another ideology, not with the content of faith itself.

This view of the matter gives liberation theology greater freedom to move, in principle, through the Scriptures and to work with the faith. . . . [Segundo, 1976:116–17]

So that there may be no mistaking his point, let us see how the deutero-learning process approaches the practical problem of violence as discussed in Christian ethics. Consistent with his distinction of faith and ideology, Segundo rejects the opinion that "the risk of wholly gratuitous love" is normative for Christian faith: "The concrete kind of love proclaimed by Jesus constitutes an *ideology*—that is, a concrete system conditioned by history" (Segundo, 1976:155). Faced with today's problems of the "institutionalized violence" and "counter-violence" accompanying the struggle for liberation, Segundo argues that Jesus' ideology of love does not entail an ethic of nonviolence for his disciples. On the contrary, he reasons that love and egotism are opposed as ends and that violence may accompany the realization of either. In fact, *"violence is an intrinsic dimension of any and all concrete love,"* since love is "efficacious" only within the context of the laws and conditions of "inertia" and "energy" operative in history (Segundo, 1976:161). Efficacious love presupposes discrimination of priorities, organization of energy, and struggle against inertia; and each of these activities require some degree of violence.[6] The dynamism of love does not seek to eliminate violence—which is impossible in any case—but "tends in the direction of reducing the quantum of violence required for efficacy to the lowest possible level" (Segundo, 1976:162).

This particular result of the deutero-learning process then is generalized. The dynamism of love does not warrant any set of rules or moral precepts for Christian faith. In fact, the only moral rule Segundo is willing to formulate is *"the end justifies the means"* (Segundo, 1976: 171). Christian ethics is primarily concerned to evaluate ends, and once the end is morally approved, then the appropriate means are best known in reference to "a concrete situation."[7] When liberation, for example, is accepted as the ultimate end for human action, then any means that promotes liberation is also acceptable. In principle there are no means that are intrinsically inappropriate to the struggle for liberation. Not surprisingly, given this view of Christian morality, Segundo has no problem advocating the manipulation of the masses by an elite dedicated to the goal of liberation.[8] None of Jesus' moral teaching stands in the way, since each is "ideological" and therefore relevant only to Jesus' immediate historical context. Nor does any consideration of the intrinsic morality of various means offer a valid basis for criticism, since such considerations are theoretically impossible. Given Segundo's view of means and ends, the only relevant consideration is "efficacy," or success in promoting the end in view.

Segundo's total conscientization thus not only results in the identification (no longer a "correlation") of Christian faith with the deutero-learning process, but also in an interpretation of biblical moral teaching as ideology. The authority of such teaching thereby is relativized so that the process of conscientization may become truly liberated and liberating. Far from shrinking away from this conclusion, Segundo points out that all teachings—including those of liberation theologians—are ideological in the sense that they are not sanctioned by an Absolute, but are subject to the relativities of history. Indeed, one sign of Christian maturity is the ability to recognize the universality of the relationship of faith and ideology, and a willingness to live and die by one's ideology despite its contextual limitations. Segundo's Christian "elite" thus is not called upon to reject ideology and affirm faith—as if this were possible—but to reconstitute faith in new ideologies ever again appropriate to new contexts. The liberation of theology, in short, means incorporating a principle of permanent liberation into theology as the one absolute of faith.

Consistent with his biblical perspective on the deutero-learning process, Segundo finds the decisive warrant for liberating theology summarized in St. Paul's reformulation of the teachings of Jesus:

(a) Only concrete love gives meaning and value to any kind of law existing in the universe (Rom. 13:8–10).

(b) Any and every type of law represents a decisive element for Christian conduct insofar as it points up more or less constant relationships between things and persons. But such laws are not decisive as moral laws (Rom. 14:14). They are decisive as constants in the service of the love-based plans and projects of human beings (1 Cor. 6:12ff; 10:23ff.), since they furnish these projects with criteria for judging what is or is not *expedient* in carrying them out (1 Cor. 10:23–29; Rom. 14:7–9).

(c) Since this desacralizes the law as a static inventory of questions concerning the morality of a given line of conduct, the conduct of the Christian must undergo a basic change. *Faith* rather than the law must serve as the springboard for launching into a new adventure. One's destiny will depend on this venture, but it possesses no *a priori* criteria established in advance. The Christian must accept the riskiness of projects that ever remain provisional and will often go astray (Gal. 5:6 and *passim*; Rom. 14:1ff.).

(d) Therefore this faith does not consist in intellectual adherence to a certain body of revealed content as the definitive solution to theoretical problems. Nor does it consist in having confidence in one's own salvation, thanks to the merits of Christ. Instead it entails the freedom to accept an educational process that comes to maturity and abandons its teacher to launch out into the provisional and relative depths of history (Gal. 4:1ff; Rom. 8:19–23; 1 Cor. 3:11–15). [Segundo, 1976: 122)]

Ultimately, then, Segundo is proposing a total conscientization of St. Paul's understanding of faith and freedom. The freedom characteristic of an elite of mature Christians is "the freedom to accept an educational process that . . . abandons its teacher." Only in this case, the teacher abandoned is the figure of Jesus as represented in the New Testament. The moral teachings of the New Testament need no longer be regarded as "*a priori* criteria established in advance" for Christian praxis. Mature Christians place their faith in the "educational process" of conscientization with an eagerness to follow it out wherever it leads in the struggle. If Segundo's intention in calling for the liberation of theology is to maximize the scope of action for Christian elites, then he has succeeded completely. But one wonders at what price comes this success.

Beyond Gutiérrez and Niebuhr

The point can be made by comparing Segundo's proposal first with that of Gutiérrez, and then with Niebuhr's. In relation to Gutiérrez's position, Segundo clarifies the central ambiguity of liberation theology by resolving the antagonism between the themes of salvation and liberation. Gutiérrez's political interpretation of salvation-history is no longer normative for liberation theology, but now is regarded as one more ideology to be surpassed in the process of total conscientization. His ambivalent Christology of Christ the Liberator gives way to an allegedly historical Jesusology that retains a relation to the New Testament only by affirming Jesus as the occasion for a deutero-learning process. Gutiérrez's almost mystical identification with the masses of the oppressed is passed over in favor of a tough-minded recognition of the elitist nature of the basic communities, which suggests that for liberation theology the difficult transition from romanticism to realism is now underway. But while Segundo's theory and praxis are more internally consistent, and logically follow from the method of conscientization, such consistency comes at the price of abandoning any lingering illusions of continuity with the mainstream of Catholic life and thought.

Even though fully aware of the radical implications of his position, Segundo does try to minimize his differences with Gutiérrez. Most evident in the area of ecclesiological praxis, these differences have been the object of controversy in Latin America. In an analysis apparently similar to the one presented here, the Uruguayan sociologist Cesar Aguiar, for example, has noted the split within the ranks of liberation theologians, between those whose praxis is based on the "masses" and those based on "elites" (Segundo, 1976:232). In this view, Gutiérrez's theology is oriented strategically to the masses, while Segundo's is geared to elites. Segundo's response is to criticize Aguiar for failing to understand how liberation theology has matured through critical reflection on its struggle against conservative elements in the church and society. He insists that his differences with Gutiérrez are only a matter of emphasis: "There is no politics without masses. But neither is there any politics without minorities" (Segundo, 1976:234). But surely it is disingenuous to dismiss their differences in this way. Segundo has accepted the radical implications of conscientization in his consistently dialectical interpretation of "faith" and "ideologies"; while Gutiérrez, perhaps naively, sees conscientization as a way of emphasizing the political implications of Christian faith, but a faith still substantively informed by the epiphanic vision of Catholic incarnational theology. The difference, in other words, is that by following the logic of conscientization Segundo—perhaps unwittingly—has cut the ground out from under Gutiérrez's position.

A comparison between Segundo's position and Niebuhr's Christian realism yields an important similarity as well as irreconcilable differences. The important similarity is that both positions respond to the essential problematic of modern theology. The irreconcilable difference is that Niebuhr bases his theology on a paradoxical vision of God and humanity, which he claims is in substantive continuity with biblical tradition, while Segundo seeks to liberate theology in favor of a dialectical vision of the struggle for liberation, which is linked to biblical tradition only through the formal indentification of faith with a deutero-learning process.

The essential problematic of modern theology is the relationship of the Absolute and the relativities of history.[9] How can theology understand the Absolute and communicate its meaning and truth if theology itself is limited by the relativity of its own historical context? Both Niebuhr and Segundo seem acutely aware of this problem in a way that Gutiérrez does not. Both agree that an honest solution to the problem requires some sort of distinction between faith and ideology, and a frank recognition of the ideological character of any theology, including their own. But they understand that distinction differently.

For Niebuhr, Christian faith is not a deutero-learning process leading toward liberation, but a "moment of prayerful transcendence" that inspires repentance and humility in the face of a Hidden God. Faith, in other words, is not an open-ended commitment to the future, but an apprehension of the paradoxical relationship of Eternity and history. Christian faith, furthermore, has a specific content whose meaning may be recognized in "the heights and the depths of human existence." Niebuhr affirms that the image of Jesus Christ represented in the New Testament is the ultimate symbol of faith, especially as it is given definitive expression in the Atonement. This symbol expresses a substantive content that cannot be abandoned or set aside in a deutero-learning process; if it could, Christian faith would cease to be Christian. Moreover, since no theology—not even the theologies of the New Testament—is exempt from "the conflict of grace and pride," Niebuhr also recognizes the ideological character of all Christian theology. Nevertheless, to the extent that the theologies of the New Testament actually succeed in conveying certain abiding truths concerning the paradoxical situation of humanity before God, they remain normative for all subsequent Christian theology and ethics.

A practical example may help clarify Niebuhr's differences with Segundo on this point. Recall that Niebuhr characterized Jesus' teaching about love as an "impossible possibility," while Segundo sees it as an "ideology" that does not necessarily bind the consciences of "mature Christians." Niebuhr and Segundo thus agree that Jesus' ethic in its own context requires nonresistance toward evil. But they differ as to the relevance of this ethic. Segundo says that it is not necessarily relevant to the present situation, since it is a part of Jesus' ideology. "Mature Christians" are free to create a new ethic in response to the need for "efficacious love" in the present situation. Niebuhr, however, characterizes Jesus' ethic of love as an "impossible, but relevant ideal." It is impossible because a consistent and single-minded attempt to practice it is morally irresponsible. But it is relevant because it serves not only to lure persons on toward greater moral aspirations and achievements, but also to illuminate the paradoxical situation of human nature, thereby suggesting that humanity is justified before God, not through action but by faith. Were Jesus' ethic to be relativized as an "ideology," these "meta-ethical" considerations would be obscured. Thus in Niebuhr's view the ethic of Jesus remains the norm for any possible future Christian ethics. Although it does not dictate the actions of Christians, still it does illuminate them by providing a pattern for shaping Christian dispositions. Niebuhr's effort to sustain a Christian imagination faithful to the substantive perspectives of the New Testament is undermined by Segundo's formalized interpretation of Jesus' faith and ideology. In response to Segundo, Niebuhr would insist that even the ideology of Jesus remains relevant, and in some sense normative, for Christian ethics today.

Skeptics might reply that Niebuhr's effort to sustain a Christian imagination doesn't amount to much, since in the end Niebuhr and Segundo come to similar conclusions about an ethic of nonresistance, or religious pacifism. But this observation is only superficially correct. Although Niebuhr recognized that religious pacifism and political responsibility are incompatible, he did not dismiss religious pacifists as irrelevant. He saw them as living witnesses to the ideal of love, whose continued presence was a necessary goad to the consciences of Christian realists. When he criticized such pacifism as a form of "Christian perfectionism," his main concern was to dispel the illusions of those who thought that it could serve as a morally realistic guideline for the exercise of political responsibility.

Segundo's argument against religious pacifism is based on a different perspective. He does not consider its ethical merits as a means toward the end of liberation but discusses it as an ideology that favors the *status quo*. An ethic of nonresistance distracts people from the struggle by failing to recognize the situation of "institutionalized violence" and the logic of liberating "counter-violence." Were the pacifist to object that he or she is responding to religious imperatives that transcend the immediate situation, Segundo would have to dismiss this objection as illusory. He might invite the pacifist to participate in the deutero-learning process in order to overcome such illusions and their unwitting service to reactionary political forces.

This example should suggest that although Niebuhr and Segundo agree in rejecting an ethic of nonresistance, they do so for significantly different reasons. Over and above the general differences separating Christian realism and liberation theology, Niebuhr and Segundo disagree about the substantive content of Christian faith. Is it a world-vision definitively expressed in Christian myth and capable of being interpreted as a norm for human nature and history, or is it a deutero-learning process compatible with any number of historically efficacious ideologies? Although both thinkers respond to the problematic of modern theology by distinguishing faith from ideology in the historical consciousness of Christians, the one insists that Christian faith has substantive meaning, the other implies that it is purely formal. Assuming that meaning, Niebuhr's mythical method seeks to interpret it; even as Segundo's total conscientization of liberation theology decodes it so that the deutero-learning process might become formal and explicit. But once this total conscientization has been accomplished, is liberation theology still recognizable as theology?

The Dilemma of Liberation Theology

This review of the praxis of liberation theology suggests that a fateful moment of truth has been reached. If, as I have argued, liberation theology is plagued from the beginning by a crucial ambiguity, stemming primarily from an incompatibility between its method and its content, then its subsequent development since Gutiérrez's Magna Charta may be seen as transforming that ambiguity into a dilemma. The dilemma is that liberation theologians must choose between either the method or the content as outlined by Gutiérrez. If they choose the method, then liberation theology becomes increasingly distant from the mainstream of Catholic life and thought; if they choose the content, then liberation theology becomes increasingly indistinguishable—methodologically, if not thematically— from the progressivism of Vatican II. In either case its distinctive program, the new way of "doing theology in a revolutionary situation," is sacrificed.

That liberation theology initially exhibited this crucial ambiguity is not surprising. Anything genuinely creative will usually seem unstable in comparision to what has gone before. But the shape of things in the post-Medellín period meant that this ambiguity would unfold in particularly adverse circumstances: polarization within the church and political repression within society. These circumstances have tended to marginalize the basic communities; thus, instead of the creative synthesis that Gutiérrez hoped for, their "critical reflection on praxis" was radicalized.

Of the two options that typically have emerged in this situation, Sobrino's Christological treatise retains the thematic content but not the method of liberation theology. The appeal to praxis is generalized and idealized, and thus the effects of marginalization cease to inform critical reflection. Instead, critical reflection is exhausted in a dialogue with European progressives resulting in a verbal reconciliation between the theme of liberation and the project of a historical Christology. This option represents one horn of the dilemma, because in it the meaning of liberation theology is trivialized.

The other option, Segundo's proposal for the liberation of theology, critically reflects the *new* Latin American reality. With a tough-mindedness that is rare among theologians, he responds by developing the method of conscientization to its logical conclusion. But in so doing, he may have dissolved even the minimum continuity necessary to sustain a substantively Christian identity for the basic communities. This option represents the other horn of the dilemma, because in it the meaning of liberation theology is completely politicized.

Without a substantively Christian identity clearly reflected in their praxis, these communities in the end may serve only as recruitment centers for secular liberation movements. That may well be an acceptable outcome from the perspective of those involved in such movements, but it is impossible to reconcile with the original intention of liberation theology. Given the events since Medellín, this dilemma cannot be resolved by continuing to assume that "salvation" and "liberation" have been synthesized in a new way of doing theology.

NOTES

1. The fundamental illusion in this case is the idea of "man" considered formally as such, and not as manifest in the various substantive definitions given to it. "Man" is an idealizing abstraction that obscures, if not precludes, a critical awareness of the dynamic structural relationships that constitute history. This, I take it, is also the issue raised by Alves's denunciation of the "revolt against transcendence." By allowing the dynamics of human history to be reduced to such an abstraction, idealists unwittingly have closed off certain possibilities and therefore have paved the way for positivism and pragmatism. Alves's protest is reflected in the fact that liberation theologians typically repudiate "anthropological" analyses in favor of allegedly "eschatological" perspectives. This theological shift, in part, is a reflection of the debate among social theorists and philosophers concering the "abolition of man" or the nature of humanism. Judging from their citations, the Latin Americans have been influenced most by Louis Althusser's discussion of this topic in *For Marx*. In short, Althus-

ser's critique of the ideological character of humanism provides philosophical justification for rejecting theological anthropology. While this conclusion is consistent with the method of conscientization, it makes theological ethics difficult, if not impossible, by precluding theoretical reflection on the normative implications of human nature.

2. For an account of how the strategy of isolation is carried out and its demoralizing consequences, see Charles Antoine's *Church and Power in Brazil* (1973:142–57). Despite its lack of objectivity, Antoine's book is very useful as a guide to the logic of praxis as typically understood in the perspective of liberation theology.

3. The various allegations concerning Vekemans's activity were presented in *The National Catholic Reporter,* July 29, 1977, and May 19 and 26, 1978.

4. In this review of the praxis of liberation theology, I have tried to take account of events leading up to but not including the third general conference of the Latin American Episcopal Council (CELAM), which met at Puebla, Mexico, in January–February 1979. Since the Puebla conference did not resolve the theological issues that are central to this book, the analysis of liberation theology presented here remains essentially unaffected by the results of that meeting.

5. By failing to be more explicit about the relationship between praxis and truth, liberation theologians in general and Sobrino in particular seem to hold a position similar to Niebuhr's reflections on religion's meaningful "illusions," as presented in *Moral Man and Immoral Society* (1932b: 81). The parallel breaks down, however, since Niebuhr affirms the nonstraightforward nature of religious "illusions," while Sobrino apparently denies it. As a consequence, thanks to its greater epistemological sophistication, Christian realism remains a promising way to understand the relationship between truth and praxis, whereas liberation theology appears to have insuperable theoretical difficulties. In any case, Niebuhr's brief flirtation with religious fictionalism ended with his abandonment of "the frank dualism in morals." In its mature form, Christian realism offers a theological anthropology in order to provide a theoretical reference point that will allow for verification of truth claims logically distinct from considerations of practical meaningfulness.

6. In working out his position, Segundo speaks of "structural violence" as "not opposed to love." This is the violence that is objectively present in social relationships, whether exercised "personally" or "indirectly." Apparently, what makes violence moral or immoral is not something intrinsic to its nature, but the moral worth of the ends for which it is employed. Nevertheless, the theoretical warrant for Segundo's view of the dynamic of love, namely, its tendency to reduce "the quantum of violence required for efficacy to the lowest possible level," remains unclear. While the criterion of "efficacy" of itself does not seem to require this reduction, in theory it is the only possible source for this imperative—if Segundo is to remain consistent. Otherwise the tendency to minimize violence may represent the residual impact of the "ideology" of Jesus. If so, given Segundo's assumptions, it still needs some sort of rational justification. This, and similar difficulties in Segundo's position, is indicative of what happens when liberation theologians try to take a stand on complex moral issues involved in praxis without the benefit of ethical reflection.

7. Segundo accepts the label "situation ethics" as a fair description of his position (Segundo, 1976: 173). As in the case of "sectarianism," the label has a pejorative sense for Segundo, which he tries to overcome by denouncing the "verbal terrorism" that makes this position taboo in some Roman Catholic circles. Be that as it may, the fact that Segundo identifies himself with situation ethics does not count against what I argued in the first section of this chapter concerning the lack of theological ethics in liberation theology. On the contrary, it is precisely the absence of sustained reflection in the area of theological ethics that inevitably makes Segundo a radical situationist. By contrast, Niebuhr's position may be characterized as moderately contextualist, since he does attempt to formulate an illuminative use of moral principles for shaping the pattern of a distinctively Christian way of life. Here it is appropriate for me to acknowledge my debt to James M. Gustafson for helping me to understand the practical consequences of liberation theology's neglect of theological ethics. While some of the opinions concerning perspectives discussed in this book echo his own, the errors of interpretation and analysis are entirely mine.

8. On this point Segundo apparently disagrees with Paulo Freire's insistence that conscientization entails strategies based on "trust in the people." Freire's understanding of the forms of "dialogical action" implies that there are some means that are intrinsically appropriate to the struggle for liberation, and some that are not. He offers descriptions of the positive values of cooperation, unity, organization, and cultural synthesis, and an analysis of the

pathologies of "activism" and "bureaucracy" to provide guidance to the question of means. It is hard to see how Segundo's elitism escapes the pattern of activism/bureaucracy that Freire denounces. Nevertheless, Segundo's theology still completes the logic of conscientization insofar as it makes the deutero-learning process itself the meaning of Christianity. Their difference lies presumably in diverging attitudes toward the Leninist conception of the role of a revolutionary vanguard, a question of enormous importance for praxis and ethics.

9. The definitive formulation of this problem was given in Ernst Troeltsch's *The Absoluteness of Christianity and the History of Religions,* which first appeared in 1902. From the beginning Niebuhr was deeply influenced by his reading of Troeltsch, and among liberation theologians Segundo has been influenced through his reading of some of Troeltsch's major interpreters.

10

Another "Unscientific Postscript"

In his recent book *Christianity and the World Order,* Edward Norman denounced the "politicization" of Christianity and called for a return to a properly "spiritual interpretation" of it based on faith in "the indwelling Christ." Since Norman includes not only Latin American liberation theology but also most every other form of contemporary practical theology in his indictment of politicized Christianity, it is appropriate to conclude this comparative analysis by relating it to his thesis. The question is whether this analysis merely provides additional evidence for his indictment, or calls for a somewhat different view of Christianity and politics.

Norman defines the process of politicization as "the internal transformation of the faith itself, so that it comes to be defined in terms of political values—it becomes essentially concerned with social morality rather than with the ethereal qualities of immortality." Elaborating the point a bit, he says that politicization occurs when Christianity "is reinterpreted as a scheme of social and political action, dependent, it is true, upon supernatural authority for its ultimate claim to attention, but rendered in categories that are derived from the political theories and practices of contemporary society" (Norman, 1979:2).

This definition of politicization has two corollaries: one, concerning the nature of contemporary society and its dominant ideology; the other, concerning the nature of authentic Christianity. In Norman's view, the process of politicization has transformed "*all* moral values in our society," and thus has resulted in (1) "the extension of the social competence of the government": "the entry of the state into areas which were formerly the traditional preserve of the Churches—education, for example, and very many other aspects of social welfare"; and (2) the development of an ideology to justify this transformation: the "new Humanism" based on a "view of man as morally autonomous and capable of progressive development" (Norman, 1979:11). By contrast, authentic Christianity for Norman "points to the condition of the inward soul of man":

In Christianity, as it was delivered by the saints and scholars of the centuries, men are first directed to the imperfections of their own

234

natures, and not to the rationalized imperfections of human society. An awareness of social values is actually involved in this however, as a necessary preliminary for comprehension of the conditioning that spirituality receives as it filters through the screens of human society. This should not lead, as, alas it now often does, to the Christian espousal of social *principles,* but to an awareness of the relativity of *all* human values. [Norman, 1979:76–77]

On a more positive note Norman confesses the Incarnation of God in Christ as the essence of Christianity, describing its meaning in the following terms: "The crude and relative inclinations of men towards a knowledge of the Infinite . . . were shown to have a real basis. The visible and the unseen world were briefly joined, and the supervening force of the divine flowed down upon the earth" (Norman 1979:77).

Despite its seeming clarity, Norman's description of the problem has only limited usefulness. His notion of authentic Christianity apparently is so narrow as to exclude all but a surprisingly unhistorical version of Anglo-Catholic orthodoxy, and his understanding of "politicization" is so broad as to include virtually the whole of modern Christianity. The difficulty with his description is that it becomes almost impossible to distinguish varying degrees of politicization on any other basis than Norman's own standard of Christian authenticity. Thus the only degree of political involvement apparently acceptable to Norman is one in which "a Christian knowledge of politics [is] acquired in order to serve the interests of the Church as an institution" (Norman, 1979:3). But if that is the case, then all of the positions discussed in this analysis—including Maritain's Integral Humanism—stand under indictment.[1] Just how large a net he casts is evident from the fact that even the Christian churches' recent concern for human rights comes in for criticism.

Not surprisingly, Norman singles out Latin American liberation theology as a typical example of politicization: "To the Church's real and important concern with the conditions in which people live has been added a succession of ideological superstructures whose content has been acquired, not from a distinctively Christian or religious source, or from a particularly Christian understanding of the nature of man and his social state, but from ideas current within the educated classes of the western world in general" (Norman, 1979:56). Among these ideas he lists Marxism and conscientization, neither of which is compatible, of course, with his view of authentic Christianity. Consistent with his sweeping generalization of the problem, Norman denounces not just theologians like Gutiérrez and Segundo, but also the bishops' conference at Medellín. Indeed, he regards the politicization of Latin American Christianity as well advanced and traceable, at least in part, to the influence of fascism in the 1930s (Norman, 1979: 47). Thus, in Norman's view, the whole spectrum of Latin American theology stands guilty as charged.

By now the divergences between my position and Norman's should be apparent. While I conclude that politicization—more or less as Norman defined it: "the internal transformation of the faith . . . in terms of political values"—is one horn of the dilemma facing liberation theology, I do not regard it as pervasive a phenomenon as he does, even among Latin Americans. Nor have I based my argument on any presumed standard of Christian orthodoxy. On the contrary, I assume an irreducible plurality of Christian religious visions, two of which—namely, the paradoxical vision and the epiphanic vision—are involved in the conflict between Christian realism and liberation theology.[2] That conflict, as I described it, does not directly concern the perspectival differences distinctive of these two visions; but it does concern the way in which they have been interpreted as models for practical theology. Thus I argued that, on the one hand, Christian realism—despite its theoretical weakness—is a consistent reflection of one form of authentic Christian spirituality, namely, the paradoxical vision; while on the other hand, liberation theology—despite its rhetorical impressiveness—is only an ambiguous reflection of the equally authentic epiphanic vision, and ambiguous precisely because it tries to synthesize this religious perspective with the dialectical vision, which is incompatible with it. In other words, although my conclusion coincides in part with Norman's, the argument for it proceeds on an entirely different basis.

This point should be clear from my assessment of the implications of the differences between the two models. While both theologies have serious difficulties, the dilemma of liberation theology is of a different order from the weaknesses of Christian realism. At this point, Norman's concern about politicization—however ill-focused—is relevant, for liberation theology's adoption of conscientization as its methodological principle inevitably does politicize its epiphanic vision. As I have argued, conscientization is not simply a corrective for what is properly criticized as the "excessive spiritualization" of traditional Catholic "academic theology"; left to its own logic, conscientization inevitably empties the epiphanic vision of its essentially religious meaning. In that sense, Norman is right in denouncing "the internal transformation of the faith." But he is wrong in failing to recognize not only how unwitting this transformation was initially, but also to what extent it tragically undermines the basic intention of liberation theology. However advanced its politicization, liberation theology's intention is to confront the Latin American reality on the basis of a genuinely Christian commitment. But given the way in which the epiphanic vision theologically defines that commitment for Catholic Christians, the question is whether or not liberation theology can faithfully reflect the content of this vision and still use conscientization as its method. In short, has liberation theology successfully reconciled the meanings of salvation and liberation in a new way of doing theology? I conclude that it has not and most likely cannot. Consequently, I see liberation theology as faced with a dilemma: politicization or trivialization.

The weaknesses of Christian realism, however serious, are not quite so severe. In general they are a consequence of Niebuhr's failure to develop a fully explicit model for practical theology. While he successfully interpreted the paradoxical vision's meaning for human selfhood, he was less successful in relating it to the historic vicissitudes of human societies. Specifically, his approach to problems of ideological and social conflict—however religiously meaningful and morally illuminating—fails to sustain the critical perspective required to fulfill Christian realism's prophetic intention. Because he was unable to develop a critical social theory consistent with the paradoxical vision, his later work suffers from ideological drift. This represents a weakness rather than a fundamental flaw in Christian realism because, in my opinion, it may be corrected without politicizing the paradoxical vision, which defines the Christian commitment for Niebuhr.[3]

Another view of the conflict is possible. Supporters of liberation theology might argue that the problem of ideological drift is not peculiar to Christian realism but is inevitable in any theology not based on praxis or solidarity with the oppressed. Indeed, they might insist that the so-called politicization of which they have been accused represents not just the only valid way to ensure this solidarity but also the authentic meaning of the teachings of Jesus. In other words, they might respond by saying that if the paradoxical vision and the epiphanic vision are incompatible with a conscienticizing evangelization, then so much the worse for these visions. At any rate, assuming that the teachings of Jesus are adequately rendered in a conscienticizing evangelization, liberation theologians might criticize these visions as ideologies that obscure the radical political implications of authentic Christianity.

While this argument is based, in my opinion, on a fundamentally mistaken view of the nature of practical theology, it does serve to raise the central issue at stake, not only in the controversy over politicization but also in the conflict between Christian realism and liberation theology. That issue concerns the role of religious transcendence in political action: what it is and what its consequences are. If religious transcendence in its Christian forms is indistinguishable from the revolutionary enthusiasm promoted by liberation theology, then in principle there is no conflict between Christianity and the dialectical vision, and the problem of politicization is meaningless. But if religious transcendence in its Christian forms is distinguishable as a spirit of disinterestedness, a heightened sense of humility born of faith, hope, and love, as Niebuhr experienced it in his paradoxical vision, then in principle there is a conflict between these theologies regarding the substantive meaning of Christianity for politics, and the problem of politicization is a serious one for practical theology.

A number of years ago, in a different context, Lucien Goldmann addressed this issue in his book *The Hidden God: A Study of the Tragic Vision in the* Pensées *of Pascal and the Tragedies of Racine*. In clarifying his assessment of these writers, Goldmann compared this tragic vision (a theological perspective fundamentally similar to Niebuhr's paradoxical vision) with the dialectical vision of Marxism. Goldmann argued that the two visions exhibit important similarities and differences. The similarities are (1) that each is based on a "wager," that is, on "an act of faith in the present or future existence of certain values" (Goldmann, 1964:303), and (2) that each affirms "the existence of a force that transcends the individual." They differ, of course, not only regarding the nature of that transcendent force, but also concerning its practical consequences: (1) the tragic vision wagers that the Hidden God exists and eternally is triumphant over evil, and "that, unless he is to lose his soul, man can never be satisfied with a good that is purely finite" (Goldmann, 1964:301), while (2) the dialectical vision wagers on the future triumph of "Humanity or the Proletariat," and that "both the finite goods and even the evil of terrestrial life . . . will receive a meaning inside the framework of faith and of hope in the future" (Goldmann, 1964:302). In short, the two visions are based on two different forms of transcendence; and along with Goldmann, I have no hesitation in recognizing the one as essentially religious and Christian, and the other as essentially secular and Marxist.

Beyond this point, however, we must agree to disagree. For although Goldmann is more than generous in his appreciation of the tragic vision, in the end he sees it as only "an essential stage" in the emergence of the dialectical vision. His words are worth quoting:

> And finally to resume and synthesize all these reasons, Christianity is the only religion which not only fully and consistently recognizes the ambiguous and contradictory nature of all reality but which also makes this characteristic into an element of God's plan for this earth. For it transforms ambiguity into paradox, and makes human life cease to be an absurd adventure and become instead a valid and necessary stage in the only path leading to goodness and truth.
>
> One could certainly show today that the historical wager on the future existence of the human community (in socialism) also possesses all these qualities; that, like Pascal's Christianity, it is incarnation, the joining up of opposites, and the fitting of ambiguity into a pattern which makes it clear and meaningful.
>
> But Pascal lived in France in the seventeenth century. For him, there was therefore no question of a historical dialect. . . .
>
> Subsequently Hegel, and especially Marx and Lukacs, have been able to substitute for the wager on the paradoxical and mediatory God of Christianity the wager on a historical future and on the human community. . . . [Goldmann, 1964:308]

Moreover, Goldmann asserts that wagering on the tragic vision necessarily entails the view that "the finite goods of this world have no value at all, and that the only human life which has real meaning is that of a reasonable being who seeks God." Perhaps this is what Norman has in mind when he says that authentic Christianity "points to the condition of the inward soul of man." Be that as it may, Goldmann finds this view a sufficient reason for wagering instead on the dialectical vision and its faith in the human future. The point of our disagreement, in short, concerns not the nature of the two visions, but their practical consequences.

Against Goldmann's interpretation, Christian realism must count as an impressive restatement of the tragic vision. While it wagers on the Infinite, it certainly does not render the finite valueless. Christian realism is not an invitation to otherworldliness; on the contrary, Niebuhr's rediscovery of one authentic form of Christian spirituality provided him with a way of sustaining his political commitment amid the frustrations of radical politics. Only a religious spirit of disinterestedness, he claimed, could overcome the malaise represented by the swinging pendulum of "fanaticism" and "cynicism" among social activists. Far from being "an essential stage" on the way toward the dialectical vision, the paradoxical vision for Niebuhr was just the opposite. Once experience had demonstrated the demonic consequences of wagering on the dialectical vision, it became an essential stage in Niebuhr's rediscovery of an authentic Christianity. The desire for human community, and the recognition of the proper value of the "the finite goods of this world," can be sustained only if the Hidden God is recognized in humility and faith. As Niebuhr remarked at the time:

> It is only religion, the high religion which worships a holy God before whom all men feel themselves sinners, that can maintain the elements of decency, pity, and forgiveness in human life and can resist the cruelty and inhumanity which flows inevitably from the process that absolutizes some human values and identifies others with the very source of all evil. [Niebuhr, 1934b:379]

If that is the case, then Goldmann has both overestimated the practical consequences of wagering on the dialectical vision, and underestimated those of the tragic vision.

Nevertheless, with Goldmann's analysis the central issue in this conflict of practical theologies in principle is resolved. The nature of religious transcendence is clearly exhibited in the paradoxical vision; and just as clearly, it is not in the dialectical vision. To see it otherwise is to do justice to the claims of neither Marxism nor Christianity. But Goldmann to the contrary, the paradoxical vision does not render a commitment to the human community meaningless; it simply bears witness to the fact that such a commitment can be sustained only if it is not confused with humanity's essentially religious longing for reconciliation with the Hidden God. For practical theologians still claiming loyalty to Christianity, there can be no question, then, of how this conflict is resolved: since the paradoxical vision does represent an authentically Christian form of religious transcendence, it is not to be abandoned in favor of the dialectical vision, which does not. The result of this analysis of the conflict in practical theology therefore may be summarized as follows: on the one hand, the weaknesses of Christian realism are not sufficient reason to reject the spirituality that inspired it; on the other hand, even as a timely protest against those weaknesses, liberation theology is faced with a dilemma that undercuts its status as a promising alternative.[4]

NOTES

1. Maritain, perhaps the most conservative of all the theologians discussed in this analysis, distinguished Integral Humanism from medieval Christianity by allowing the temporal sphere its own autonomy "as an *intermediate or infravalent* end" (Maritain, 1973:176). By contrast medieval Christianity allowed the temporal sphere no autonomy, and recognized it as having only an "instrumental" value relative to the spiritual. What Maritain criticizes as the medieval view apparently is the only basis for political action compatible with Norman's view of authentic Christianity.

2. When pressed to define this pluralism further, I find myself roughly in agreement with the five ideal types outlined in H. Richard Niebuhr's *Christ and Culture* (1951). Like the visions mapped out in this analysis, Niebuhr's types represent substantively different perspectives. His third type, "Christ above Culture," overlaps with what I've identified as the "epiphanic vision"; and his fourth type, "Christ and Culture in Paradox," with the "paradoxical vision." There are differences, however, in the way we assess the merits of these perspectives; but such are irrelevant in this context.

3. In this analysis, for the most part, I have merely illustrated the weaknesses of Christian realism; I have not shown how they might be overcome. My sense that they can be corrected is based on a reading of the work of the German neo-Marxist Jürgen Habermas, who has managed—in my opinion—to demythologize the Frankfurt School's critical social theory in a way that makes it a promising resource for reconstructing Christian realism. I hope to have more to say about this possibility in the future.

4. Since this book was written on the assumption that the conflict of practical theologies is not reducible to the confessional differences between Roman Catholics and Protestants, I have not found it necessary to outline a distinctively Catholic alternative to the Catholic liberation theology. There may be some readers, however, who find Christian realism too "Protestant" to be of much use to Catholic theologians and social activists. My advice in that case is to consider Niebuhr's work as a model for creating a Catholic agenda in practical theology. Where he is most illuminating is in seeing that the rediscovery of an authentic spirituality (for him, a Reformation spirituality) is the key to theological renewal. Catholic theologians therefore would do well to rediscover an authentically Catholic spirituality, and then go from there. My hunch is that Jacques Maritain's work, once allowance is made for its neoscholastic philosophical foundation, is still a good place to begin. For an indication of how his work compares with Niebuhr's see McCann, 1978.

Bibliography

Althusser, Louis
  1970   *For Marx*. Trans. Ben Brewster. New York: Vintage Books.
Alves, Rubem
  1973   "Christian Realism: Ideology of the Establishment." *Christianity and Crisis*
          33:173-76.
Antoine, Charles
  1973   *Church and Power in Brazil*. Trans. Peter Nelson. Maryknoll, New York: Orbis
          Books.
Arias, Mortimer
  1978   "Contextual Evangelization in Latin America: Between Accommodation and
          Confrontation." *Occasional Bulletin of Missionary Research* 2:19-28.
Assmann, Hugo
  1976   *Theology for a Nomad Church*. Trans. Paul Burns. Maryknoll, New York:
          Orbis Books.
Baum, Gregory
  1975   *Religion and Alienation: A Theological Reading of Sociology*. New York:
          Paulist Press.
Bennett, John C.
  1956   "Reinhold Niebuhr's Social Ethics." In *Reinhold Niebuhr: His Religious,
          Social, and Political Thought*. Ed. Charles W. Kegley and Robert W. Bretall.
          New York: The Macmillan Company, pp. 46-77.
  1973   "Liberation Theology and Christian Realism." *Christianity and Crisis* 33:197-
          98.
  1975   *The Radical Imperative: From Theology to Social Ethics*. Philadelphia:
          Westminster Press.
Berger, Peter
  1976   *Pyramids of Sacrifice: Political Ethics and Social Change*. Garden City, New
          York: Doubleday Anchor Books.
Berryman, Phillip E.
  1976   "Latin American Liberation Theology." In *Theology in the Americas*. Ed.
          Sergio Torres and John Eagleson. Maryknoll, New York: Orbis Books, pp.
          20-83.
Brown, Robert McAfee
  1973   "Liberation Theology and Christian Realism." *Christianity and Crisis* 33:199-
          200.
Chrystal, William G.
  1977   "Introduction." In *Young Reinhold Niebuhr: His Early Writings—1911–1931*.
          Ed. William G. Chrystal. St. Louis: Eden Publishing House.
Dulles, Avery
  1977   *The Resilient Church: The Necessity and Limits of Adaptation*. Garden City,
          New York: Doubleday.
Fierro, Alfredo
  1977   *The Militant Gospel: A Critical Introduction to Political Theologies*. Trans.
          John Drury. Maryknoll, New York: Orbis Books.
Frankena, William K.
  1973   "Is Morality Logically Dependent on Religion?" In *Religion and Morality*. Ed.
          Gene Outka and John P. Reeder, Jr. Garden City, New York: Doubleday
          Anchor Books, pp. 295-317.
Frei, Eduardo
  1978   *Latin America: The Hopeful Option*. Trans. John Drury. Maryknoll, New York:
          Orbis Books.

Freire, Paulo
1970   *Pedagogy of the Oppressed*. Trans. Myra Bergman Ramos. New York: Seabury Press.
1973   *Education for Critical Consciousness*. New York: Seabury Press.
Geertz, Clifford
1971   *Islam Observed: Religious Development in Morocco and Indonesia*. Chicago: University of Chicago Press.
1973   "Religion as a Cultural System." In *The Interpretation of Cultures*. New York: Basic Books, pp. 87-125.
Gilkey, Langdon
1975   "Reinhold Niebuhr's Theology of History." In *The Legacy of Reinhold Niebuhr*. Ed. Nathan A. Scott. Chicago: University of Chicago Press, pp. 36-62.
Goldmann, Lucien
1964   *The Hidden God: A Study of Tragic Vision in the* Pensées *of Pascal and the Tragedies of Racine*. Trans. Philip Thody. London and Henley: Routledge and Kegan Paul.
Granfield, Patrick
1967   "Interview with Reinhold Niebuhr." In *Theologians at Work*. New York: The Macmillan Company.
Gremillion, Joseph, ed.
1976   *The Gospel of Peace and Justice*. Maryknoll, New York: Orbis Books.
Gustafson, James M.
1971   "Christian Ethics in America." In *Christian Ethics and the Community*. Philadelphia: Pilgrim Press, pp. 23-82.
1975   *Can Ethics Be Christian?* Chicago: University of Chicago Press.
Gutiérrez, Gustavo
1973   *A Theology of Liberation*. Trans. Sister Caridad Inda and John Eagleson. Maryknoll, New York: Orbis Books.
Gutiérrez, Gustavo, and Shaull, Richard
1977   *Liberation and Change*. Atlanta: John Knox Press.
Habermas, Jürgen
1970   *Toward a Rational Society: Student Protest, Science, and Politics*. Trans. Jeremy J. Shapiro. Boston: Beacon Press.
1974   *Theory and Practice*. Trans. by John Viertel. Boston: Beacon Press.
Harvey, Van A.
1966   *The Historian and the Believer*. New York: Macmillan.
Herberg, Will
1960   *Protestant, Catholic, Jew*. Garden City, New York: Doubleday Anchor Books.
Hopkins, C. Howard
1940   *The Rise of the Social Gospel in American Protestantism, 1865–1915*. New Haven: Yale University Press.
Houtart, Francois, and Rousseau, André
1971   *The Church and Revolution*. Trans. Violet Neville. Maryknoll, New York: Orbis Books.
King, Rachel Hadley
1964   *The Omission of the Holy Spirit from Reinhold Niebuhr's Theology*. New York: Philosophical Library.
Lehmann, Paul
1956   "The Christology of Reinhold Niebuhr." In *Reinhold Niebuhr: His Religious, Social, and Political Thought*. Ed. Charles W. Kegley and Robert W. Bretall. New York: The Macmillan Company, pp. 252–80.
Lonergan, Bernard
1972   *Method in Theology*. New York: Herder and Herder.
Long, Edward LeRoy, Jr.
1967   *A Survey of Christian Ethics*. New York: Oxford University Press.
Mannheim, Karl
1936   *Ideology and Utopia*. New York: Harcourt, Brace, and World.
Mannix, Daniel P., in collaboration with Cowley, Malcolm
1962   *Black Cargoes: A History of the Atlantic Slave Trade*. New York: The Viking Press.

Maritain, Jacques
 1973   *Integral Humanism: Temporal and Spiritual Problems of a New Christendom.*
           Trans. Joseph W. Evans. Notre Dame: University of Notre Dame Press.
Marx, Karl, and Engels, Friedrich
 1964   *On Religion.* New York: Schocken Books.
McCann, Dennis P.
 1978   "Reinhold Niebuhr and Jacques Maritain on Marxism: A Comparison of Two
           Traditional Models of Practical Theology." *The Journal of Religion* 58:140–68.
Merkley, Paul
 1975   *Reinhold Niebuhr: A Political Account.* Montreal and London: McGill-Queen's
           University Press.
Metz, Johannes
 1969   *Theology of the World.* Trans. William Glen-Doepel. New York: The Seabury
           Press.
Miranda, José
 1977   *Being and the Messiah: The Message of St. John.* Trans. John Eagleson.
           Maryknoll, New York: Orbis Books.
Niebuhr, H. Richard
 1951   *Christ and Culture.* New York: Harper and Brothers.
Niebuhr, Reinhold
 1927   *Does Civilization Need Religion?* New York: The Macmillan Co.
 1929   *Leaves from the Notebook of a Tamed Cynic.* Chicago: Willett, Clark, and
           Company. All quotations taken from this book are as cited in the pages of the
           new edition issued by Meridian Books, New York: Meridian Books, 1957.
 1932a   *The Contribution of Religion to Social Work.* New York: Columbia University
           Press.
 1932b   *Moral Man and Immoral Society.* New York: Charles Scribner's Sons.
 1934a   *Reflections on the End of an Era.* New York: Charles Scribner's Sons.
 1934b   "The Problem of Communist Religion." *The World Tomorrow* 17:378–379.
 1934c   "Why I Leave the F.O.R." In *Love and Justice: Selections From the Shorter
           Writings of Reinhold Niebuhr.* Ed. D. B. Robertson. Cleveland: Meridian
           Books, 1967, pp. 254–259.
 1935   *An Interpretation of Christian Ethics.* New York: Harper and Brothers. All
           quotations taken from this book are as cited in the pages of the new edition of *An
           Interpretation of Christian Ethics* issued as part of The Seabury Library of
           Contemporary Theology. New York: The Seabury Press, 1979.
 1937a   "The Truth in Myths." In *Faith and Politics.* Ed. Ronald H. Stone. New York:
           George Braziller, 1968, pp. 15–32.
 1937b   *Beyond Tragedy.* New York: Charles Scribner's Sons.
 1939   "Ten Years That Shook My World." *The Christian Century* 56:542–46.
 1940   *Christianity and Power Politics.* New York: Charles Scribner's Sons.
 1941   *The Nature and Destiny of Man, Volume I.* New York: Charles Scribner's Sons.
 1943   *The Nature and Destiny of Man, Volume II.* New York: Charles Scribner's
           Sons.
 1944   *The Children of Light and the Children of Darkness.* New York: Charles
           Scribner's Sons.
 1946   *Discerning the Signs of the Times.* New York: Charles Scribner's Sons.
 1949   *Faith and History.* New York: Charles Scribner's Sons.
 1952   *The Irony of American History.* New York: Charles Scribner's Sons.
 1953   *Christian Realism and Political Problems.* New York: Charles Scribner's Sons.
 1955   *The Self and the Dramas of History.* New York: Charles Scribner's Sons.
 1956   "Intellectual Autobiography." In *Reinhold Niebuhr: His Religious, Social, and
           Political Thought.* Ed. Charles W. Kegley and Robert W. Bretall. New York:
           The Macmillan Company, pp. 3–23.
 1959   *The Structure of Nations and Empires.* New York: Charles Scribner's Sons.
 1964   "Introduction." In *On Religion.* By Karl Marx and Friedrich Engels. New
           York: Schocken Books, pp. vii–xiv.
 1965   *Man's Nature and His Communities.* New York: Charles Scribner's Sons.
 1977   *Young Reinhold Niebuhr: His Early Writings—1911–1931.* Ed. William G.
           Chrystal. St. Louis: Eden Publishing House.

Niebuhr, Reinhold, and Heimert, Alan
  1963   *A Nation So Conceived.* New York: Charles Scribner's Sons.
Niebuhr, Reinhold, and Sigmund, Paul E.
  1969   *The Democratic Experience: Past and Prospects.* New York: Frederick A.
            Praeger.
Norman, Edward
  1979   *Christianity and the World Order.* New York: Oxford University Press.
Ogden, Schubert M.
  1979   *Faith and Freedom: Toward a Theology of Liberation.* Nashville: Abingdon
            Press.
Pendle, George
  1963   *A History of Latin America.* Harmondsworth, England: Penguin Books.
Perrin, Norman
  1974   *The New Testament: An Introduction.* New York: Harcourt, Brace, Jovano-
            vich.
Plank, John
  1973   "Liberation Theology and Christian Realism." *Christianity and Crisis* 33:198–
            99.
Quigley, Thomas
  1973   "Liberation Theology and Christian Realism." *Christianity and Crisis* 33:200–
            202.
Richard, Pablo
  1978   "The Latin American Church: 1959–1978." *Cross Currents* 28:34–46.
Rovere, Richard
  1962   *The American Establishment.* New York: Harcourt, Brace and World.
Sanders, Thomas G.
  1973   "The Theology of Liberation: Christian Utopianism." *Christianity and Crisis*
            33:167–73.
Segundo, Juan Luis
  1976   *The Liberation of Theology.* Trans. John Drury. Maryknoll, New York: Orbis
            Books.
  1978   *The Hidden Motives of Pastoral Action: Latin American Reflections.* Trans.
            John Drury. Maryknoll, New York: Orbis Books.
Smith, Donald Eugene
  1970   *Religion and Political Development.* Boston: Little, Brown and Company.
Smith, T. Lynn
  1976   *The Race Between Population and Food Supply in Latin America.* Albuquer-
            que: University of New Mexico Press.
Sobrino, Jon
  1978   *Christology at the Crossroads: A Latin American Approach.* Trans. John
            Drury. Maryknoll, New York: Orbis Books.
Stone, Ronald H.
  1972   *Reinhold Niebuhr: Prophet to Politicians.* Nashville: Abingdon Press.
Thompson, Kenneth W.
  1975   "Niebuhr as Thinker and Doer." In *The Legacy of Reinhold Niebuhr.* Ed.
            Nathan A. Scott. Chicago: University of Chicago Press, pp. 100–110.
Torres, Sergio, and Eagleson, John, eds.
  1976   *Theology in the Americas.* Maryknoll, New York: Orbis Books.
Tracy, David
  1975   *Blessed Rage for Order: The New Pluralism in Theology.* New York: The
            Seabury Press.
Troeltsch, Ernst
  1971   *The Absoluteness of Christianity and the History of Religions.* Trans. David
            Reid. Richmond: John Knox Press.
Weber, Max
  1964   *The Theory of Social and Economic Organization.* Trans. A. M. Henderson
            and Talcott Parsons. Ed. Talcott Parsons. New York: The Free Press.
Weil, Simone
  1973   *Waiting for God.* New York: Harper and Row.

Index

245